For Richard and Joanne

The Conquest of Jerusalem
and the Third Crusade

Crusade Texts in Translation

Titles in this series include:

The Conquest of Jerusalem and the Third Crusade
Sources of Translation
Peter Edbury

The Song of the Cathar Wars
A History of the Albigensian Crusade
Janet Shirley

Chronicle of the Third Crusade
A Translation of the
Itinerarium Peregrinorum et Gesta Regis Ricardi
Helen J. Nicholson

and forthcoming:

Walter the Chancellor's 'Antioch Wars'
Tom Asbridge and Susan Edgington

The Templar of Tyre
Paul Crawford

Crusader Syria in the Thirteenth Century
Janet Shirley

The Conquest of Jerusalem and the Third Crusade

Sources in Translation

PETER W. EDBURY

Ashgate

Aldershot • Brookfield USA• Singapore • Sydney

© Peter Edbury, 1998

First published under the Scolar Press imprint, Ashgate Publishing Ltd, 1996.

Published by
Ashgate Publishing Ltd.
Gower House, Croft Road
Aldershot
Hampshire GU14 9DD
Great Britain

Ashgate Publishing Company
Old Post Road
Brookfield
Vermont 05036-9704
USA

ISBN 1 84014 676 1

British Library Cataloguing-in-Publication Data

Edbury, Peter W.
   The Conquest of Jerusalem and the Third Crusade: Sources in Translation.
   1. Crusades – Third, 1189–1192. 2. Jerusalem—History—Latin Kingdom, 1099–1244.
   I. Title. II. William, of Tyre, Archbishop of Tyre, c. 1130–c. 1186. Historia rerum in partibus transmarinis gestarum. English.
   940.1'82

US Library of Congress Cataloging-in-Publication Data

Edbury, Peter W.
   The Conquest of Jerusalem and the Third Crusade: Sources in Translation / Peter W. Edbury
      p. cm.   Collection of works translated from the Old French and Latin. Includes bibliographical references and index.
   1. Crusades – Third, 1189–1192—Sources. 2. Jerusalem—History—Latin Kingdom, 1099–1244—Sources. I. Edbury, Peter W. II. William, of Tyre, Archbishop of Tyre, c. 1130–c. 1186. Historia rerum in partibus transmarinis gestarum. English.
   D163.A3C66   1997   95–26600
   909.07–dc21   CIP

This volume is printed on acid-free paper.

Printed and bound in Great Britain by Nuffield Press Ltd., 21 Nuffield Way, Abingdon, Oxon OX14 1RL

Crusade Texts in Translation 1

Contents

Foreword

This is a collection of sources in English translation, few of which have been translated previously. Most of this work comprises a rendering of the 1184-97 section of a major narrative source for the period under consideration, the Old French Continuation of William of Tyre. It has been taken from the edition prepared by the late M.R. Morgan and published in 1982 as *La Continuation de Guillaume de Tyr (1184-1197)*. The second and much shorter part of this book consists of a selection of texts and excerpts, chosen because they illustrate further the events handled by the main narrative. The Continuation of William of Tyre has been translated in its entirety from Morgan's edition. Most of the shorter texts similarly are unabridged, but where they have been shortened for any reason this is made clear. A special word of thanks is due to my colleague, Dr Helen Nicholson, both for introducing me to the publisher and for reading and commenting on a substantial section of the translation. She has saved me from many blunders. Jonathan Osmond, John Percival and Jonathan Phillips have all in their different ways given me much needed help and encouragement. I should also like to thank Ian Dennis for preparing the maps and Geoff Boden for helping get the text ship-shape.

Peter Edbury
Cardiff, 1995

Abbreviations

B/K	William Archbishop of Tyre: *A History of Deeds Done Beyond the Sea*. Translated and annotated by E.A. Babcock and A.C. Krey. 2 vols. New York, 1941.
Diceto	Ralph of Diceto, *Opera Historica*. Ed. W. Stubbs. 2 vols. RS 68. London, 1876.
'Ep. Cant.'	'Epistolae Cantuarienses', ed. W. Stubbs in *Chronicles and Memorials of the Reign of Richard I*. Ed. W. Stubbs. Vol. 2. RS 38. London, 1865.
'Eracles'	'L'Estoire de Eracles empereur et la conqueste de la Terre d'Outremer', *Recueil des historiens des croisades. Historiens occidentaux*. Vol. 2. Paris, 1859.
Howden, *Chronica*	Roger of Howden, *Chronica*. Ed. W. Stubbs. 4 vols. RS 51. London, 1868-71.
Howden, *Gesta*	*Gesta Regis Henrici Secundi Benedicti Abbatis*. Ed. W. Stubbs. 2 vols. RS 49. London, 1867.
Outremer	*Outremer: Studies in the history of the Crusading Kingdom of Jerusalem*. Ed. B.Z. Kedar, H.E. Mayer and R.C. Smail. Jerusalem, 1982.
PL	*Patrologiae cursus completus. Series Latina*. Compiled by J.P. Migne. 217 vols with 4 vols of indexes. Paris, 1844-64.
RRH	*Regesta Regni Hierosolymitani (1097-1291)*. Compiled by R. Röhricht. Innsbruck, 1893. *Additamentum*. 1904.
RS	Rerum Brittanicarum Medii Aevi Scriptores (Rolls Series). 251 vols. London, 1858-96.
WT	*Willelmi Tyrensis Archiepiscopi Chronicon*. Ed. R.B.C. Huygens. 2 vols. Corpus Christianorum Continuatio Mediaevalis. 63-63A. Turnhout, 1986.

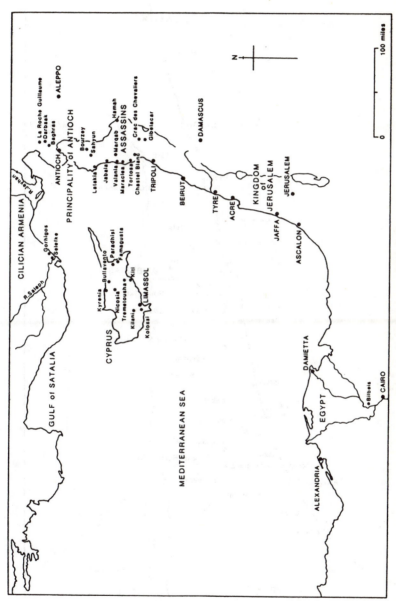

Map 1 The Eastern Mediterranean

Map 2 The Kingdom of Jerusalem

Introduction

On 4 July 1187 the army of the kingdom of Jerusalem suffered a crushing defeat in the hills a few miles to the west of the Sea of Galilee. The victor was that most famous of all medieval Muslim rulers, Salah al-Din Yusuf, better known in the English-speaking world as Saladin. The king of Jerusalem and many of his barons were taken captive on a hill called the Horns of Hattin, and it is from that hill that the battle is named even though the actual engagements were spread over a much wider area. Saladin's victory was so complete that few of the cities or fortresses of the kingdom could offer any resistance. Jerusalem itself surrendered on 2 October, leaving only Tyre and a handful of isolated castles in Christian control.

Jerusalem had been in Christian hands for almost 90 years. It had been won by the army of the First Crusade in 1099, and the kingdom of Jerusalem dated from Christmas Day 1100 and the coronation of the first king. Until 1187 the kingdom had been reasonably successful in resisting Muslim attack, and its collapse sent shock-waves through the whole of western Europe. The two reasons usually given for this collapse can be stated simply: the Muslims were stronger than previously; the Christians weaker. Divisions in the Muslim world of the Near East had contributed to the successes of the First Crusade and its aftermath, but since 1174 Saladin had controlled both Egypt and Damascus, and so for the first time a single hostile ruler governed all the lands adjacent to the Christian-held territories. What was more, Saladin's military resources outstripped those of any of his predecessors. On the other hand, since 1174 the kingdom of Jerusalem had experienced an extended period of political uncertainty which had entailed division and rivalry among the leading figures. Between 1174 and 1185 the king was chronically ill with leprosy; there was then a brief period of minority followed by the accession in 1186 of Guy of Lusignan, a man who was already deeply unpopular with a substantial section of the nobility. Guy needed a major victory to silence his critics; he could not afford to allow Saladin's build-up of troops and incursions into Christian territory to go unchallenged. But even when he committed his forces to what has to be regarded as a military gamble on a huge scale, the rivalries and divisions among his advisers only served to confuse his conduct of operations.

The defeat at Hattin and with it the loss of the most precious relic in the kingdom, the Holy Cross on which Jesus had been crucified, together with the Muslim conquest of Jerusalem and the other places associated with Christ's life on earth, led directly to the Third Crusade. Individual groups of warriors from western Europe began arriving quite soon after the initial catastrophe, but the rulers from the West were slower to respond. In the summer of 1190 the ageing emperor Frederick Barbarossa died en route for the Holy Land while crossing a river in Asia Minor. The kings of France and England, Philip Augustus and Richard the Lionheart, managed to set aside their rivalries in time to start out in 1190, but neither monarch reached the East until the summer of 1191, four years after Hattin.

What they found was a situation in which the Christians, who had managed to retain the two crucial ports of Tripoli and Tyre, were seeking to wrest a third major port from the Muslims. The siege of Acre (the present-day Akko in northern Israel) had begun two years earlier, and it required the arrival of the kings to give the operations the necessary boost to bring them to a successful conclusion. They also found political divisions among the leadership. Guy had been released in 1188, but he had discovered that Conrad of Montferrat, whose timely arrival in 1187 had put heart in to the defenders of Tyre and who had warded off Saladin's attack later in the year, refused to allow him into that city, let alone take control there. Guy, relying heavily on the crusaders from the West, had then begun the siege of Acre, but his authority had been further undermined in 1190 when his wife, through whom he had derived his rights to the throne of Jerusalem, died.

There was clearly much to be done. King Philip of France returned to the West at the beginning of August, almost as soon as Acre had surrendered, but Richard remained in the East until October 1192. Would Richard be able to win back Jerusalem? Could he achieve a situation in which the political disputes were settled and the Christians had a reasonable chance of retaining their territory once the crusaders had departed? The siege of Acre had weakened the Muslims' resolve, and Richard was able to continue grinding down their morale with the result that they agreed to a truce shortly before his departure. This truce was to hold until 1197. But winning back Jerusalem was not feasible. Thanks partly to the naval superiority the Christians enjoyed, Richard was able to occupy the coastal regions south of Acre. But he was less confident inland, largely because he could see that any major military action at Jerusalem would leave his supply-lines dangerously exposed. So although he made two military demonstrations in the direction of Jerusalem and actually came within sight of the holy city, he made no attempt to lay siege to it. As for the political situation, events conspired to make a workable solution possible. Conrad was assassinated in April 1192; at about the same time Richard installed Guy in Cyprus, which he had conquered the previous year on his journey to the Holy Land, and he then arranged for his kinsman, Count Henry of Champagne, to rule over those parts of the kingdom of Jerusalem that the Christians had managed to salvage.

What I have set out to do in this book is to present an account of the events outlined above taken from the writings of people who themselves were either eye-witnesses or who had spoken to people who were. The major part of this book consists of a translation into English of a narrative compiled in the Holy Land sometime in the thirteenth century. It is an anonymous work, originally written in French, and known as the Old French Continuation of William of Tyre. Its great merit is that it provides a view of what had happened from the standpoint of the western European settlers in the East. It therefore has a different slant to those histories written in the West, several of which were explicitly intended to praise the achievements of King Richard. It almost goes without saying that it is even less like the other major group of accounts for this period, the eulogistic biographies written after Saladin's death by members of his entourage. The other documents and passages that are translated here are intended to provide further information and, in places, offer corrections to the main narrative. A few are drawn from alternative versions of this source or other histories of the period, but most are contemporary letters which contain descriptions of what was going on and at the same time reveal something of the attitudes and assumptions of their authors.

The Old French Continuation of William of Tyre

The text that I have translated was edited by Margaret Ruth Morgan as *La Continuation de Guillaume de Tyr (1184-1197)*,[1] and it is to be found in a single manuscript now in the Bibliothèque municipale in Lyon. During the 1170s and early 1180s Archbishop William of Tyre wrote a history in Latin of the kingdom of Jerusalem from the First Crusade down to his own day. It breaks off with the events of 1184 and has long been recognized as being of fundamental importance for understanding the affairs of the East in the twelfth century.[2] At some point in the early decades of the thirteenth century it was translated into French, and many of the manuscripts of the French translation have continuations tacked on to the end.[3] In several instances the continuations take the history of the Crusades and the Frankish East well into the second half of the century. The Lyon manuscript stops in 1248, but, while the section from 1197 to the end is found elsewhere, that for the years 1184 to 1197 is unique.

---

1 Paris, 1982.

2 The standard edition of the Latin text is *Willelmi Tyrensis Archiepiscopi Chronicon*, ed. R.B.C. Huygens (Turnhout, 1986). For an English translation: William Archbishop of Tyre: *A History of Deeds Done Beyond the Sea*, trans. E.A. Babcock and A.C. Krey (New York, 1941).

3 For the most recent discussion of the date of the translation, see J.H. Pryor, 'The *Eracles* and William of Tyre: An Interim Report' in B.Z. Kedar (ed), *The Horns of Hattin* (Jerusalem and London, 1992), pp. 288-9. For what follows, see M.R. Morgan, *The Chronicle of Ernoul and the Continuation of William of Tyre* (Oxford, 1973).

William's history began by noting that the seventh-century Byzantine emperor, Heraklios, brought the relic of the Holy Cross back to Jerusalem. Because the emperor's name appeared in the first sentence of the text, the French translation came to acquire the title *L'Estoire de Eracles* (*The History of Eracles* i.e. Heraklios), and it is for that reason that this version has been christened the 'Lyon *Eracles*'.

This is a useful label as there are a number of other recensions from which it needs to be distinguished. In the nineteenth century the editors of the *Recueil des historiens des croisades* employed a different version as the principal text in their edition,[4] and that text is often known from the former owners of the manuscripts as the 'Colbert-Fontainebleau *Eracles*'. Two other versions need to be mentioned. The overwhelming majority of the manuscripts with continuations for the period 1184-97 have a text that is shorter than either the Lyon *Eracles* or the Colbert-Fontainebleau *Eracles*, and for that reason Morgan designated this text the *abrégé* (or abridgement). Finally there is the Florentine *Eracles*. This survives in a single manuscript, now in the Biblioteca Medicea-Laurenziana in Florence, and traces the history of the East as far as 1277. For the period 1184-97 it falls into two parts. Until 1191 and Richard and Philip-Augustus's sojourn in Sicily en route for the Holy Land it follows the *abrégé* and is of no particular interest, but from there until 1197 it contains a unique text which is closely related to the Lyon *Eracles* but which is generally more concise. Morgan edited this 1191-97 section in parallel to her edition of the Lyon text.[5]

All these versions are broadly similar in content and tone, but the relationship between them for the period 1184-97 is nevertheless complex. This complexity is increased by the fact that in addition to the William of Tyre continuations there is a separate narrative which owes nothing to William's work and which in the nineteenth century was edited as *La Chronique d'Ernoul et de Bernard Le Trésorier*.[6] This starts with the founding of the Latin states in the East after the First Crusade and ends in 1227 or, in some manuscripts, in 1231. For the period 1184-97 the text is almost identical to the *abrégé* version of the Continuations. It would appear that after William's history had been translated into French, someone had taken this other text, lopped off the first part at the point in 1184 where William had finished, and tacked on the section from 1184 onwards at the end, thereby bringing the narrative closer to his own day. At the same time, this editor had preserved a few episodes from the earlier section by repositioning them later in the text.

---

4 'L'Estoire de Eracles empereur et la conqueste de la Terre d'Outremer', *Recueil des historiens des croisades. Historiens occidentaux*, 2 (Paris, 1859).

5 For this text, see *La Continuation de Guillaume de Tyr*, pp. 9-12, 14. The parallel section begins at para. 107.

6 Ed. L. de Mas Latrie (Paris, 1871).

One group of manuscripts of the *Chronique d'Ernoul* contains a valuable piece of information concerning the authorship. On 1 May 1187 Balian of Ibelin, an important nobleman in the kingdom of Jerusalem, sent his squire into the Templar castle of La Fève in southern Galilee to find out why its garrison had left it unoccupied. According to these manuscripts, this squire's name was Ernoul and it was he who had first put this story into writing.[7] Ernoul himself is otherwise unknown,[8] but the partisanship for the Ibelin family is unmistakable in this section of the narrative, and so the idea that it was written by one of Balian's retainers is highly plausible. The question then arises: what exactly did Ernoul write? Morgan argued that his chronicle followed broadly the narrative as it appears in the *Chronique d'Ernoul* to 1197, but that the text preserved in the Lyon *Eracles* is closer to Ernoul's original for the 1184-97 period than the *Chronique* or any of the other recensions of the Continuation. She published her views on this subject in 1973, and since then the only scholar to have challenged her to my knowledge is Professor John Gillingham, who has proposed that Ernoul's authentic writings did not extend beyond the end of 1187 and that what followed are reworked versions of a text dating from the 1220s.[9] The idea that the surviving texts incorporate a pro-Ibelin source as far as the end of 1187 but no further seems to me to have much to recommend it. The account of the years 1186 and 1187 gives the impression that Balian was the one man who came through this period of calamity with his reputation untarnished. But thereafter the favour shown him ceases, and he largely disappears from the narrative. Another feature of the 1186-87 account that is not echoed later concerns Conrad of Montferrat. In 1186-87 he is presented as the divinely ordained saviour of Tyre, a righteous man who through the workings of God's providence salvaged a remnant of the kingdom. This view culminates in his successful defence of Tyre at the end of 1187. But after that he too almost disappears from sight. When in 1190 he engineered the divorce of Isabella, the heiress to the throne, so that he himself could marry her, the text is highly critical, and when in 1192 he died there is not a word of praise for him.[10]

To return to the Lyon *Eracles*. In all probability the sections describing the events of the years 1186 and 1187 incorporate much that was written by Ernoul and so can be accepted as a reworking of his eye-witness account. But whether it is closer to Ernoul's original than any of the other

---

7 See below, para. 27.

8 Morgan (*The Chronicle of Ernoul*, pp. 44-5) revived the idea that he was a man named Arneis of Jubail who was still alive in the 1230s. This is unconvincing on both onomastic and historical grounds.

9 John Gillingham, 'Roger of Howden on Crusade' in *Richard Coeur de Lion: Kingship, Chivalry and War in the Twelfth Century*, (London and Rio Grande, 1994), p. 147, n. 33.

10 Below, paras. 104-6, 137-8.

5

versions is open to doubt. Those passages in which it is identical to the other versions - the Colbert-Fontainebleau *Eracles* and the *abrégé* - probably preserve a version of the narrative that is as near as we can get to the original, but where the Lyon *Eracles* diverges from the others it is just as likely that the passages it contains are themselves later interpolations or reworkings of existing material.[11] The most substantial section in which all three versions are virtually identical is represented by paragraphs 4-28 in the text translated here. There are also a number of shorter identical sections scattered through paragraphs 49-75, but here the Lyon *Eracles* frequently introduces material of its own. But even this common material contains an allusion to the Fourth Crusade of 1204,[12] and so either Ernoul was writing after that date and thus is not as close to the events as might be hoped, or someone else had already been adapting his text before the various versions went their separate ways.

The Lyon *Eracles* provides the fullest version of the narrative for 1184-97. It is much closer to the Colbert-Fontainebleau *Eracles* than it is to the *abrégé* and the *Chronique d'Ernoul*. The first major divergence between the Lyon and Colbert-Fontainebleau texts comes in paragraphs 40-49 which describe the battle of Hattin and its immediate aftermath. (Part of the equivalent Colbert-Fontainebleau text is translated as document 4a in Part II of this book.) Between paragraphs 49 and 81 there are a number of short passages for which the Lyon *Eracles* has a unique version, including two longer sections at paragraphs 66-71 and 75-81. Until paragraph 81 the Colbert-Fontainebleau *Eracles* has on the whole been close to the *abrégé*, but from paragraph 82 (the beginning of the siege of Acre) these two versions go their own way. On the other hand the Colbert-Fontainebleau *Eracles* and the Lyon *Eracles* remain close to each other from paragraph 82 until paragraph 131, the lone exception being paragraphs 116-19 which deal with Richard's conquest of Cyprus (the equivalent Colbert-Fontainebleau text is translated below as document 7a). However, from paragraph 131 (the beginning of Richard's march south from Acre in the summer of 1191) the Colbert-Fontainebleau *Eracles* and the Lyon *Eracles* are totally separate.

The passages that are unique to the Lyon *Eracles* (or to the Lyon *Eracles* together with the Florentine *Eracles*) are of particular interest. But there is no good reason to prefer its accounts of events to those found in the other versions. Indeed, on occasion, as in the case of the account of Saladin's supposed 1187 invasion of the principality of Antioch (paragraphs 45-6), the Colbert-Fontainebleau text is much to be preferred.[13]

---

11 This point is further explored in P.W. Edbury, 'The Lyon *Eracles* and the Old French Continuation of William of Tyre' in B.Z. Kedar et al (eds), *Montjoie: Studies in Crusade History in Honour of Hans Eberhard Mayer* (Aldershot, 1997), pp. 139-53.

12 See below, para. 16. Cf 'Eracles', p. 24; *Chronique d'Ernoul*, p. 96.

13 For a discussion of this point, see below, p. 164 and doc. 5a.

What we have is a compilation containing the handiwork of several contributors. The Lyon text incorporates material that would have been in Ernoul's original account, but there is much else besides, and it would appear to have reached the form in which it has been transmitted to posterity in the 1240s if not later. Paragraph 70 contains a reference to the crusade of Thibaut, king of Navarre and count of Champagne, which took place in 1239-40. On the other hand, as Frederick II is still emperor and the descendants of al-Adil are still ruling in Egypt (paragraphs 148, 165), the text would seem to have reached completion before 1250. How much more of the unique material was incorporated at the same time as the reference to Thibaut's crusade cannot be known, but there is a scattering of references to events dating to around 1230 which could suggest that the late revisions may have been extensive.[14]

But although the Lyon *Eracles* reached its present form half a century after the events it describes, the other versions cannot be much earlier. Both the Lyon *Eracles* and the Colbert-Fontainebleau *Eracles* share an identical reference to the Fifth Crusade of 1217-21 and would seem to imply that it was not a particularly recent event (paragraph 97). On the other hand, writing of Richard's time spent in Sicily in the winter of 1190-91, the *abrégé* alludes to the Peace of Paris of 1229 which marked the end of the Albigensian crusades.[15] In short, although I do not accept Morgan's view that the Lyon text is inherently superior to the others and closer to the putative original, nor do I believe that, taking it as a whole, it should in any way be regarded as inferior.

Like all narrative accounts of past events, the Lyon *Eracles* version of the Continuation of William of Tyre presents a story that is flawed and distorted. Fallible memories, carelessness and unreliable informants have all contributed to a range of mistakes. Often evidence from other sources provides strong corroboration for the statements it makes, but elsewhere the information is demonstrably false. Where no other evidence exists for a particular episode or anecdote and so no verification is possible, the historian is left to ponder. But on a different level the authors have also sought to place their own interpretation on events. Whether in ascribing praise or blame or simply in seeking to understand how their own present situation had come about, they have built into their narrative their own interpretations of the past. It is in trying to discern their views and through them something of the mentality of their time and environment that much of the fascination of this history lies.

---

14 Allusions to late events include the Treaty of Jaffa (1229); Aimery Barlais (leader of the anti-Ibelin faction in the civil war in Cyprus, 1229-33), and Patriarch Gerald's tower at Jaffa (1229). Paras. 71, 181, 184.

15 'Eracles', pp. 160-1 variants; *Chronique d'Ernoul*, p. 269.

Notes on the Translations

Cross-references to 'paragraphs' or 'paras.' relate to the translation of the Continuation of William of Tyre from Morgan's edition (I have retained her numbering of the paragraphs), and cross-references to 'documents' or 'docs.' relate to the texts and excerpts in the second part of this book. Biblical references are to the Authorized Version. Personal names have been anglicized where appropriate, but for placenames I have adopted no consistent policy (even if such a thing were possible) but have used the form which I consider to be the most readily identifiable. The Continuation is translated in full (except for paragraph 189 of Morgan's edition which, as she explains, does not belong there anyway). In the few instances where I have omitted passages from the documents, these omissions are clearly indicated.

The perennial problem facing any translator lies in achieving a balance between a literal rendering of the text and producing something which approximates to acceptable English. The result is inevitably going to be a compromise. In the case of the Continuation, the poverty of vocabulary and expression to be found there have necessitated a modicum of paraphrasing; I have tried hard to be faithful to the original, but I am also well aware that it is all too easy for a translator to impose his or her own interpretation on the text.

Part I

The Old French Continuation of William of Tyre, 1184-97

1   The hatred between the king and the count of Jaffa was so great that it increased from day to day until it reached the stage where the king sought grounds for separating him from his sister.[1] He asked the patriarch to summon them, saying that he wanted to challenge the validity of the marriage and demonstrate that it was neither good nor legal. The count got to hear of it and secretly slipped away from the barons and went to Jerusalem where his wife was then staying and implored her to leave the city before the king came back with his host. He feared that if the king found her he would not allow her return to him. Accordingly he begged her to come with him to Ascalon straight away. The king heard that the count had left the host, and so he sent messengers after him to summon him to his court. He replied that he would not go because he would be disinherited. Many messengers were sent, one after another, but they could not bring him back, as he excused himself through illness. The king said that since he would not come he would go and summon him himself. He went straight to Ascalon accompanied by his barons, but he found the gates firmly shut. He called out and ordered them to be opened. Three times he struck the gate with his hand. But no one came forward to do his command. The burgesses of the town had climbed on the walls and turrets, but none dared move, waiting to see how the affair would end. The king left in a great rage and set off for Jaffa where he was met by knights and sergeants who escorted him in without any opposition. He took possession of the town and installed his own governor.

   Then he left to go on to Acre. He summoned a great *parlement* of all the barons and prelates. When they were assembled the patriarch, accompanied by the masters of the Temple and Hospital, went directly into the king's presence and, falling at his feet, begged him most humbly to set aside his anger at the count of Jaffa and have him come before him.[2] The king would not listen to them, and made it clear that he would do no such thing. They were greatly offended by the fact that a man who was in so

---

1   Para. 1 is the last chapter of William of Tyre's history. For a translation of William's Latin text, B/K, 2, pp. 507-9 (WT, pp. 1062-4). These events belong to the early part of 1184. The king is the Leper King, Baldwin IV (1174-85), and the count is Guy of Lusignan, count of Jaffa and Ascalon since 1180 when he had married the king's sister Sibylla. See below, docs. 1a-c.

2   The patriarch is Eraclius (1180-90), the master of the Templars, Arnold of Torroja (1181-84), and the master of the Hospitallers, Roger des Moulins (1177-87). These three were sent as envoys to the West later in 1184.

feeble a physical state should bear such hatred in his heart. They angrily left the court and departed from the city. The *parlement* was supposed to have been called to send envoys overseas to the princes of France and other lands asking them to aid the land of Jesus Christ and the people of the kingdom. But, though they should have discussed this need first, the patriarch began by raising the other matter as I have described. Because he could not get his own way, he and the two masters left and so nothing could be done about the business for which they had been assembled.

The count of Jaffa learned that the king would have no mercy on him, and that for neither love nor prayer would he grant him his peace. So he thought up a way of angering him. He collected as many knights as he could, and they went directly to the castle of Daron where the Turks of Arabia who are called bedouins had gathered and were pasturing their flocks.[3] In return for payment the king had allowed them to do this, and he kept them under his protection. As they trusted to this protection, they had not bothered to post guards. The count and his knights came upon them and surprised them. Some they killed, and they seized all their flocks and carried off to Ascalon as much of their money and goods as they could find. On his return from Acre to Jerusalem the news reached the king of how Count Guy of Jaffa had raided the bedouins who were under his safe-conduct in the land of Daron, and he was so incensed by it that afterwards he fell victim to the illness from which he died. He immediately sent for the count of Tripoli because he had faith in his good sense and loyalty, and he entrusted to him all his power and the government of the land. There was great joy at this among the barons and the lesser people, for they had been saying for some time that, since neither of the two kings was capable, there was no way for the land to be properly governed unless all the affairs of state were handed over to the count of Tripoli.[4]

2   When King Baldwin was on his death bed, he had all the liege men of the kingdom of Jerusalem come before him, and he insisted that they be bound by their oath to accept Count Raymond of Tripoli as regent of the kingdom until Baldwin his nephew should come of age. It was this nephew, the son of his sister Sibylla and the marquis William,[5] whom he

---

3   Daron was a town belonging to the royal domain and lay beyond Ascalon on the route to Egypt.

4   Raymond III count of Tripoli (1152-87) was also, by virtue of his marriage, lord of Tiberias. The allusion to Baldwin IV's death is not in William of Tyre's original, but a later addition, unique to this version of the text. (William was writing before his death had occurred.) The 'two kings' are Baldwin IV and his nephew, Baldwin V, who had been crowned in 1183.

5   William Longsword, son of William III marquis of Montferrat, had married Sibylla in 1176 and had died the following year.

had had crowned king in his own lifetime, thereby making him his heir in much the same way as his uncle, Baldwin III, had made him his.[6] It had been agreed that if ill fortune befell the young Baldwin and he died without an heir, they should choose Raymond of Tripoli to be king of Jerusalem if they wanted someone from within the kingdom, and, if they wanted to have a foreigner from overseas as king, they should act in accordance with the count's advice and wishes. For King Baldwin was well aware that there was no one else in the kingdom of Jerusalem who had as much right as the count of Tripoli, since he was the first cousin of King Baldwin (III) on the side of the family through which the inheritance passed. For when Baldwin (III) was dying, he had arranged that his brother Amaury (1163-74) should have the kingdom of Jerusalem because he was the rightful heir and that after him his son Baldwin should have it because he was his nephew and godson.

3   After the death of King Baldwin III, Amaury his brother went to the patriarch of Jerusalem and the barons of the kingdom and requested the crown because it was his right and had passed by inheritance to him and to no one else. In reply the patriarch said that he was not worthy to have the crown of the kingdom of Jerusalem, for he was in a state of mortal sin and so should not have the crown or any other honour. The sin for which the patriarch reproved him and which formed this obstacle to his accession was that Amaury had married Agnes, the sister of Count Joscelin and his cousin's daughter. Amaury made his reply to the patriarch and said that he would place himself at God's mercy and at the mercy of the Holy Church and of the patriarch, and that he would do whatever he was commanded. The patriarch said that if he would separate himself from his cousin whom he had married in defiance of God and the law he could have the crown of Jerusalem. He promised the patriarch that he would leave the lady and would send word to Rome on this matter requesting pardon from the pope and a dispensation to legitimize the lady and her children. So he parted from her and was then crowned king and had the lordship of the kingdom of Jerusalem. While King Amaury was sending his messengers to the court of Rome, Agnes, who had been his wife, married Hugh of Ibelin.[7] King Amaury later married Maria, the niece of the emperor Manuel (1143-80), and by her he had a daughter named Isabella who subsequently became queen of Jerusalem.

That is why the conscience of King Baldwin the Leper was touched so that he did not want any foreigner to acquire the kingdom of Jerusalem

---

6   Here and later the text reads 'Baldwin IV' for Baldwin III.

7   For a discussion of the circumstances surrounding Amaury's accession in 1163, see H.E. Mayer, 'The Beginnings of King Amalric of Jerusalem' in B.Z. Kedar (ed), *The Horns of Hattin* (Jerusalem and London, 1992), pp. 121-35.

without the assent of the rightful heir of the kingdom. Because he knew that Guy of Lusignan would not be suitable to govern or sustain the kingdom and that his sister did not have any right to it (for when her mother separated from her father the children were not declared legitimate),[8] he ordered his men to be steadfast to their oath of the count of Tripoli and give him the regency of the kingdom of Jerusalem because he had a greater right to it than anyone else.

4   Count Raymond of Tripoli replied that he would willingly take the regency, but on condition that he did not have charge of the child during the next ten years so that if any misfortune such as death befell him no one could say that it was his doing. He wanted the fortresses and castles to be in the keeping of the Temple and the Hospital, for he did not want to be open to suspicion on any matter nor held to account for any ill deed. Also he wanted to be compensated so that what he spent on the kingdom would be at no cost to himself. For at that time he had no truces with the Saracens, and he had no income in the land with which he could sustain the host against them. Furthermore, he wanted to be assured that he would control the regency for ten years and that if the child died within those ten years the regency would pass to whoever was the closest heir until such time as by the counsel of the pope at Rome, the emperor of Germany and the kings of France and England the kingdom was adjudged to one of the two sisters, either to Sibylla who was the daughter of the Countess Agnes or to Isabella who was the daughter of Queen Maria. King Amaury had separated from the mother of the elder sister before he became king, and the younger was the child of the king and the queen. Because of this the barons were not in agreement that the elder sister should have the throne if the child died unless on the advice of the four[9] that I have just named. That was why the count of Tripoli made these stipulations, for he did not want there to be discord in the land if the child died, and for that reason he wanted to be in charge until the four should give their ruling.

5   The king and the barons were in full agreement with the count's conditions. It was thereupon arranged that Count Joscelin who was the uncle of the child's mother should have charge of the young Baldwin,[10] and that

---

8   This directly contradicts William of Tyre's statement. WT, p. 869 (B/K, 2, p. 301). For the constitutional problems surrounding the succession to the throne in the mid-1180s, see J. Riley-Smith, *The Feudal Nobility and the Kingdom of Jerusalem, 1174-1277* (London, 1973), pp. 104-8.

9   Here and in the next sentence the text reads 'three'.

10 Joscelin of Courtenay, titular count of Edessa and brother of Agnes, King Amaury's first wife.

the count of Tripoli should hold the city of Beirut and should garrison it, because if what had been laid upon him by the barons of the land was going to cost him money, he would recover his expenses if Beirut were assigned to him. When he had thus arranged matters, the king ordered that the child should be crowned. He was taken to the Sepulchre for his coronation, and then, because he was small and they did not want him to be overshadowed by them, he was carried in the arms of a knight to the Templum Domini. This knight was a big, tall man named Balian of Ibelin, and he was one of the barons of the land.[11] Now it is customary in Jerusalem that when the king wears his crown he receives it at the Sepulchre and wears it on his head as far as the Temple where Jesus Christ was offered. There he offers his crown but then buys it back. For it used to be the custom that when a mother had her first male child she would offer him at the Temple and buy him back with a lamb or with two pigeons or two turtledoves.[12] When the king has offered his crown, tables are set out for a meal at the Temple of Solomon which is where the Templars live.[13] There the king and his barons and all those who wished to eat sit down, with the exception only of the burgesses of Jerusalem who serve. For they owe this duty to the king that, when he has worn his crown, they wait on him and his barons at their meal.

Not long after the king had worn his crown the Leper King died. Before he died he ordered all his men to come to him at Jerusalem. They all answered his call, but just as they were arriving, the king departed this life, and all the barons of the land were present at his death.[14] On the next day they buried him in the church of the Sepulchre where the other kings had been buried since the time of Godfrey of Bouillon. He was buried between the hill of Mount Calvary where Jesus Christ had been put on the cross and the Sepulchre where He was laid. All the kings are buried between the place of the Sepulchre and Mount Calvary and Golgotha.

6   Before the king died and the younger Baldwin had worn his crown, he had all the barons of the land do fealty and homage to the child as lord and king. Afterwards he had them do homage to the count of Tripoli as regent, and he made all the barons and knights of the realm swear that they would abide by the settlement concerning his two sisters and that they would obey the count of Tripoli and help him govern and protect the land

11   Baldwin V's coronation was in 1183 and had already been noted by William of Tyre.
12   The allusion is to the offering of Christ in the Temple. Luke 2 vv. 22-4. Cf Leviticus 12 v. 8.
13   The Templum Domini was the Augustinian canonry established in the Dome of the Rock. The Templar headquarters were in the adjacent al-Aqsa mosque, the so-called 'Temple of Solomon'.
14   Baldwin IV died in March 1185.

if the child died within ten years. After the Leper King had died and the child had been crowned, he was entrusted to the keeping of Count Joscelin, who took him to Acre where he looked after him as well as he could, while the count of Tripoli acted as regent of the kingdom.

7   In the first year after the death of King Baldwin the Leper it did not rain at all in the kingdom of Jerusalem with the result that in Jerusalem there was no water and hardly anything to drink. It so happened that there was there a burgess named Germain who was very eager to do good for the sake of God. Because of the shortage of water he had marble basins set into the walls in three places in Jerusalem, and at each of these basins he had two cups attached by chains, and he always kept them full of water. Any man or woman could go there to drink. When Germain saw that there was hardly any water left in the cisterns and that it had not rained at all, he was very sad because he would not be able to sustain this work of charity that he had begun. Then he remembered that he had heard tell from the old men of the land that at the side of the Spring of Siloam there was an ancient well that Jacob had made and that was now covered over and choked and had fallen into disuse. It would be difficult to find. So the good man went and prayed to Our Lord that he would enable him to find this well and would help him continue the good that he had begun, so that by His will it would be possible for the poor people to have water. On the following morning he got up and went to the church and prayed God to help him. Then he went to the square and took workmen and went to the place where he had been told the well was and had them dig until they found it. When he had found it, he had it cleaned out and refurbished at his own expense. Then he had a wheel set above it with pots attached which a horse turned in such a way that the pots that were full came up and the empty ones went down. He had stone basins made where the water that he took from this well would fall, and all who needed water could take it into the city. The burgess had his horses draw water night and day and replenish the basins for all who wanted it and all at his own cost until the Lord God sent rain and they had water in their cisterns. Even then the good man did not stop. He had three packhorses and three servants who did nothing else but carry water to the basins that he had in the city so as to satisfy the thirst of the poor people. This well from which he had the water drawn was at least 50 *toises*[15] deep. Later the Christians of the land broke it and filled it in when they heard that the Saracens were coming to besiege the city.

---

15   A *toise* was slightly less than 2 metres.

8 The Spring of Siloam which was close by this well was not good to drink because it was salt. They used this water for tanning hides in the city, for washing clothes and watering the gardens that were down in the valley. This spring did not flow on Saturdays but remained still. Now I will tell you what happened at this spring. One day at the time Jesus Christ was going about the land, Our Lord was in Jerusalem with his apostles and they were going down a road when they saw a man who had no eyes. Then the apostles came to Jesus and asked Him whether it was because of the sin of his father or his mother or some other relative that he had no eyes. Jesus replied that it was nothing to do with the sin of his father or mother or other relative but because He would be revealed in him. So Jesus Christ went and scooped up some earth and took a piece of mud and put it on the place where his eyes should have been and told him to go to the Spring of Siloam and wash. He went and washed, and he acquired both eyes and sight. Then he went back into the city of Jerusalem and went to his relations who were amazed when they saw that he had his sight, and they asked how it had happened. Later, when the Jews, the masters of the law, heard tell that he who had never had sight was healed, they demanded to know how it was that he could now see. He told them everything that had happened, and they did not want to believe him but sent to his parents and asked if they were certain that it was the same person and they answered that they were.[16]

9 Now I shall tell you about Count Raymond of Tripoli who was regent of the kingdom of Jerusalem. When he saw that there was no rain in the land and that the corn that had been sown was not growing, he feared that there would be shortages, and so he called the barons of the land and the masters of the Temple and Hospital and said to them, 'Lords, what advice will you give me seeing as there is no rain and the corn will not grow? I fear that the Saracens will realize that we are in difficulties and will attack us. What counsel will you give me? Should I make truces with the Saracens through fear of famine?' The barons advised him to make truces with the Saracens and especially with Saladin. Saladin willingly agreed to a four-year truce. After the truce had been concluded between the Christians and the Saracens, the Saracens brought the Christians as many supplies as they would normally have had in good times. If there had been no truce, they would all have died of hunger. So the count of Tripoli was much loved by the people of the land, and because of the truce he had made with the Saracens they greatly honoured him and gave him their blessings.

I forgot to tell you when I was describing the Spring of Siloam of an act of charity that the burgesses of Jerusalem did, but I shall tell you now. They did it in Lent, on the day on which the gospel for the day tells of the

---

16   John 9.

poor man to whom Jesus Christ restored his sight with some mud and ordered him to go the Spring of Siloam which he did. He received his sight and could see. In remembrance of this they did the act of charity of which I shall tell you. They had basins carried to the spring, and they had them filled with wine. They loaded pack animals with bread and wine, and they brought so much that all the poor people who came to that place had bread and wine a plenty, and they also had money. Thus it was that the men and women went out in procession that day to do this charity.

10   I shall now tell you about an important man from Lombardy whose name was William,[17] and he was the marquis of Montferrat. This marquis was the grandfather of the King Baldwin who was a child and was father of William Longsword, the child's father. When he heard that his grandson was king of Jerusalem he was delighted, and he went and took the cross and left his land to his eldest son and went off overseas. After he had arrived in the land of *Outremer*, the king and the count of Tripoli and all the barons of the land received him most honourably and they rejoiced at his coming. Then the king went and gave him a castle which is above the river on this side near to where Jesus Christ fasted for 40 days. This castle is on a high mountain seven miles from Jerusalem and three miles from the river and is called Saint Elias. It is named after Elias because it is said that this is the mountain where he fasted 40 days and then slept and where God sent him a piece of bread and water in a vessel and had him woken by an angel so that he might drink and eat and he drank and ate.[18] Because it had happened there where the castle is, the people of the country call it Saint Elias. In ancient times it was called Ephraim, and it was where God sent his angel to Gideon who was winnowing at his threshing floor to tell him that he would vanquish the Midianites who were coming to destroy the land of Jerusalem. So Gideon said to the angel that he should show him a sign by which he could believe him. He replied thus because he was of humble lineage. God afterwards gave him a sign which was that a fleece that he had on his threshing floor was full of dew and the ground around was dry. Then the ground was wet and the fleece was dry.[19] This signified Our Lady.

11   Marquis William had a son named Conrad. This man took the cross to follow his father to the land of *Outremer* and see his nephew who was

---

17   Here and elsewhere all the versions of our text erroneously call this man Boniface. Boniface was the marquis William's son, later famous as the leader of the Fourth Crusade.

18   1 Kings 19.

19   Judges 6.

the king of Jerusalem. He set off to cross the sea, but Our Lord did not want him to make the journey and sent him for a time to Constantinople because He had foreseen the loss of the land that was coming about as the result of His anger at the sins of the people of Jerusalem and foresaw that through this same Conrad part of the land would be preserved. For despite their sin of extravagance Our Lord did not want to destroy everything. But because of this one good man He left them a remnant, as you will hear.

It was just the same as had happened to Solomon's son when God's wrath descended on Solomon because of the sin that he had committed for the sake of a pagan woman whom he had taken unrighteously. Playing on the love that he had for her, she had him build three pagan shrines[20] on three mountains each of which were three miles from Jerusalem, the third being on the Mount of Olives. The Lord God was more angry because of the shrine that he had built on the Mount of Olives than because of any previous sin, since it was from the Mount of Olives that He rose to heaven in the sight of His apostles after He had been raised from death to life. So the Lord God told Solomon that he had angered Him, but that because of the great love that He had had for his father David He would not destroy him but would bear with him for as long as he should live. However, he should know that after his death his son would not hold the kingdom except for only a small part. This small part He would leave him because of the love that He had for his father David. Similarly for the sake of the one good man who was in the land, Our Lord did not want to deprive Christendom of the whole land. Just as He left something for Solomon's son for David's sake, so also He left a city named Tyre because of Conrad who was then in Constantinople, and you will hear later how he preserved it.[21]

At the time of Conrad's arrival, Isaac was emperor in Constantinople, and he had not yet been blinded. There was an important man there named Lyvernas[22] who had been a cousin of the emperor Manuel. He had been in hiding while Andronicos was emperor, and because he had remained hidden Andronicos had not mutilated him as he had his other relatives. When he learned that Andronicos was dead and that Isaac had become emperor and had freed the world from Andronicos, as I shall describe, he was overjoyed, and from then on he plotted to gain the empire of Constantinople for himself. But for as long as Isaac was emperor he made no move.[23]

---

20 Here and in the next sentence the text has 'mahomeries', i.e. mosques.
21 For God's dealings with Solomon, see 1 Kings 11. Christ's Ascension from the Mount of Olives is recounted in Acts 1 vv. 9-12.
22 Alexios Branas.
23 Andronicos Comnenos reigned in Constantinople 1183-85. He was succeeded by Isaac II Angelos (1185-95) whose rule ended with his overthrow and blinding by his brother Alexios III Angelos (1195-1203). The chronicler errs in his belief that Branas rebelled against Alexios III (below, para. 16). In fact he had been loyal to Andronicos and rebelled against Isaac in 1187. There are a number of inaccuracies

12   Andronicos executed Alexios who controlled the empire of Constantinople and had charge of the emperor Manuel's infant son.[24] That same night he devised a treacherous scheme with the advice of his secretary, a man named Langosse.[25] One night Andronicos had the young child, who was husband to King Louis of France's daughter and whom he should have looked after in good faith, seized and taken out in a boat on the sea in a sack and thrown in and drowned. Then, before this deed became known, he sent for the emperor's relatives, and as soon as they had come he had them imprisoned and their eyes gouged out. There were some whose noses and lips he had cut off. That was how he treated most of the emperor's relatives - all those he could find. After that he became emperor and wore the crown and did such evil as you shall hear.

13   While Andronicos was emperor of Constantinople there was not a beautiful nun in an abbey nor the daughter of a knight or burgess whom he did not lie with by force. He was so hated because of his evil that everyone in Constantinople longed for his destruction and death. It happened one day that Andronicos was out of Constantinople on campaign. There was a young nobleman of the emperor Manuel's kindred with him named Isaac.[26] This man was the son of a poor widow and was extremely impoverished. He served Andronicos at his court and was held in scorn. Andronicos had given him a day's leave to go to Constantinople to change his clothes and go to the baths. After Isaac had gone off, Andronicos took it into his head to find out when he himself would die. He sent for his astronomers and asked them how long he would live. The astronomers withdrew and went aside and found by their astronomy that he would only live for three days. The oldest of them said to the others that he feared that if they said he had only three more days to live he would do some great evil. 'Let us say that he has five more days to live,' and so they agreed. They came before him and told him that they had found that he would live for five days. He was extremely terrified and asked who would be the next emperor. They asked for leave until the following day when they would tell him. When they came back they said that the name of the man was Isaac. On hearing this Andronicos assumed

---

in this account of Byzantine politics. For a reliable modern account, see C.M. Brand, *Byzantium Confronts the West, 1180-1204* (Cambridge, MA, 1968).

24   Manuel Comnenos (1143-80) was succeeded as emperor by his young son Alexios II (1180-83). Power rested with a kinsman, Alexios Comnenos the protosebastos, until April 1182 when he was blinded. Alexios II, who had married Agnes, a daughter of Louis VII of France, was murdered in September 1183.

25   Stephen Hagiochristophorites.

26   Isaac Angelos was descended from one of Manuel's aunts.

that they meant the duke of Cyprus.[27] So he had his host prepared by land and sea, and it was announced publicly that the traitor Isaac had rebelled against his lord the emperor and intended to seize the empire.

After he had given these orders, Langosse went to him and said that there was an Isaac in Constantinople who was of no account and of vile birth, and he advised him that if he were killed he would be freed from his fear. Andronicos gave him permission to do as he wished with him, so he went to the man's house in Constantinople and called for him. When he heard Langosse's voice, Isaac said to his mother, 'Mother, that man is calling me to my death. Tell him that I am sleeping.' The people of Constantinople were well aware that whenever Langosse went in search of anyone it was to kill him. Isaac's mother told Langosse that Isaac was asleep. He pressed him to come quickly to the emperor. He took leave of his mother and his relatives and took a sword and put it under his surcoat. As soon as he came before Langosse he taunted him and said, 'Why do you hate me? I always obey the command of the emperor.' Langosse replied, 'Are you complaining about what I have said to you? I shall do worse things to you yet.' He raised his hand and struck him with his whip. Isaac took great offence because Langosse had struck him. He took hold of his sword and promptly cut off his head.

14   As soon as Isaac had cut off Langosse's head, the people of Constantinople gathered round him and carried him with his still blood-stained sword to the Boukoleon. There they took the crown and went to Saint Sophia and had him crowned. They then had the place put into a state of defence. The cry went through the city: 'The devil is dead! The devil is dead!' Andronicos who was at his camp heard that Isaac had been crowned emperor. He got on a galley to pass the Arm of Saint George so as to go to Trebizond. All night they were at sea, and they worked hard but they could not pass through, and so he had to go back to Constantinople.[28] He made his way to the Blachernai palace.[29] Andronicos was a good archer, and he thought that when Isaac was crowned and passed before the Blachernai he could shoot him with an arrow and kill him. In this way he would free himself and so would be emperor and have the empire in peace. But when Isaac was passing wearing the crown and Andronicos took his bow in his hand and fitted an arrow, the bow broke just as he was

---

27 Isaac Ducas Comnenos took the imperial title and usurped power in Cyprus at about this time.

28 Sailing northwards through the Bosphorus from Constantinople to the Black Sea has always been difficult because of the strong contrary current.

29 The Boukoleon was the palace-complex in the heart of Constantinople near Saint Sophia. The Blachernai palace was at the northern extremity of the city.

taking aim. Then the people of Constantinople besieged him and he was taken.

Isaac went and had him put in the Boukoleon and decided to make him suffer a vile death because he had drowned his rightful lord, the son of the emperor Manuel, and because of the great evils that he had done. So Isaac had him stripped naked and made him wear a chaplet of garlic stalks. Such was the crown he had made for him, and thus was he crowned king. Then he had his hair cropped and shaved in a cross, and he gouged out one of his eyes but let him keep the other so he would see the shame and the punishment he was to receive. He had an ass brought and they had him mounted on it backwards with him holding its tail like a rein. And so he was led through all the streets of Constantinople and he wore his crown. Now I shall tell you what the women did. They had prepared urine and excrement and threw it in his face, and those who could not reach climbed up on the terraces with urine and excrement ready and threw it on his head. This they did in every street. In this manner did Andronicos wear his crown in Constantinople. When he came outside the city, he was left to the women, and they fell on him like starving dogs on a rotting corpse and tore him in pieces. Any who could have a bit as large as a bean ate it; they took a knife to the bones and removed the flesh and ate it. There was not a bone or piece of tendon left that they did not eat. It was said that all those who had eaten any of him or who had been at his death would be saved because they had helped avenge the evil that he had done. The place to which they had dragged him and put him to death was close to the pillar from which Mourtzouphlos was cast down.[30] There they dug into a dung hill and buried him in that foul place. They found there a vase of green porphyry on which was inscribed in Greek, 'When the evil emperor dies a shameful death, here shall he be interred.'

15   As a consequence of the evil of Andronicos and Langosse, Isaac, the new emperor, was greatly loved by the people of the land. He was especially loved by the abbeys, and there was not a monastery in Constantinople that did not have his image painted above the entrance. He was not married at the time of his accession, and on the advice of his men he sent to the king of Hungary asking for his sister to be his wife. The king was delighted and sent her to Constantinople. Isaac married her and had her crowned empress. Later she bore a son who was named Alexios.[31]

It happened that Isaac was travelling through his empire and was staying near Philippi, the city where, so it is said, King Alexander was

---

30   Alexios V Mourtzouphlos, emperor in 1204, was executed in 1205 by being forced to jump from a column in the Forum of Theodosius.

31   Isaac married Margaret, the daughter of the then king of Hungary, Bela III (1173-96). Alexios was the son of Isaac's previous marriage.

born. It is about five days journey from Constantinople. It is said that Saint Paul addressed one of his letters there, and this epistle is still known as the Epistle to the Philippians. They used to make good silk there, and the city is now called Thebes.[32] When Alexios, Isaac's brother, discovered that Isaac was staying at a certain abbey, at the prompting of his wife who had told him that if she were not to be empress she would never sleep with him, he quickly set off to join him. As he had always served and honoured him, Isaac was not on his guard against his brother's malice and treason. When Alexios entered the room where his brother was, he attacked him and, grabbing him by the hair, took his knife and gouged out his eyes. Then he went to Constantinople and had himself crowned as emperor and his wife as empress.[33]

16   After Alexios had been crowned, the empress who had been Isaac's wife married her daughter to Philip, duke of Swabia, the son of the emperor Frederick. She took her son by Isaac and sent him to her brother, the king of Hungary, and he brought him up and looked after him until the coming of the men of France as you will find later in this history.[34]

Lyvernas of whom I have spoken already and who was closer to the emperor Manuel than to Alexios, gathered a large number of people and came before Constantinople. When Alexios learned that Lyvernas was coming against him with his army, he begged the marquis Conrad who was then in Constantinople that he and his men should stand by him until the war was brought to a close. The marquis agreed that he would be happy to stay. Lyvernas led his forces to Constantinople in readiness for battle. The emperor Alexios did not want to come out against him because of Lyvernas's extensive family connections within the city. So it was the marquis who went against Lyvernas. He was pointed out to him, and he rode towards him. Lyvernas and the men in his squadron assumed that he had left the city and was joining their side, but as he drew near to Lyvernas he spurred his horse violently and struck him in the middle of his body so that he fell down dead. He then turned back to Constantino-

---

32   There are several errors here. The place referred to is Philippi in Thrace which was indeed where Saint Paul's epistle was addressed. The text wrongly calls it 'Caesarea Philippi'; Alexander the Great was not born there but at Pella, and Thebes, famous for its silk production, is in another part of Greece altogether.

33   This occurred in 1195. The chronology of what follows is seriously awry: the Branas revolt and Conrad's sojourn in Constantinople had been in 1187 in the reign of Isaac II.

34   Philip of Swabia (died 1208), the son of the western emperor Frederick Barbarossa (1152-90), married Isaac's daughter by his previous marriage. Isaac's son, Alexios, was kept in confinement in Constantinople until his escape, probably in 1201. The reference to the coming of the men of France is an allusion to the Fourth Crusade of 1202-04.

ple. When those who wanted to lay siege to Constantinople saw that their lord was dead, they turned and fled. The emperor summoned Conrad to his palace, and kept him with him because he did not want Lyvernas's partisans in the city to do him shame or ill. Conrad stayed with the emperor until the moment that he was destined to come to the land of *Outremer* to save that city which God had ordained He would leave in Christian hands.

17   Now let us return to King Baldwin the child who was at Acre in the keeping of Count Joscelin, his mother's uncle. He fell ill and died. Then Count Joscelin devised a great act of treachery. One night he told the count of Tripoli to go to Tiberias rather than accompany the king to his funeral, and added that he should not let any of the barons of the land go but should entrust the king's body to the Templars who would take it to Jerusalem for burial. Like a fool the count of Tripoli followed this advice. The Templars carried the body of the king to Jerusalem, and the count went to Tiberias. Count Joscelin thereupon came and seized the city of Acre. He then went to Beirut, which the count of Tripoli had in his keeping, and he entered it treasonably and garrisoned it with knights and sergeants. After that he sent word to the countess of Jaffa who was his niece, telling her to take all her knights and go to Jerusalem; once the king her son was buried, they should seize the city and garrison it, and she should have herself crowned as queen.

    When the count of Tripoli found out that Count Joscelin had betrayed him, he summoned all the barons of the land to join him at Nablus. They all came except for Count Joscelin and Prince Reynald.[35] Count Joscelin would not leave Acre, and the countess of Jaffa was in Jerusalem with her husband and their knights. There she had her son the king buried. Among those present were the marquis William his grandfather, the patriarch, and the masters of the Temple and the Hospital. When the king had been buried, the countess of Jaffa went to the masters of the Temple and the Hospital and begged them to give her their advice. The master of the Temple[36] came and told her not to worry for they would crown her in spite of all the men of the land - the patriarch out of love for her mother, and the master of the Temple out of hatred for the count of Tripoli. They summoned Prince Reynald who was at Acre[37] to come to Jerusalem which he did.

---

35   Reynald of Châtillon had at one time been prince of Antioch by virtue of his marriage to Princess Constance. He was now lord of Outrejourdain thanks to his marriage to the heiress.
36   Gerard of Ridefort (1185-89).
37   Other versions say that Reynald was at Kerak, the principal castle in his lordship of Outrejourdain.

They then took counsel as to what they should do. They advised the countess to summon the count of Tripoli and the barons who were at Nablus to come to her coronation as the kingdom had fallen to her by inheritance. She immediately sent messengers telling them to come. The barons at Nablus refused. Instead they sent two Cistercian abbots to Jerusalem to the patriarch and to the masters of the Temple and Hospital, forbidding them in the name of God and of the pope to crown the countess of Jaffa before they had taken counsel concerning those matters about which they had sworn the oath in the time of the Leper King. The abbots went to Jerusalem with two knights, John of Bellême and William Le Keu who was the father of Thomas of Saint Bertin, and delivered their message.

The patriarch and the master of the Temple and Prince Reynald said that they would not keep faith nor abide by the oath, but would crown the lady. The master of the Hospital wanted no part in it, and said that he would have nothing to do with it for they would be acting against God and against their oaths. Then they shut the gates of the city, so that no one could come in or go out, for they were afraid that the barons, who were about 12 miles away at Nablus, would enter the city before they could crown the lady and there would be a riot.

18   When the barons heard that the city was shut up so that no one could go in or out, they dressed up a sergeant who had been born there as a monk and sent him to Jerusalem to spy on the lady's coronation. He set off but could not enter by any of the gates. He came to the 'Madeleine' of the Jacobites of Jerusalem that adjoins the city walls. It had a postern by which the city could be entered, and he persuaded the abbot there to let him in.[38] Then he went to the Sepulchre and stayed there until he had seen and learned what he had been sent to find out.

The master of the Temple and Prince Reynald took the lady and brought her to the Sepulchre to be crowned by the patriarch. Prince Reynald stood up and said to the people, 'Lords, you are well aware that King Baldwin and his nephew whom he had had crowned are dead, and that the kingdom is now without an heir and without a governor. We wish with your approval to crown Sibylla, the daughter of King Amaury and sister of King Baldwin. For she is the closest heir to the kingdom.' The people who were there said with one voice that they loved King Amaury[39] more than anyone else. They had all forgotten the oath that they had sworn to the count of Tripoli, and because of this it went ill for them later.

---

38   The Jacobite church of Saint Mary Magdalene was near the eastern end of the northern wall of Jerusalem.

39   Perhaps this should read 'loved the daughter of King Amaury ... '.

When the lady had come to the Sepulchre, the patriarch went to the master of the Temple and requested the keys to the treasury where the crowns were kept. The master of the Temple willingly handed them over. Then they ordered the master of the Hospital to hand over his key. He replied that he would neither send it nor bring it to them unless it was by the counsel of the men of the kingdom. So the patriarch, the master of the Temple and Prince Reynald went to the master of the Hospital to get the key. But when he heard that they were on their way, he hid himself in his house, and it was almost noon before they found him and could speak with him. When they did find him, they begged him to give them his key. He replied that he would never give it to them. He was holding the key in his own hand out of fear that some monk of his household might take it and give it to the patriarch. They kept on cajoling and threatening him until he grew angry and threw it into the middle of the house.

So the master of the Temple and Prince Reynald came and took the key, and they went to the treasury and got out two crowns and brought them to the patriarch. The patriarch placed one on the altar and with the other he crowned the countess of Jaffa.[40] When the countess was crowned and was queen, the patriarch addressed her with these words: 'Lady, you are a woman; it is fitting that you should have a man by you who can help you govern your kingdom. You see that crown there. Now take it and give it to such a man as can govern your kingdom.' She took the crown and called her husband who was before her and said to him: 'Sire, come up and receive this crown, for I do not know where better I can bestow it.' He knelt before her, and she placed the crown on his head. The master of the Temple put his hand on it and helped her to place it and said, 'This crown is well worth the marriage of Botron.'[41] After this the patriarch anointed him. Thus was he king and she queen. This was done on a Friday in the year of the incarnation of Jesus Christ 1186. Never before had the coronation of a king in Jerusalem been on a Friday or with the gates shut.

When the sergeant, who had come in the habit of a monk to watch what would happen, had seen the coronation, he left by the postern by which he had come in and returned to Nablus to tell the count of Tripoli and the barons who had sent him all that he had seen. As soon as Baldwin of Ramla heard that Guy of Lusignan was king of Jerusalem he said, 'This is one thing for certain: he will not last a year as king.' Nor did he, for he was crowned in mid-September and lost the kingdom on Saint Martin *Calidus* which is at the beginning of the month of July.[42] Then Baldwin of

---

40   For the coronation, see below, docs. 2a-b.

41   See below, para. 33.

42   I.e. at the battle of Hattin which took place on 4 July 1187. Saint Martin *Calidus* is the feast of the ordination and translation of Saint Martin of Tours, so-called to distinguish it from the saint's other feast-day which falls on 11 November.

Ramla addressed the count of Tripoli and the barons of the land: 'Good lords, now do the best you can, for the land is lost. I shall go into exile for I do not want to bear the blame or reproach for having been present at its loss. For I know only too well that this man who is now king is a madman and a fool. He will in no way follow my advice nor yours but will want to go astray by the counsel of those who know nothing. Because of this I shall leave the country.'[43] Then the count of Tripoli said, 'Sir Baldwin, for God's sake have pity on Christendom. Let us consider how we can protect the land. We have here the daughter of King Amaury and Humphrey her husband.[44] We shall crown her and go to Jerusalem and take control, for we have the support of the master of the Hospital and all the barons, except for Prince Reynald who is with the king in Jerusalem. I have truces with the Saracens and shall have for as long as I want. So we shall not be attacked by them, but rather they will help us if we have need.' Everyone agreed to this, and they pledged themselves to crown Humphrey the next day.

19 When Humphrey heard that they wanted to crown him, he decided that he could not bear so great a responsibility. Once darkness had fallen he mounted his horse, and he and his knights rode through the night and so fled to Jerusalem. In the morning, when the barons had risen and were getting ready to crown him, they were told that he had fled. Humphrey came before the queen whose sister he had as wife and greeted her. But she would not greet him because he had been opposed to her and so had not been at her coronation. He began to scratch his head like a shamefaced child and said, 'Lady, I cannot do otherwise, for they wanted to make me king by force.' The queen said, 'Sir Humphrey, you have done right. Since you have acted thus I will pardon you my anger. Now go and do homage to the king.' Humphrey thanked the queen because she had set aside her anger and did homage to the king and remained with the queen in Jerusalem.

When the count of Tripoli and the barons who were at Nablus learned that Humphrey had fled to Jerusalem and had done homage to the king, they were downcast and did not know what to do. Then the barons came to the count of Tripoli and said, 'Sire, for God's sake, advise us about the oath which the Leper King made us swear, for we do not want to do anything that will bring us shame or reproach.' The count said that they should keep the oath that they had made, for he did not know what other advice to give.

---

43 Baldwin of Ibelin, lord of Ramla and Mirabel, was the elder brother of Balian of Ibelin.

44 Isabella, King Amaury's daughter by Maria Comnena, had married Humphrey IV of Toron in 1183.

20   Then the barons took counsel among themselves and came to the count and said, 'Sire, since it has come to pass that there is a king in Jerusalem, we cannot set up in opposition to him for this would only invite censure. So we beg you for God's sake not to bear us ill will, but to go to Tiberias and stay there, and we shall go to Jerusalem to the king and do homage; we shall give you all the help we can, saving our honour, and we shall see to it that you get back all the money you have spent on the land in return for which the Leper King gave you Beirut in pledge.' Baldwin of Ramla dissented from this advice.

When the count of Tripoli saw that all the barons had failed him, he went off to Tiberias, and the barons, with the sole exception of Baldwin of Ramla, went to Jerusalem to do homage to the king. But Baldwin sent his young son there and told the barons to petition the king to put him in seisin of his land and accept his homage. After the barons had done homage, they pleaded with the king to put Baldwin of Ramla's son in seisin of his father's land and accept his homage. The king replied that he would not put him in seisin of the land nor receive his homage until his father did homage. But if his father would do homage, he would certainly give his son seisin of his lands, and he made it plain that unless Baldwin of Ramla came and did homage he would seize his land.

21   After this the king summoned Baldwin of Ibelin and the other barons to a *parlement* at Acre. They assembled in the cathedral church of the Holy Cross, and at once the king got up at the lectern and began to speak. He told how he had been crowned king of Jerusalem and how God had granted him so great a favour and so worthy a crown; even though he was unworthy, they should not hold him in scorn. He then requested that they pay him their homage and fealty as vassals should to their lords. And so he ended his address. When he had finished he told Prince Reynald who was standing nearby to summon Baldwin of Ibelin to do homage. Prince Reynald summoned him three times. But he, being a wise and stalwart man, would not reply to this summons. When the king saw that Baldwin would not answer to the prince's summons, he himself summoned him and said, 'Dear friend, come forward if you will give me your homage and fealty, and show good will to these high-born men who are here.' He replied, 'My father never did homage to yours, and I will not do it to you. I commend my fief to you until Thomassin, my son who is here, comes of age. He will come to you as to his good lord and will do to you what he ought, but I will quit your kingdom within three days.'

Then he took leave of Balian his brother and entrusted his son to him to look after until he should reach his majority. After that he got on the road and, setting off with the other knights who had commended their fiefs, went to the prince of Antioch.[45] When the prince of Antioch heard that Baldwin of Ibelin and so many knights were coming, he was delighted. He went out to meet them and received them with great joy.[46]

22 While all this was going on, a spy came to Prince Reynald and told him that a great caravan was travelling from Cairo to Damascus and would have to pass by the land of Kerak. The prince immediately got on his horse and went to Kerak and assembled as many of his men as he could, and they went and took the caravan and with it the sister of the sultan Saladin. When Saladin heard that Prince Reynald had seized the caravan and his sister, he was extremely angry and distressed. He immediately sent messengers to the new king demanding the return of the caravan and his sister and claiming that he had no wish to break the truce that he had concluded in the time of the little king. King Guy ordered Prince Reynald to return the caravan and the sultan's sister to Saladin. He replied that he would not do so, for he was lord of his land, just as Guy was lord of his, and he had no truces with the Saracens. The pretext for the loss of the kingdom of Jerusalem was the seizure of this caravan that we have just described.

23 King Guy, who was in Jerusalem, took counsel with the master of the Temple as to what he could do about the count of Tripoli who would not come to do homage. The master of the Temple advised him to summon his host and go to besiege Tiberias. When the count of Tripoli heard tell that the king had summoned his host to come against him, he was very pleased. He sent to Saladin who was lord of Damascus telling him that King Guy was gathering his troops to make war on him, and Saladin replied that if he should need help he would come to his aid. Saladin sent him knights, sergeants and crossbowmen with a plentiful supply of arms, and told him that if he were besieged in the morning he would be with him that same evening. Then Saladin came and called up his own forces and mustered them five miles from Tiberias at Banyas.[47]

King Guy had assembled his men at Nazareth. Balian of Ibelin went to him and said, 'Sire, why have you raised this host? Where are you going? Winter is coming on and this is no time to keep up an army.' The king said that he intended besieging Tiberias. 'On whose advice, sire,' said Balian, 'do you wish to do that? It is a bad decision. No wise man would ever have given you such counsel, and you well know, sire, that you

---

45 Bohemond III (1163-1201).
46 Baldwin is known to have been in Antioch in February 1187. Nothing is known of his career after that date.
47 Banyas and Tiberias are about 40 miles apart.

would never have brought the men here on my advice nor on the advice of the barons. There is a great force of knights inside Tiberias, both Christians and Saracens, and you have few people to besiege them. You should know that if you go there not a man will escape, for as soon as you start the siege Saladin will come to its aid with a great army. Break up your host, and I and some of our people from among the leaders of our forces will go to the count of Tripoli and make peace between you if we can, for hatred is no good for anyone.'

Then the king dispersed his host and sent messengers to Tiberias as he had been advised. When they came to the count and spoke about peace, the count said that he would make no peace until he had possession of the castle of Beirut which had been taken from him, but if the castle were returned he would behave in such a way that everyone would have his good will. The messengers returned to the king and recounted what he had said.

24 After this things remained the same all winter, almost until Easter. When it was nearly Easter King Guy learned that Saladin was assembling his host to enter his land. He ordered all the barons and the archbishops and bishops to come to him in Jerusalem. When they had come before him, he asked their advice as to what he should do about Saladin and his threatened invasion. The barons advised and counselled him to reach an agreement with the count of Tripoli, since unless he did so he would not be able to put his own forces in the field against the Saracens. For the count of Tripoli had a large number of knights with him, and he was such a wise man that if he were on good terms with him and would accept his advice he need have no fear of the Saracens. 'Sire, you have lost Baldwin of Ramla, the best and wisest knight in your land, and if you lose the aid and counsel of the count of Tripoli then you will have lost everything.'

The king replied that he would gladly make peace with him and would agree to whatever they advised. Then he called the master of the Temple, Brother Gerard of Ridefort; the master of the Hospital, Brother Roger des Moulins; Joscius, archbishop of Tyre;[48] Balian of Ibelin and Reynald of Sidon,[49] and commanded them to go to the count of Tripoli to make peace; whatever terms they agreed he would accept.

So the envoys set off. Four of them spent the first night of their journey at Nablus, though Reynald of Sidon went by another road. Then Balian of Ibelin told the masters of the Temple and Hospital and the archbishop of Tyre that their journey the next day would be short and that he would stay back at Nablus as he had some small thing to do; he would set out at night and travel on through the dark and so be with them at day-

---

48 1186-1202.
49 Reynald, lord of Sidon, c.1171-c.1200.

break. So they resumed their journey the next morning[50] while Balian stayed behind.

25   Nur al-Din, Saladin's son who was newly armed, was encamped on the other side of the river. He was known as Nur al-Din Amir 'Ali and was later lord of Damascus.[51] His father had ordered him to enter the Christians' territory and challenge them because of the caravan that Prince Reynald had seized together with his sister whom he had captured and was holding in prison. His only route into the Christian lands was via the territory of Tiberias. Because the lordship of Tiberias at that time belonged to the count of Tripoli and because the count had truces with Saladin and had given him much help and shown him much love, Nur al-Din had no wish to enter Christian territory without his leave. He knew that there was a quarrel between him and the king, and so he told the count of Tripoli to let him enter the land of the Christians through his lordship to make a raid.

When the count heard this demand he was very sorrowful. He realized that if he refused the favour he was requesting he would lose the help and counsel of his father Saladin, and that if he agreed to it he would thereby bear great shame and reproach in Christendom. He decided to arrange things so that the Christians would be warned and so would lose nothing, while at the same time Saladin's son would take no offence. He sent word to Nur al-Din that he would certainly give him leave to pass through his land and to enter the land of the Christians on the undertaking that he would cross the river at sunrise, return to his own land at sunset and not stop at the river towards sunset; he would take nothing from any town or house and would do no damage. This he swore to do. On the following morning he crossed the river, went past Tiberias and entered the land of the Christians. The count of Tripoli had the gates of Tiberias shut so that those inside could not go out to do him damage.

Now the count had known the day before that the envoys were on their way, and so he wrote letters and got messengers and sent them to the knights who were at Nazareth in the garrison and to everywhere else he knew the Saracens would have to go: on no account were they to move from their towns or houses, for the Saracens would enter the land and had bound themselves so that so long as they did not come out of their towns they need have no fear, but if they were found in the fields they would be

---

50   The text says 'night' for 'next morning'.

51   al-Malik al-Afdal Nur al-Din Abu'l-Hasan 'Ali (al-Afdal to most modern writers) was Saladin's eldest son and ruler of Damascus 1193-96. This was apparently his first command, and other versions of the text anachronistically speak of him being 'newly dubbed knight'. They also make it clear that his forces were on the east bank of the Jordan at Jacob's Ford, a few miles to the north of the Sea of Galilee.

taken and killed. Thus did the count of Tripoli warn the people of the land. Then the messengers came to the masters of the Temple and Hospital and to the archbishop of Tyre who were at the castle of La Fève bringing letters addressed to them from the count of Tripoli.

When the master of the Temple heard that the Saracens would enter the land the next day he sent post haste to a convent of his order that was four miles from there at a town name Caco.[52] In his letter he commanded his men to set off and come to him immediately, since the Saracens would enter the land the next morning. As soon as the convent received their master's order they rode out and, arriving before nightfall, lodged outside the castle. The following morning they set off and came to Nazareth. There were 80 Templar knights plus ten Hospitallers who were escorting their master, and there were 40 knights in the royal garrison at Nazareth. They all left Nazareth and went a good two miles towards Tiberias before finding the Saracens at the springs that are called the Springs of Cresson. They were returning so as to cross the river without having done any damage to the Christians, for the Christians had been left in peace as the count of Tripoli had ordered.

The master of the Temple was a good knight and physically strong, but he treated all the other people wrongly as he was too presumptuous. He would not accept the advice of the master of the Hospital, Brother Roger des Moulins, nor of Brother James of Mailly, who was the marshal of the Temple, but scoffed at him and told him that he was speaking like someone who was wanting to flee.[53] The marshal replied that he would not flee the battle but would remain on the field like a man, but *he* would flee like an evil coward. Then the master of the Temple and the knights who were with him together with the master of the Hospital charged at the Saracens. The Saracens withstood them joyously and closed in on them so that the Christians could not pass through. There were at least 7,000 armed Saracen knights, and the Christians had only 140. There the master of the Hospital had his head cut off, and so did all the knights of the Temple. Only the master of the Temple together with just three knights escaped. The 40 knights who were in the royal garrison were all taken. When the squires of the Temple and Hospital saw that the knights were being cut down by the Saracens, they turned in flight with all the baggage so that none of the Christians' baggage was lost.[54]

26 Now I shall tell you what the master of the Temple did. As he was passing through Nazareth and was going out against the Saracens, he sent

---

52 La Fève (al-Fula in southern Galilee) and Caco (Qaqun between Nablus and Caesarea) were both Templar castles.
53 It may be that part of this altercation is missing from the text.
54 For this battle, see doc. 3.

back one of his sergeants post haste on horseback and had him proclaim in Nazareth that all those who could bear arms should come after him for booty, for they would defeat the Saracens. So the people came out from Nazareth, all who could go, and they ran until they came to where the battle had been. There they found the Christians dead and defeated, and the Saracens bore down upon them and took them all. After the Saracens had defeated and killed the Christians, they took the heads of the Christian knights and attached them to the points of their lances, and they led the prisoners bound, and so passed before Tiberias. When the people of Tiberias realized that the Christians had been vanquished and that the Saracens were carrying their heads on their lances and that they had the others captive and bound, they grieved greatly for they recognized the heads of their friends and the others who were being taken away into captivity. They were so grief-stricken that they came close to killing themselves. So Saladin's son crossed the river at sunset and duly kept his promise to the count of Tripoli. They did no damage in any castle, town or house, only to those whom they encountered on the field of battle. This battle was on a Friday, the day being the feast of Saint Philip and Saint James, 1 May. It had come about because of the caravan that Prince Reynald had taken in the land of Kerak, and it was the beginning of the loss of the kingdom.

27   Balian was at Nablus, and at nightfall he left to follow the masters of the Temple and Hospital as he had promised. When he had gone two miles he came to a city called Sebastea. He remembered that it was an important festival and decided not to go on until he had heard Mass. So he turned aside to the house of the bishop and got him up and they talked together until the watchman announced the day. Then the bishop had his chaplain vested and had him sing Mass.

When Balian had heard Mass he set off at great speed after the master of the Temple and travelled until he came to the castle of La Fève. Outside the castle he found pitched the tents of the convent, but there was no one there. He was very surprised to find no one who could tell him what had happened.[55] Then he had his squire enter the castle to see whether he could find someone to let him know what was going on. The squire went and called out in the castle, but he did not find anyone who could give him the news he sought except two sick people who were lying in a room and they did not know anything. So he reported that he had found no one who could tell him what was happening. Balian told him to remount and ride behind him and so they continued towards Nazareth.

---

55 One group of manuscripts of the *Chronique d'Ernoul* (p. 149) adds here that the squire 'was called Ernoul (or Ernous); it was he who first put this tale into writing'.

When they were a short distance from the castle, a brother of the Temple came out on horseback and called to them to wait, and so they waited until he came up to them. Balian of Ibelin asked him what the news was, and he said, 'It's bad.' He then told them how the master of the Hospital had had his head cut off, how of all the brothers of the Temple only four, the master and three others, had escaped, and how the knights whom the king had left to garrison Nazareth were all captured. When Balian heard this he was very distressed, and called one of his sergeants and sent him back to Nablus to his wife the queen to bring her the news and tell her to order all his knights at Nablus to come to him at Nazareth that night.[56] Then he met the squires who had escaped the defeat with the Templar knights' baggage. And you must know in truth that if Balian had not turned aside at Sebastea to hear Mass, he would have arrived easily in time for the battle.

When Balian came to Nazareth there was great sorrow in the city for those who had been killed or taken in the battle, for there were few families that had not had someone killed or taken. There he found the master of the Temple who had escaped. Balian stayed and waited until his knights came from Nablus, for he dared not go on until his knights had arrived. Then he sent word to Tiberias to tell the count that he was at Nazareth. When the count of Tripoli heard that Balian had not been in the battle he was very glad, and the next day he sent as many as 50 knights to escort him.

28   When Balian had found the master of the Temple at Nazareth, he asked him what had happened in the battle. He told him that they had acquitted themselves well, and the Christians had killed many of the Saracens but had then been defeated when an ambush that they had laid in a mountain cut them off. Then they decided to send to the battlefield so that the bodies of the knights might be buried. They requisitioned all the packhorses of the city and put them to work carrying the corpses to Nazareth for burial.

The next day Balian, the archbishop of Tyre and the master of the Temple started off for Tiberias. When they had come outside the city, the master of the Temple went back because he could not ride, so painful and grievous were the wounds he had received in the battle the day before. But Balian and the archbishop of Tyre went on to Tiberias. The count learned that they were coming and went to meet them, very sorrowful and greatly angered at the events of the day before, and all because of the pride of the master of the Temple. When the count met the envoys he greeted them with great honour and took them to his lodging. At that point Reynald of Sidon arrived. While the envoys were at the castle with the count, they

---

56   Balian had married Maria Comnena, the widow of King Amaury, in 1177.

told him their mission. The count then said that he was much grieved and shamed by what had happened, and whatever they might decide among themselves he would do, for he well knew that they would not counsel him ill. They told him that he should expel the Saracens from his city and then come with them to the king; just as he had left it up to the three of them to arrange terms, so too had the king. Then they sent a messenger post haste to tell the king that they would be bringing the count with them.

When the king heard that the count of Tripoli was coming to him he was very glad, for he had been very sorrowful at the loss suffered by the Templars. So he left Jerusalem and went out to meet the count of Tripoli, and they met outside a castle that is called Saint Job, for it was said in the country that Job had lived there and that it had been his dwelling place.[57] As soon as the king saw the count he got off his horse and went to greet him. When the count saw that the king was coming to him on foot, he too dismounted and went to him. As the king was approaching, the count fell on his knees before him. The king raised him up and threw his arms around his neck and embraced and kissed him. Then they went back to Nablus and lodged there. The king apologized to the count for many things - for his coronation and other deeds that you have heard tell of already. Then the count said to him that if he would act on his advice his kingdom would be secure and stable and well governed; but factiousness and envy which would lead them to hate what they should love would prevent the king from doing anything that he advised.

After this they left Nablus and went to Jerusalem where they were received by a big procession, and that day the people had a grand celebration to mark the peace between the king and the count. There the count took his leave of the king. The king ordered him to assemble his host and muster it at the Springs of Saffuriya,[58] for he was well aware that Saladin was massing his men to enter the land. The count advised him to send to the prince of Antioch for help especially as he had lost his knights and the convent of the Temple and the master of the Hospital. The king did as the count advised, while the count went to Saffuriya and brought together his host. The prince of Antioch dispatched Raymond, his eldest son, with 50 knights.

Then the king sent to the patriarch in Jerusalem telling him to bring the Holy Cross. So he brought it forth from Jerusalem and entrusted it to the prior of the Sepulchre, instructing him to carry it in the host with the king, for he had an excuse and could not go. It was most unfortunate that it accompanied the host, for the prophecy spoken by the archbishop of Tyre when they elected Eraclius to be patriarch came true: an Eraclius had won the True Cross in Persia and had taken it back to Jerusalem, and an

---

57 A Hospitaller property between Nablus and La Fève.
58 In Galilee, a short distance north of Nazareth.

Eraclius would take it out and it would be lost in his time.[59] From that moment when Eraclius took the cross out of Jerusalem it has never been back, for it was lost in the battle as you will hear. When the Holy Cross was with the king and his host, the master of the Temple came and advised the king to send throughout all the land announcing that all who would take his pay should come to him and would be given good wages, and he would let the king have the money in the house of the Temple that belonged to King Henry.

29 When King Henry of England had had Saint Thomas of Canterbury martyred, he realized that he had done wrong and decided to go overseas and do so much good in the service of God that he would reconcile himself to Him for this and other crimes. So it was that after Saint Thomas had been martyred, he would send each year in the passage[60] great wealth to be placed in the treasury of the houses of the Temple and Hospital in Jerusalem. He intended that when he arrived he would find a great store with which he could aid and succour the land. The master of the Temple gave the money that he had to King Guy, saying that he wanted him to lead as many men as could be mustered against the Saracens so as to fight against them and avenge the shame and loss that they had inflicted on him and on Christendom. The king took the money from the Temple and hired knights and sergeants so that he had at least 1,200 knights and 30,000 other men.[61]

The count of Tripoli asked leave to go and to put Tiberias in a state of readiness, for he had heard truly that the sultan Saladin had assembled 180,000 mounted men and was now intending to engage the king in the greatest wager of battle he had ever had, especially now that he had heard that the count of Tripoli was reconciled with him. The king agreed that the count should go and fortify Tiberias. He provided those inside with arms and provisions and ordered his wife and his officers to take to the boats and protect themselves on the sea if they saw that Saladin's forces were so great that they could not defend themselves, and he would soon come to their aid.

30 Then the king went from Jerusalem to Acre and the count came by a different route from Tiberias. When they had arrived in Acre, a messenger

---

59 See below, para. 37.

60 The twice yearly sailing to the East.

61 Thomas Becket had been martyred in Canterbury cathedral in 1170. For King Henry II's treasury, see H.E. Mayer, 'Henry II of England and the Holy Land', *English Historical Review*, 97 (1982); C. Tyerman, *England and the Crusades, 1095-1588* (Chicago and London, 1988), pp. 45-8, 54-6.

came hurriedly from Tiberias, from the countess, and informed the king that Saladin had entered the kingdom and had besieged Tiberias with a great force of men. She was very frightened and distressed. The king immediately ordered the knights and barons to be summoned to take counsel concerning the news he had received. When they were assembled in *parlement* the king asked for the aid and counsel of the vassals and of all those who were there. The master of the Temple and Prince Reynald and many others counselled the king to go and chase Saladin out of the kingdom at the first opportunity: he was in the early days of his kingship, and, if he let himself appear as a fool in the eyes the Saracens, Saladin would take advantage of him, and thereafter he would not be able to hold out against him but would lose the kingdom.

When they had finished speaking the king then asked the count of Tripoli for his counsel and advice, and the count, having heard those who were there, said, 'Sire, I counsel and urge you to have your cities and castles provided with food, men and armour and other equipment. Even though the prince of Antioch has sent you his son, send to him again, and tell Baldwin of Ibelin how Saladin has entered the kingdom in great strength and that they should come to the aid of the kingdom. I know that Saladin will enter at Gor. You know that we are in the height of the summer, in the hottest part of the year. The strength of the place and the heat will assail them, and by then the prince and Baldwin will have come. When Saladin makes his departure we shall be ready and shall fall on the rearguard of his host and inflict so great a loss on them that, if it please God, we and the kingdom of Jerusalem will remain in peace.'

31   When the count of Tripoli had finished speaking, the master of the Temple and Prince Reynald said to the count that his counsel was not good and was 'mingled with the hair of the wolf'.[62] On hearing this the count turned to the king and said, 'Sire, I require and summon you to go to the aid of Tiberias.' The master of the Temple and Prince Reynald answered that the king would go willingly. As soon as they were ready, the king and all the knights of the kingdom of Jerusalem left the city of Acre and went to camp at the Springs of Saffuriya. There the king had the muster taken a second time and found that he had so many knights and other men on foot or on horseback that they numbered more than 40,000. It was because the Holy Cross had been brought from Jerusalem to be carried in the host that he had so many men there. The king trusted more in his own power and in his men than in the virtue of Jesus Christ and the Holy Cross, and because of this things went ill for him later.

---

62   Evidently a popular saying denoting duplicity.

32   After he had had the muster taken, he wanted to take counsel with his men once more. Again he sent word to the count of Tripoli to give him counsel and advice. The count answered wisely and said, 'Sire, you should know that Tiberias is mine, and any damage done there falls on me and on no one else. For the lady of Tiberias, my wife, and her children are in the castle, and the last thing I would want is for any harm to come to them. I have sent provisions and advised them that, if they find that Saladin's forces are so great that they cannot resist them, they should take to the sea until we can rescue them. In view of this, Sire, if you intend to fight Saladin, let us go and camp before Acre and let us be near our fortresses. I know Saladin to be so proud and so presumptuous that he will not leave the kingdom until he has attacked you in battle. If he comes to fight you near Acre and it turns out badly for us - may God protect us from this - we can withdraw to Acre and the other cities that are nearby. But if God gives us the victory so that we defeat him and force him back to his own land, we shall have so reduced and shattered him that he will never be able to recover.'

When the count had finished speaking the master of the Temple said to him, 'Again this is the hair of the wolf.' On hearing this the count immediately said to the king, 'Sire, I summon and require that you go to relieve Tiberias.' He replied that he would go willingly. Meanwhile the countess of Tiberias had sent a messenger to the king calling on him to aid her, for she and her men were hard pressed. On hearing this news a cry went up among the knights in the host: 'Let us go and rescue the ladies and maidens of Tiberias!'

33   Now we shall leave off speaking of the king and the knights who were encamped at the Springs of Saffuriya and explain the ill-feeling and hostility between the master of the Temple, Brother Gerard of Ridefort, and the count of Tripoli. When the master of the Temple first came to the land of Jerusalem he was a lay knight, and on several occasions King Amaury and the count employed him as a mercenary. The count promised to give him the first good marriage that should fall within his patronage. He did not have long to wait before William Dorel, the lord of Botron, died. He had been married to Stephany, the daughter of Henry Le Bufle whom Hugh of Jubail married after William's death and by whom he had Guy of Jubail. William had had a daughter by his first wife. After his death a rich Pisan named Plivain came to the land bringing with him great wealth. He asked the count of Tripoli for this maiden, who was the heiress to Botron, to be his wife. Although the count had promised her to Gerard of Ridefort, he preferred to give her to Plivain rather than to Gerard because Plivain had given him a lot of money in return for this marriage. It was said that he put the maiden on a balance with gold on the other side, and that the gold she weighed, and more, was given to the count; in exchange for this great sum the count granted her to Plivain.[63]

When Gerard of Ridefort saw that the count had refused him this marriage, he was extremely angry because, as he said, the count had given her to a peasant (*vilain*).[64] For the men of France hold those of Italy in scorn. However rich a man may be, he will not be so noble that they will not regard him as a peasant, since most of the men of Italy are usurers, corsairs, merchants or seafarers, and because the men of France are knights they treat them with contempt. Then Gerard insulted the count of Tripoli and angrily left him and went to Jerusalem. There he fell ill and in consequence entered the house of the Temple. Not long afterwards Brother Arnold of Torroja who had been master of the Temple died, and the brothers of the Order elected Brother Gerard of Ridefort as his successor.[65] When he attended the coronation of King Guy and the queen placed the crown on her husband's head, the master assisted her. Once it was set in place, he said, 'This crown is well worth Botron'.[66] Such was the origin of the hatred that existed between the master of the Temple, Brother Gerard of Ridefort, and the count of Tripoli.

34 After these altercations the king called the count of Tripoli and the barons and the master of the Temple to come to him at evening and asked their advice. The count of Tripoli counselled the king not to move from the springs but to stay put and keep his camp there, for Saladin had too great an army and the king did not have enough men to oppose him and drive him from Tiberias: if Saladin destroyed Tiberias he would bear the full cost. The king and the barons who were present were happy to take the count's advice and stay where they were.

When night fell the master of the Temple went to the king and said, 'Sire, do not trust the advice of the count for he is a traitor, and you well know that he has no love for you and wants you to be put to shame and lose the kingdom. I advise you to move off immediately together with the rest of us, and let us go and defeat Saladin. This is the first crisis that you have encountered since you became king. If you do not leave this camp, Saladin will come to attack you, and if you withdraw at his attack the

---

63 Botron was a lordship in the county of Tripoli between Jubail and Tripoli itself. William Dorel is last known to have been alive in 1174; Plivain was Raymond of Tripoli's vassal by 1179 and lord of Botron by 1181. Henry Le Bufle, an important lord in Jerusalem, had died before 1171; Hugh (III) lord of Jubail flourished 1177-86 and his son, Guy (I), 1186-1233.

64 A play on words in the original.

65 Arnold died in 1184. For Gerard's rise to prominence, see M. Barber, *The New Knighthood: A History of the Order of the Temple* (Cambridge, 1994), pp. 109-10.

66 Above, para. 18.

shame and reproach will be all the greater for you.' The king commanded the host to start off.

When the barons of his host heard that the king was commanding them to move they were amazed. They said to the king, 'Sire, our advice was that we should all stay put and remain here at least for tonight. By whose counsel are you making the host set off?' To this he replied, 'You have no right to ask me by whose counsel I am doing this. I want you to get on your horses and leave here and head towards Tiberias.' They, as good and loyal vassals, obeyed the king and did as he ordered. Maybe if they had countermanded the order that he had given it would have been better for Christendom.

I must tell you about a miracle that happened in the host. During the previous day and on the night they set out from the Springs of Saffuriya the horses of the Christian host showed no desire to drink nor to taste water despite the great heat, but acted like sad and sorrowing men. Then on the morrow they began to fail their masters in the heat of the day and falter and die under them.

35 I must tell you about an incident involving the men of the host, even though it seems foolish and the Holy Church has forbidden people to believe it. When the host had left the Springs of Saffuriya and had passed two leagues beyond Nazareth, some sergeants in the host found an old Saracen woman riding on a donkey. They thought she was a slave fleeing from her lord and detained her. Some of them knew she was from Nazareth. They asked her where she was going at that hour, but she was unable to give them an adequate reply. So they threatened and tortured her, and she admitted that she was the slave of a Syrian of Nazareth. Then they asked where she was going. She told them that she was going to Saladin to collect the reward for the service she had done him. They tortured her further to discover what this service was. She revealed that she was a sorceress and had cast a spell on the men of the host; for two nights she had encircled them and had cast her spells by the devil; had they stayed and not moved from the camp she would have bound them so strongly by the devil's art that Saladin would have taken every one of them and no one would have escaped. She told them that things would go badly for them and that few of them would survive. It was indeed true that few knights escaped and avoided being killed or taken. The men who had found her asked, 'Can you free the host from this spell by which you have bound it?' She replied that she could, but only if they returned to the camp from where they had started. They regarded this as a lie since she was a Saracen and had admitted to being a sorceress. Then they collected brushwood and dry grass and made a big fire and pushed her on it. Twice or three times she jumped out of the fire. There was a sergeant there with a Danish axe, and he struck her on her head and split it in two. Then they threw her on the fire and she was burnt. Saladin came to hear of it and was very sorry; he would have rewarded her richly had she not been burnt.

36   No one should wonder at this tale for we find written in the Fourth Book of Moses that, when the Children of Israel had crossed the desert of Sinai and entered the land of Moab which we nowadays call the land of Kerak and Montreal, the king of that land was called Balak. Because of the fear he had of the Children of Israel in the light of what they had done to the other people of that land who were his neighbours, he sent his men and entrusted them with great wealth and commanded them to go to Balaam the sorcerer who was beyond the river Euphrates in the land of Edessa; they were to give him this wealth and promise him far more if he would come to curse and cast a spell on the Children of Israel so that they could not cause him any trouble.

The envoys came to him and gave him their message and the gift. He agreed to come with them. That night he made an offering to the devil as was his wont. It was told him in a vision that he should go and that he should be careful not to curse the Children of Israel. However, as he was going on his way, he turned against the command that God had given him and decided he would curse them. Our Lord sent his angel with a drawn sword to meet him on the road along which he was travelling. His ass saw the angel and the drawn sword and took fright and bolted off the road into a field. Balaam started beating the ass and returned to the road. When he was back on the road he came to a narrow place between two vineyard walls, and the angel again came before him with a drawn sword. The ass was so frightened that she threw off her wicked master, and he hurt his foot in the fall. While the ass was cowering and he was hitting her, Our Lord opened the ass's mouth and had her speak to Balaam and say, 'Sire, am I not still your ass on which you are used to ride? Why do you hit me?' He said to her, 'If I had a sword I would gladly kill you.' At these words Our Lord opened his eyes and he saw the angel and immediately worshipped him. Then the angel said to him, 'Your road is against me.' 'Sire, I will turn back if you like.' The angel said to him, 'No, I want you to go on, but you must see to it that you do not curse the Children of Israel.'

Balak received him honourably and took him to a high mountain from which he could see the Children of Israel the better to curse them. When he arrived he said to Balak, 'How can I curse those whom God has blessed?'. Then he spoke his prophecy of Our Lady Saint Mary and the nativity of Jesus Christ: 'A star shall be born of Jacob and a man of Israel shall rise up and strike and destroy the captains of Moab.'[67] Since he could not conquer the Children of Israel by his curses and sorceries, he advised him to chose the most beautiful maidens in all his land and give them each a quantity of wine and send them to the camp, for the Children of Israel were tired and weary. They would see the beauty of the young girls and would want to lie with them and drink their wine. 'And so they will sin and anger God and God will be angry with them. But if they throw them out so that they return to you, you may know that they will destroy you.' The Children of Israel kept the young girls and lay with them and drank their wine. No one should wonder that the land of Jerusalem was lost, for they committed so much sin in Jerusalem that Our Lord was extremely angry. They did service to the devil in return for which he deceived them by putting hatred between them so that the kingdom was destroyed.

37   Now we shall tell you about the election of the patriarch Eraclius who had been archbishop of Caesarea.[68] When the patriarch Amaury was dead, William, archbishop of Tyre, a very good man who both feared and loved God greatly, went to the canons of the Sepulchre and spoke to them and won some of them over, saying, 'Sirs, God has taken our father, the patriarch, to himself, and you are about to make the election. I advise you in good faith not to elect any prelate who is from this side of the sea. For you could elect such a man that you could be grieved and the kingdom would suffer, for it would be between me and Eraclius, archbishop of Caesarea. If you elect him and present him to the king, the king will accept him willingly, for his mother loves him greatly and you know how she had him made archbishop of Caesarea. You know what the manner of his life is like as well as I do. If you want to elect a wise man from overseas, I and the other prelates in the kingdom will be willing to advise you, and if you are worried about the expenses, we will gladly bear them for you. This is why I am speaking these words to you and giving you this advice: I have found in a book that an Eraclius brought the Cross from Persia and placed it in Jerusalem and an Eraclius will take it from

---

67   Thus far we have a summary of the story of Balaam more or less as found in Numbers 22-4 (the quotation here is derived from Numbers 24 v. 17). What follows is not in the biblical account, but was recorded by Josephus and was current in both Rabbinic and Islamic tradition.

68   These events relate to the year 1180. Paras. 37-9 would appear to have been moved from their original location in the narrative for that period. Amaury of Nesle was patriarch 1158-80; William, the celebrated historian, was archbishop of Tyre 1175-c.1184; Eraclius was archdeacon of Jerusalem by 1169 and became archbishop of Caesarea in 1175. See P.W. Edbury and J.G. Rowe, 'William of Tyre and the Patriarchal Election of 1180', *English Historical Review*, 93 (1978).

Jerusalem and in his time it will be lost.[69] Because of this I want you to take my advice.'

The canons of the Sepulchre agreed with him. The archbishop left them and they went to their chapter meeting. The king's mother had already entreated them to elect Eraclius. When they were in the chapter meeting, they departed from the archbishop of Tyre's advice. Some of them there she had corrupted, and as a result they elected William, archbishop of Tyre, and Eraclius, archbishop of Caesarea, as patriarch and presented them both to the king. The king received them favourably, and his mother begged him to accept Eraclius as patriarch. He granted his mother's wish and agreed to the election they had made.

Some people say that the king of Jerusalem has this prerogative in the election of the patriarch, that when the canons of the Sepulchre have elected a patriarch they must present him to the king (for confirmation). If they have elected someone at vespers, they present him to the king, and the king can delay replying until the next day at the hour of prime; if they elect at the hour of prime, they present him to the king, and he should reply at vespers. This is the right which it is said the king should have in the election of the patriarch of Jerusalem, but I have never found or heard tell of it and because of this I do not want to say whether it is correct. If the king has this privilege, he should be well able to prove it when the need arises. It is said, and it is found in Holy Scripture, that when the apostles were staying on Mount Zion after Pentecost and after the death of Judas they chose two men; one was called Joseph the Just and the other Matthias, and they threw lots and the lot fell upon Matthias.[70] Because of this some people would say that the canons of the Sepulchre represent the apostles and the king the lots; they elect and the king chooses.

38 We shall now tell what Eraclius's life was like both before and after he became patriarch. He had little sense and had only a smattering of learning but was handsome in his appearance. He was extremely dissolute and intent only on wallowing in luxury. Agnes, the mother of the Leper King, loved him excessively, and because of the great love she had for him she made him archdeacon of Jerusalem, then archbishop of Caesarea and finally, as has been described, patriarch. The patriarch took as his mistress a woman named Pasque de Riveri. She was the wife of a draper of Nablus, which is 24 miles distant from Jerusalem. He often had her come to Jerusalem, and she would stay with him for 15 days or more. He gave her and her husband so much that he made them rich, and because of this her husband let him have his way with her. Not long afterwards the

---

69   The allusion is to Heraklios, the Byzantine emperor (610-40) who recovered the Cross from the Persians. William of Tyre's history opens with this incident.

70   Acts 1 vv. 23-6. The election of Matthias was before, not after, Pentecost.

43

draper died. The patriarch took his wife to be with him all the time and bought her property and had precious stones cut for her. She went about in the city of Jerusalem so richly that any stranger would have imagined her to be a countess or baroness, so much gold, precious stones, cloth of gold and pearls did she have to adorn her body. People who knew her would say as she passed, 'Look! There goes the patriarchess!'

39 On one occasion the patriarch and the king and the barons of the kingdom were holding a *parlement* at the patriarch's palace to attend to the needs of the land. Lo and behold, a servant came in to the place where these lords were assembled and shouted, 'Sir patriarch, I bring you good news; if you will give me a good reward, I will tell it you.' The patriarch and the king and the others who were gathered there thought he was going to relay news of some benefit for Christendom, since it was normal when any good tidings came to Jerusalem for him to go and tell the patriarch. So the patriarch said to him, 'Wretch, tell us your news, but only if it is good!' 'Lady Pasque de Riveri has given birth to a daughter.' The patriarch answered, 'Shut up you fool, say no more.' It was because the archbishop of Tyre knew about his life that he made that request to the canons of the Sepulchre of which you have already heard. But they did the opposite of what he had asked, for Our Lord had allowed it to happen because of the sins of the men of Jerusalem.

After Eraclius had become patriarch, he was on Mount Zion on Maundy Thursday to make the chrism, and there he excommunicated the archbishop of Tyre without prior warning and without right to appeal before him to obtain justice. The archbishop therefore appealed to Rome, and he should have gone to answer for his faith before Pope Alexander and the council he was holding. He was preparing to go, but the patriarch hired a physician and gave him a large sum of money to go with Archbishop William and poison him. The physician did what was asked and poisoned the archbishop.

The patriarch crossed the sea and went to Marseilles and from Marseilles he journeyed to Gévaudan, his homeland. When he heard that Archbishop William was dead, he returned and went to Jerusalem and his life was worse than before.[71] So all the laity and clergy had the bad example of the life of an evil leader. Because of the sin of those who lived in the kingdom of Jerusalem, Our Lord was greatly angered and cleansed His land of sin and of those who had committed it. And so it happened

---

71 This blackening of Eraclius's character has been challenged by B.Z. Kedar, 'The Patriarch Eraclius' in *Outremer*, pp. 177-204. The story of excommunicating and then poisoning Archbishop William is almost certainly fictitious. For a discussion, see P.W. Edbury and J.G. Rowe, *William of Tyre: Historian of the Latin East* (Cambridge, 1988), pp. 20-2.

that when Saladin took Jerusalem he found in the city two aged men; one was called Robert of Coudre who had been with Godfrey of Bouillon at the conquest, and the other was Fouchier Fiole who was born in Jerusalem just after it was conquered. Saladin found these two in Jerusalem and because they were elderly he had pity on them. They asked him to let them stay and finish their lives in the city of Jerusalem. He willingly agreed and ordered that they should be given their requirements for as long as they should live. So they lived out their lives.

40   Now I shall tell you about King Guy and his host. They left the Springs of Saffuriya to go to the relief of Tiberias. As soon as they had left the water behind, Saladin came before them and ordered his skirmishers to harass them from morning to midday. The heat was so great that they could not go on so as to reach water. The king and all his men were too spread out and did not know what to do. They could not turn back for the losses would have been too great. He sent to the count of Tripoli, who led the vanguard, to ask his advice. The message came back that he should pitch his tent and make camp. The king gladly accepted this bad advice, though when he gave him good advice he would never take it. Some people in the host said that if the Christians had pressed on to meet the Saracens, Saladin would have been defeated.[72]

41   As soon as they had made camp, Saladin ordered his men to collect brushwood, dry grass, stubble and anything else that could be used to light fires, and to make palisades all round the Christian host. This command was carried out in full. Early next morning he ordered the fires to be lit. This was quickly done. The fires burned vigorously and made an enormous amount of smoke, and this, in addition to the heat of the sun, caused the Christians considerable discomfort and harm. Saladin had commanded caravans of camels loaded with water from the Sea of Tiberias to be brought up and had the water jars positioned near the camp. They were then emptied in the sight of the Christians with the result that they and their horses suffered even greater anguish through thirst.

A strange thing had happened in the Christian host the day they had been encamped at the Springs of Saffuriya, for the horses refused to drink the water either at night or in the morning, and because of their thirst they were to fail their masters when they most needed them.[73]

Then a knight named Geoffrey of Franclieu went to the king and said, 'Sire, now is the time for you to make the *polains* with their beards dear to the men of your country.' One of the causes of the hatred between King

---

72   For other accounts of the battle of Hattin, see below, docs. 4a–b.
73   Repeated from para. 34.

Guy and his Poitevins and the people of this land was that when he became king the Poitevins sang a song in Jerusalem which greatly incensed the men of the kingdom. The song went:

> Maugré li Polein,
> Avrons nous roi Poitevin.

This hatred and scorn gave rise to the loss of the kingdom of Jerusalem.[74]

42   When the fires were lit and the smoke was great, the Saracens surrounded the host and shot their darts through the smoke, thus wounding and killing men and horses. When the king saw the torments that were afflicting his army, he called the master of the Temple and Prince Reynald and asked their advice. They counselled him to join battle with the Saracens. He ordered his brother Aimery, who was the constable, to organize the divisions.[75] He did as best he could. The count of Tripoli, who had led the vanguard at their arrival, led the first division and was out in front. In his division he had Raymond, the son of the prince of Antioch, with all his company and the four sons of the lady of Tiberias, Hugh, William, Ralph and Oste.[76] Balian of Ibelin and Count Joscelin made up the rearguard. Just as the divisions were being drawn up and the battle lines made ready, five knights from the count of Tripoli's division deserted and went to Saladin and said, 'Sir, what are you waiting for? Go and take the Christians for they are all defeated.' When he heard these words he ordered his men to advance, and they started off and drew near to the Christians.

When the king saw that Saladin was coming against him, he ordered the count of Tripoli to charge. It is a right belonging to the barons of the kingdom that, when the whole army is in their lordship, the baron on whose land the battle is to take place leads the first division and is out in front: on entering his land he leads the vanguard and on leaving leads the rearguard. Accordingly, since Tiberias was his, the count of Tripoli took the forward position. The count and his division charged at a large squadron of Saracens. The Saracens parted and opened a way through and let them pass. Then, when they were in their midst, they closed in on

---

74   'Despite the *polains*, we shall have a Poitevin king.' This passage provides clear evidence for antipathy between the Poitevins in Guy's household and the *polains*, the second or third generation Frankish settlers in the East. See M.R. Morgan, 'The Meanings of Old French *polain*, Latin *pullanus*', *Medium Aevum*, 48 (1979), pp. 40-54. Geoffrey of Franclieu is otherwise unknown, but men with this surname can be found in the kingdom of Jerusalem as early as 1129.

75   Aimery of Lusignan, the future king of Jerusalem (1197-1205) and first king of Cyprus (1196-1205), had been constable of Jerusalem since about 1181.

76   Hugh, William, Ralph and Oste were Raymond's stepsons, his wife's children by her marriage to Walter of Falconberg.

them. Only ten or twelve knights from the count's division escaped. Among them were the count of Tripoli himself and Raymond, the son of the prince of Antioch, and the four sons of the lady of Tiberias. When the count saw that they were defeated, he did not dare go to Tiberias which was only two miles away, for he feared that if he shut himself up in there and Saladin found out, he would come and take him. He went off with such company as he had and came to the city of Tyre.

After this division had been defeated the anger of God was so great against the Christian host because of their sins that Saladin vanquished them quickly: between the hours of terce and nones[77] he won the entire field. He captured the king, the master of the Temple, Prince Reynald, the marquis William, Aimery the constable, Humphrey of Toron, Hugh of Jubail, Plivain lord of Botron, and so many other barons and knights that it would take too long to give the names of all of them. The Holy Cross also was lost.

Later, in the time of Count Henry,[78] a brother of the Temple came to him and said that he had been at the great defeat and had buried the Holy Cross and knew where it was; if he could have an escort he would go and look for it. Count Henry gave him an escort and his permission to go. They went secretly and dug for three nights but could not find anything. Then he went back to the city of Acre.

This disaster befell Christendom at a place called the Horns of Hattin, four miles from Tiberias on Saturday 4 July 1187, the feast of Saint Martin *Calidus*. Pope Urban III was governing the Apostolic See of the Church of Rome, Frederick was emperor in Germany, Philip son of Louis was king of France, Henry *au Cort Mantiau* was king of England, and Isaac was emperor in Constantinople.[79] The news of it struck the hearts of those faithful to Jesus Christ. Pope Urban who was at Ferrara died of grief when he heard the news. After him was Gregory VIII, a man of saintly life, who held the papal see for two months before he too died and went to God. After Gregory came Clement III to whom Archbishop Joscius of Tyre brought a truthful account of the news as you will find written below.[80]

43　　Saladin had left the field rejoicing at his great victory and was in his camp. There he ordered all the Christian prisoners who had been taken

---

77　About 9.00 a.m. to 3.00 p.m.

78　Henry of Champagne, ruler of the remaining portion of the kingdom of Jerusalem 1192-97.

79　Pope Urban III (1185-87); Frederick Barbarossa (1152-90); Philip II Augustus (1180-1223); Henry II (1154-89); Isaac II Angelos (1185-95).

80　Gregory VIII (October-December 1187); Clement III (1187-91). For Archbishop Joscius's embassy, see below, paras. 72, 74.

that day to be brought before him. First they brought the king, the master of the Temple, Prince Reynald, William the marquis, Humphrey of Toron, Aimery the constable, Hugh of Jubail and several other knights. When he saw them all lined up in front of him, he told the king that he would have great satisfaction and would be held in great honour now that he had in his power prisoners as valuable as the king of Jerusalem, the master of the Temple and the other barons.

Then he ordered that syrup diluted with water be brought in a gold cup. He tasted it and gave it to the king to drink and said, 'Drink deeply.' The king, who was extremely thirsty, drank and handed the cup to Prince Reynald. Prince Reynald would not drink. When Saladin saw that he had handed the cup to Prince Reynald he was angered and said to him, 'Drink, for you will never drink again.' The prince answered that if it pleased God he would never drink or eat anything of his. Saladin asked, 'Prince Reynald, by your law, if you held me in your prison as I now hold you in mine, what would you do to me?' He replied, 'So help me God, I would cut off your head.' Saladin was greatly enraged at this most insolent reply and said, 'Pig, you are my prisoner and yet you answer me so arrogantly.' He took a sword in his hand and thrust it right through his body. The mamluks who were standing nearby rushed at him and cut off his head. Saladin took some of his blood and sprinkled it on his own head in recognition that he had taken vengeance. Then he ordered that Reynald's head be brought to Damascus, and there it was dragged along the ground to show the Saracens whom the prince had wronged that vengeance had been exacted.

44   Saladin had the king and the other prisoners led off to Damascus where they were held in prison in accordance with their rank. When the lady of Tiberias heard that the king was taken and the Christians defeated, she assumed that her husband and her children had been lost. She sent word to Saladin that she would surrender Tiberias if he would give her a safe-conduct to go to Tripoli. Saladin willingly agreed, and he immediately ordered the town to be occupied and had the lady and people of Tiberias conducted to safety.

The third day after the battle; Saladin charged an emir named Taqi al-Din who was lord of Hamah and the husband of his sister to hurry to Acre.[81] He set off and just as he was reaching a village called Saffran which is three leagues from Acre, Count Joscelin arrived in the city. Joscelin, who had been governor in Acre, had been in the rearguard and had escaped the defeat with Balian of Ibelin. When he heard that the emir was hastening towards Acre, he called together a group of burgesses and on their advice sent the keys to Taqi al-Din saying that he wanted a safe-

---

81   Taqi al-Din was Saladin's nephew, not his brother-in-law.

conduct and would surrender the city to the sultan if he would conduct the inhabitants and their wives and possessions to safety. The bearer of the keys and of this news was a burgess of Acre called Peter Brice.[82] When the rest of the people heard that Count Joscelin had surrendered the city and had sent the keys to the Saracens, they were all furious and there was almost a major battle between them in the city. They said that they would rather burn the town down than surrender it to the Saracens, and some people actually started fires in the city. With Acre on fire, Taqi al-Din sent news to Saladin that all the kingdom was his and he should come; the men of Acre had surrendered the city, and he had the keys. When Saladin heard this news he was very glad. He immediately started out, only to find on his arrival the fires burning in the city. He told the burgesses that he would show them all the love and courtesy they could want from a safe-conduct if they would put the fires out; those who wanted to remain could stay safe and sound paying the tax which is customary between Christians and Saracens, and he would have those who had no wish to stay taken to safety wherever they preferred to go.

45   On hearing this order, they took counsel together and put out the fires, and Saladin told his officers to take possession of the city and its strongholds. He gave the people of Acre 40 days in which to take away their wives and children and their goods.

After he had secured the city of Acre and had installed his officers and had arranged for the people to be escorted wherever they wanted, Saladin went to besiege Tyre. Balian of Ibelin, who had led the rearguard in the battle, had repaired there. He was acquainted with Saladin and sent to him requesting an escort and safe-conduct to go to Jerusalem to seek his wife and children and household and then go to Tripoli. Saladin replied that he would happily give him an escort and a safe-conduct to Jerusalem on the understanding that he would take an oath on the Christian gospels that he would spend only one night in Jerusalem and would depart the next morning. When he had taken the oath, Saladin had him conducted safely to Jerusalem. His arrival pleased many of the men of Jerusalem, both the patriarch and the inhabitants of the land.

While Balian was in Jerusalem, he held to his oath and was all set to leave the city as he had agreed with Saladin. The citizens went to the patriarch and asked him for God's sake to keep Balian in the city as they had no captain or governor who could help them. The patriarch sent to find Balian and asked him to stay. Balian replied that he had sworn an

---

82   The Brice, Briccii or Brizi were a Venetian burgess family with long associations in Acre. See J. Prawer, *Crusader Institutions* (Oxford, 1980), p. 288; D. Jacoby, 'L'expansion occidentale dans le Levant: les Vénitiens à Acre dans la seconde moitié du treizième siècle', *Journal of Medieval History*, 3 (1977), pp. 240-2.

oath to Saladin and could remain no longer. The patriarch said that he would absolve him from his oath for it would be to the benefit of Christendom. He accepted the patriarch's arguments and had himself absolved from the oath he had made and stayed in Jerusalem. He gave such advice as he could to the best of his ability, and he remained there right up to the time Jerusalem was evacuated.

Meanwhile Saladin had gone to besiege the city of Tyre. But when he got there he found that it was too well provided with men and knights who had escaped the battle and who were now forming the garrison. He saw that there was nothing to be gained there and moved on to take Sidon. Then he took Beirut.[83] Next he went to Jubail, and he brought the lord of Jubail with him before the castle and had him speak to his men so as to secure his release. The men in the castle took counsel and decided they could not hold out. So they surrendered it and thereby obtained their lord's freedom.[84] From there Saladin went on to Tripoli.[85] He found it well defended, and so he passed on further and came to the land of Cilicia. There he took the cities of Jabala and Latakia and the castles of Sahyun and *La Garde*. From there he went and took Baghras and Darbsak and went to besiege a Templar castle called La Roche Guillaume.[86]

In this castle there was a knight named John Gale who had been born in Tyre. This man had fled the kingdom and had gone to the Muslim lands because he had killed his lord. He found his way to Saladin, who entrusted him with teaching his nephew how to bear arms in the Frankish fashion and also courtesy and good manners. While this knight had the young noble in his care, he made up his mind that if he could make his peace and return to Christendom he would gladly do so. Saladin came to the region of Aleppo, bringing the knight and the young man with him, and he left them there. John Gale conducted himself well and honourably. He sent messages to the Templars at the castle of Baghras telling them that if they wanted to buy Saladin's nephew from him he would be happy to sell him to them on the understanding that he could have legal immunity and so return to the kingdom of Jerusalem. The Templars agreed to pay him 14,000 saracen bezants and gave him his immunity. When the deal with the Templars had been struck, he and the young man went off one day by themselves with their hawks. The Templars were lying in wait, and they seized the youth and brought him to the castle.

---

83 Sidon surrendered on 29 July and Beirut on 6 Aug.

84 Hugh, lord of Jubail, had been among those captured at Hattin.

85 No - Saladin turned south after occupying Jubail. See below doc. 5a for an alternative version of events.

86 These fortresses and towns are in the principality of Antioch, not Cilicia. This campaign in northern Syria took place in the summer of 1188 and so the account here is misplaced. See para. 75. The identity of *La Garde* is uncertain; the context suggests that Bourzey (taken by Saladin in August 1188 about a month after Sahyun) might be meant.

46   After Saladin had defeated the Christians and taken the king, both his sister and his brother-in-law, Taqi al-Din, began to urge him to recover their son. Since he was his nephew, Saladin was keen to comply, and that explains why he went to besiege that castle. While he was at the siege, Reynald of Sidon, who had escaped the defeat, arrived in the city of Tyre. He sent a knight to Saladin at the place where he was conducting the siege of La Roche Guillaume saying that he wanted to surrender the city of Tyre and that he should send his banners to place on the castle. When Saladin heard this news he was delighted. He gave the banners to the knight and told him to go ahead and set them up and he would soon come and take possession. The knight departed and brought the banners to Reynald who then made ready to do what he had planned. But God would not allow the city of Tyre to be delivered to the Saracens but wanted instead to save it for the Christians so that they could use it as a base in the future. Reynald of Sidon was afraid to raise the banners over the castle because of the people of the city. He sent his envoy back to Saladin who was still at the siege, saying that he dared not place his banners on the city of Tyre unless he himself should be there, and that if he wished to have the city he should make haste to come. The envoy brought Saladin this message, and as soon as he had heard it he abandoned the siege of La Roche Guillaume and set off.[87]

However, while he was on his way, God sent the marquis Conrad of Montferrat who had long been in Constantinople. He came and took possession of the Tyre and made ready for Saladin's arrival. He expelled Reynald of Sidon from the city and took the banners that he found at the castle and tore them up and threw them out of the castle as a gesture of contempt for Saladin. When Saladin came before Tyre he expected to find that Reynald would deliver it to him. But he found nothing of the sort. Instead he found the city well supplied. So he departed and went to besiege Ascalon.

47   Now I shall tell you about the marquis's arrival. As you have already heard, the marquis Conrad had left his own land to come to the kingdom of Jerusalem as a pilgrim, but he ended up in Constantinople. Isaac, the emperor, gave him his sister to be his wife. But because he had killed Lyvernas, Lyvernas's kin were threatening to kill him. He himself was so valiant that the emperor Alexios[88] greatly feared him and wanted to blind him. His wife found out, and, because she loved him so much, she told him what was going on and begged him to protect himself lest any

---

87   The story of John Gale may be entirely fictitious. Saladin cannot have been at La Roche Guillaume in 1187, and so that element at least in the story is untrue.

88   Repeating the error made at para. 16. At para. 42 it is correctly stated that Isaac II was emperor at the time of Hattin.

harm should befall. The marquis called the knights that he had brought from his land and let them know what his wife had said. He called for their cooperation, instructing them that when he went to greet the emperor they should ask his leave to go to Jerusalem to complete their pilgrimage; irrespective of any gifts or promises the emperor might make, they should on no account agree to remain, for, if they did, he would be in great danger of death or blinding. They undertook to do as he had asked.

The next morning they went to greet the emperor. Once the formalities were over, they requested leave from the marquis to resume their pilgrimage. The marquis implored them to stay, but they refused. The emperor learned from his interpreter that they were asking to be allowed to go. He pleaded with them and promised them great wealth if they would remain for the war that was currently in progress. They replied most insistently that they would not stay. The marquis told the emperor that they had promised and sworn that as soon as they had completed their pilgrimage they would return. The emperor was satisfied with this assurance and gave them leave to go.

There was a ship belonging to some Pisans there, and the emperor ordered them to carry them to Syria. He gave them provisions and paid for the ship. The marquis gave them most of the wealth that he had in Constantinople. While the ship was preparing to set sail, the emperor was at the sea-shore taking his leisure. The marquis saw that it was ready, that the sea was calm and that it was good weather for sailing, so he said to the emperor, 'Sire, I have forgotten one small matter that I want one of my knights to tell my father and nephew.' The emperor replied, 'For God's sake go and tell him.' The marquis got in a small boat and went to the ship. As soon as he was in the ship, he asked the seamen if the weather was good enough to set sail and they said it was. 'Set sail,' he said, 'and for God's sake let's get going'. So they sailed away, and God gave them good weather, and they arrived in Syria outside the city of Acre.[89] Thus did God deliver the marquis from the hands of the Greeks.

48 At that time it was the custom in the city of Acre to ring a bell when any ship came from overseas, and a small boat would go out to the ship. It was some time since any ship had arrived. When the marquis appeared no bell sounded, and so they lowered the ship's boat into the water with some of the most experienced mariners and sent them to the city to find out why they had not heard the bell and what the latest news was. The ship's boat approached the Tower of the Flies, and they asked who the city belonged to. The people in the tower told them that it belonged to Saladin and that they could land in safety relying on Saladin's safe-conduct. They replied that they would not land since the town was in Saracen hands. A renegade

---

89 13 July 1187.

who was on the tower told them, 'Go off to Tyre. There my lord Saladin who has taken your Cross and your king and the whole Christian host will take you.' When the people in the boat heard this, they returned to the ship and told the marquis the news. The marquis was most distressed, and he had them sail away and so they came to Tyre.

When they arrived before Tyre, the Christians in the city were over-joyed because God had sent them a ship at such a moment of crisis. They sent to find out who was on board and were delighted to discover that it was the marquis of Montferrat. A large section of the people of the city went and begged him to land and come to their aid, for unless the city was succoured by God and by him it would be surrendered to the Saracens as soon as he was gone, for Saladin's banners were already in the city. To this the marquis replied, 'Sirs, you tell me that if I go away the city will be delivered to the Saracens and the Christians will lose it. If you will receive me as lord so that the city shall be mine, and if you will swear to me and do homage and agree that after me my heirs shall be the lords of it, I shall land and with the help of God defend it against the Saracens.' The people of Tyre, who had lost hope and who knew that Saladin was coming to take the city and that the king was captured and that Christen-dom was defeated, were very pleased that they had found a captain who dared to take charge of the city and defend it for them. They agreed to all his demands and requests and swore the oaths to him and his heirs just as he had asked.

Then he landed and was received with honour and was taken in a great procession through the city. He was soon put in possession of the city with its castle and fortifications. Reynald of Sidon, who would have surren-dered it to Saladin, did not dare stay but took a boat and fled to Tripoli, leaving the marquis as lord of Tyre.

49   Not long afterwards three Pisan ships full of provisions and men arrived at Tyre, and so the people of the city had greater security. Saladin came to take over the city as Reynald of Sidon had arranged. When he was encamped outside he expected that someone would open the gates to him. But he found himself deceived, for the marquis, as you have heard, had already taken possession. He had discovered the banners in the castle, and he himself took them on to the wall facing Saladin's camp and tore them up and threw them into the moat or ditch as an act of defiance. When Saladin saw him making this defiance and realized that he had failed to gain the city, he sent orders to Damascus to have the marquis William brought to him. On his arrival, he had someone speak to Conrad who was in the city saying that if he would surrender Tyre he would free his father whom he had taken and give him great wealth. Conrad replied that he would not give him even so much as the smallest stone of Tyre in return for his father. 'But tie him to a stake and I shall be the first to shoot at him. For he is too old and is hardly worth anything.' They brought him before the city. The marquis cried out and said, 'Conrad, dear son, guard well the city!' And he took a crossbow in his hand and shot at his father. When Saladin heard that he had shot at his father, he said, 'This man is an unbeliever and very cruel.'

Then he went off and besieged Caesarea and took it and then went on to take Arsur and Jaffa. From there he went to besiege Ascalon. He was not able to capture it as quickly as he had expected because it was strongly fortified. He sent to Damascus and had King Guy brought over. When he arrived at Ascalon he said to him, 'King, if you will surrender the city of Ascalon to me, I shall let you go free.' The king replied that he would speak to his men who were in the city. Saladin agreed and let him go. So he went and called the burgesses of the city, for there were no knights there, and said to them, 'Sirs, Saladin has said that if I will surrender the city to him he will let me go. It would not be right for such a fine city to be surrendered for just one man, so if you think that you can hold Ascalon for the benefit of the Christians and for Christendom do not surrender it. But if you do not think you can hold it, I beg you to surrender it and deliver me from captivity.' The burgesses took counsel among themselves and perceived that they could not hold the city nor expect any help from elsewhere. Had they known that aid could come, they might well have held out. It was their opinion that it would be better to surrender and save their lives than be starved out and taken by force. So they surrendered it to Saladin on the following conditions: they, their wives, children and possessions were to be freed, and Saladin would have them conducted to Christian territory; the king was to nominate ten men who were to be released from captivity.

It is said that he chose the master of the Temple, Aimery the constable who was his brother, and the marshal. He chose nine people of this sort. As the tenth he chose a scribe instead of a knight, and it was regarded as a great wrong and evil that he should leave a knight and choose a Syrian. Saladin undertook to free the king from prison at the beginning of March. Ascalon was surrendered at the beginning of August.[90] When Saladin had possession of Ascalon, he sent the king to Nablus and told the queen that she could go and be with her husband. He did not want her in Jerusalem once he was besieging it. When the queen heard this message she went off to Nablus to be with the king, and she was there when Saladin took Jerusalem.

The day Ascalon was surrendered, some people arrived from Jerusalem at Saladin's summons to see if peace could be made with the men of the city. It was a Friday, and the sun moved in such a way that at the hour of nones it seemed like night. Saladin went to the burgesses of Jerusalem and told them that they should know that he had conquered all the land except

---

90   In fact Ascalon surrendered on 4 Sept. 1187.

for Jerusalem, and that they would do well to surrender it to him. (I forgot to say that the day that Ascalon was surrendered to Saladin, all the surrounding castles also surrendered.) The burgesses replied that if it pleased God they would never surrender the city. 'I tell you now,' said Saladin, 'that you will. I firmly believe that Jerusalem is the house of God, both in your religion and in mine. I shall not lay siege to the house of God nor shall I have siege engines bombard it if I can have it by peaceful agreement. I want this very much, and I will tell you now that I shall make you comply. I shall give you 30,000 bezants as aid to fortify the city of Jerusalem and I shall also give you an area of five miles in any direction around the city within which you can move and work freely. I shall arrange for sufficient foodstuffs to come so that nowhere in all the land will lack provisions thanks to the market that I shall let you have. So you will have a truce from now until Pentecost. If by then you have received aid, you will have defended yourselves against me, but if you do not have any aid then you will hand the city over to me and I shall have you and your possessions escorted out in safety to Christendom.' They replied that if it pleased God they would never surrender that city where God had shed His blood for them to Saracens under such terms. When Saladin saw and heard their answer he swore that he would never accept Jerusalem by treaty but instead would take it by force.

Balian of Ibelin sent to Saladin requesting him to provide an escort and safe-conduct for his wife and children so that he might send them to Tripoli. He told him that he was not able to abide by the agreement he had made, for he was so closely guarded in Jerusalem that he could not leave. Saladin sent him a knight and had his household escorted to Tripoli. He had taken all the kingdom of Jerusalem with the only exception of Tyre, Kerak and Montreal.[91]

50   Saladin left Ascalon one Thursday night and went to besiege Jerusalem.[92] On the Friday morning he laid siege to the walls from the David Gate as far as the Gate of Saint Stephen. Before he had made an assault he told the people of Jerusalem to surrender the city and he would gladly honour the terms he had given them at Ascalon; however, they should know that if they would not surrender the city to him he would begin the attack and would never let them come to terms but would take it by force. For that was his oath. The citizens replied that he could do his worst, but they would never surrender. So Saladin armed his men to attack. The Christians sallied forth and fought with the Saracens. The

---

91   The author has omitted to mention that the Christians still held the castles of Belvoir, Safed and Beaufort. See below, paras. 62, 67-70.

92   For a letter written by the patriarch shortly before the siege began, see below doc. 4c.

battle did not last long as the morning sun got in the Saracens' eyes and they withdrew until the evening; at evening they renewed the assault and they attacked until night. Saladin besieged Jerusalem in this fashion for eight days. On no occasion could the Saracens use their strength to force the Christians back into the city, but each day they confronted them outside the gates until darkness fell. On two or three occasions the Christians pushed the Saracens back to their tents. Not once could the Saracens erect a petrary, mangonel or engine on that side of the city.[93] Now I shall tell you how the Saracens attacked. They made no move until after the hour of nones had passed, but then, when they had the sun at their backs and the Christians were facing into the sun, they attacked until night. The also had skins with which they blew dust into the air so that it flew into the Christians' faces. So the Christians had to contend with both the dust and the sun in their faces.

51   When Saladin realized that he could do no harm to the Christians from that side of the city, he moved his siege operations to the area between Saint Stephen's Gate and the Mount of Olives.[94] So those who were on the Mount of Olives would see all that was done in Jerusalem. The relocation of the siege took place eight days after his arrival outside Jerusalem and meant that no one could come out. Between Saint Stephen's Gate and the Josaphat Gate which was where the siege was concentrated there was no gate or postern through which the defenders could make a sally and attack the Saracens. The only exception was the gate at the 'Madeleine' which permitted access to the space between the two walls.[95]

The same day that Saladin moved from the David Gate to Saint Stephen's Gate he had a petrary erected that threw three times at the city walls. That night he erected several petraries and mangonels so that on the morrow there were eleven large ones, all of them bombarding the walls of the city. In the morning Saladin armed his men and created a shield-wall

---

93   Petraries and mangonels were both forms of traction-lever artillary used for casting rocks. Their precise form is a matter for some dispute. See R. Rogers, *Latin Siege Warfare in the Twelfth Century* (Oxford, 1992), pp. 254-73.

94   25 Sept. 1187. The initial assaults had been from the west or north-west against the defences between the Tower of David and the Damascus Gate (here called Saint Stephen's Gate). The activities have now moved round to the stretch of wall on the northern side of the city between the Damascus Gate and the north-eastern corner. As Joshua Prawer has pointed out ('The Jerusalem the Crusaders Captured: a Contribution to the Medieval Topography of the City' in P.W. Edbury (ed), *Crusade and Settlement* (Cardiff, 1985)) the Christian army of 1099 had employed a similar change of strategy.

95   For the postern at the 'Madeleine', see para. 18. Prawer ('The Jerusalem the Crusaders Captured', pp. 2-3) demonstrated that in front of the main line of walls there was a lower *antemurale*: hence the 'two walls'.

in front of his archers who shot so quickly that it was like rain. There was not a man so brave in the city who dared show a finger above the walls. The Saracens came up to the ditch and set their sappers to work. In two days they had undermined fifteen *toises* of the wall. After they had mined and shored up their tunnel, they put in combustible material and set it on fire with the result that the wall fell outwards into the ditch. The Christians could not dig a countermine against the Saracens for they feared the petraries and the mangonels and the crossbow bolts and could not withstand them.

52 I must not omit to tell you about an act of courtesy of Saladin's during the siege of Jerusalem. When Baldwin of Ibelin left the kingdom he entrusted his own small son who was named Thomassin to the care of his brother Balian. There was also another child called Guillemin, the son of Raymond of Jubail. Both children were in Jerusalem, and when their fathers heard that Saladin was besieging the city, they sent asking him to let their children come to them so that they would not be taken into captivity. When Saladin heard this request he was happy to do what he could to comply. He immediately sent word to Balian, who was governor in Jerusalem, telling him to send him his nephew Thomassin, the son of his brother Baldwin, and Guillemin, the son of Raymond. As soon as Balian received this message he sent them to him most gladly. When the children came before Saladin, he received them honourably as the children of free men, and had them taken off and given robes and jewels and ordered them to be given something to eat. After he had had them clothed and they had eaten, he took them and sat them on his knees, the one on his right and the other on his left, and began to sob. Some of his emirs who were there asked why he was weeping. He said that no one should wonder at it because the things of this world are merely on loan and are then recalled. 'And I shall tell you the reason. For just as I am now disinheriting other men's children, my own will find that after my death they will be disinherited. And I shall say more. For I disinherit the foreigners and those who are against my faith. But my brother Saif al-Din,[96] who should take care of my children after my death, will instead disinherit them.' This was his prophesy, and Saif al-Din later did just that, as remains true to this day.

53 Because of his great desire to gain the city of Jerusalem, Saladin spared no effort in assaulting it vigorously day and night without cease.

---

96 Saif al-Din (died 1218) is more commonly known to historians as al-'Adil. From the late 1190s he and his descendants largely excluded Saladin's own children from power.

Those within were grieved and exhausted. When they realized that they could not defend themselves, the Christians in the city came together and took counsel as to what they should do. They went to the patriarch and Balian of Ibelin and told them that they wanted to sally forth at night and attack the Saracen host, for they would rather die honourably in battle than be captured shamefully in the city. They were well aware that their defence was useless and they could not hold out, but they would rather die where Jesus Christ had suffered death for them than surrender the city to the Saracens. The good knights and burgesses were all in agreement with this proposal, but the patriarch spoke against them: 'Sirs, I think this is a very bad idea. For there is another consideration. If we save ourselves by laying down our lives that we might save them, that in my opinion would not be good. For every man that is in this city, there are 50 women and children. If we are dead, the Saracens will take the women and children. They will not kill them but will make them renounce the faith of Jesus Christ, and they will all be lost to God. But if we can arrange things with Saladin so that we can all get out of the city and go to the Christian-held lands, that would seem better than going out to fight. For we can then save the women and children.' They all came over to this view, and begged Balian of Ibelin to go to Saladin to make whatever peace he could. So he went and spoke with him.

At the very time he was with Saladin, the Saracens made an assault on the city. They brought up ladders up and set them against the walls, and they were able to climb up and plant ten or twelve banners on the top. They had got up in the places where they had been mining. When Saladin saw his men and the banners on the city walls, he said to Balian, 'Why do you seek to surrender the city and make peace? You can see my banners and my people on the walls. It is too late. As you see, the city is mine. And in any case the fakirs and the hadjis and the other Muslim men of religion are pressing and urging me not to give you any terms but to take revenge for those Muslims whom Godfrey slew by shedding the blood of those who were in the streets and even at the Temple in Jerusalem.'[97] While they were talking, Our Lord granted the Christians strength and victory so that the Saracens who were on the walls and ramparts fell off, and the others were chased out of the ditch. Saladin was shamed and saddened, and he told Balian to go back to the city, for he would speak to him no more.

However, in the morning he came back to talk with him, and he was prepared to listen to what he had to say. Balian entreated him, saying, 'Sire, have mercy for the sake of God on both sides in this conflict. For the people of the city are despairing of their lives and would rather kill

---

97 An allusion to the Christian capture of Jerusalem 1099 by the crusaders under Godfrey de Bouillon.

each other than be taken by force. There will be great loss of life on both sides before you can take the city by force as you intend.'

54 I shall now tell you about a Saracen petrary. It struck the hoarding on one of the towers so that the hoarding fell and made an enormous noise. The look-outs on both sides were so frightened that each began to cry, 'Help! Help!' Those within thought that the Saracens had broken into the city, and the Saracens thought that the Christians were attacking them.

Now I shall tell you what the women of Jerusalem did. They brought basins and placed them before Mount Calvary and filled them with cold water. Then they put their children in up to their chins and cut their hair and threw it away. The monks, priests and nuns all went barefoot beneath the walls in a procession with the Holy Cross that belonged to the Syrians carried before them, and the priests carried aloft the Body of Christ. But Our Lord did not deign to hear the prayers or noise that was made in the city. For the stench of adultery, of disgusting extravagance and of sin against nature would not let their prayers rise to God. God was so very angered at that people that He cleansed the city of them. Not a single man or woman remained except for two elderly men who survived hardly any longer.

55 Now we shall leave these iniquities and tell you about Balian of Ibelin who went to Saladin and told him that the Christians of Jerusalem would surrender the city to him in return for their lives. Saladin replied that he was speaking too late: 'For when I suggested it and made them a fine offer by which they might surrender the city, they would not accept my terms. I have sworn an oath that I shall never take them by treaty, but only by force. If they want to surrender to my mercy and obey me as slaves, I shall take them, but not otherwise. You can well see that you will get no help and that the city can but fall.'

So Balian came and pleaded with him that for the sake of God he would have mercy on them. Saladin answered: 'Listen,' he said, 'out of love for God and for you I shall tell you what I will do. I shall have mercy on them in a manner that will save my oath. They will surrender to me as if taken by force. I shall leave them their goods and their wealth for them to do with what they will, but I shall take their persons into custody. Those who are able or who wish to ransom themselves I shall set free in return for a stipulated ransom. Those who lack the means to free themselves or do not want to do so will remain in my custody as if taken by force.'

Then Balian asked, 'Sir, what will be the price of the ransom?' Saladin answered that it would be the same for both rich and poor. The men would give 30 bezants, the women ten and the children five: those who could not pay the ransom would be slaves. Balian replied, 'Sire, in a city such as this there are only a few people apart from the burgesses who could manage that, and for every man who can pay the ransom there are a hundred who could not redeem themselves for even two bezants. For the city is full of ordinary people who have come in from the surrounding area for protection. Find some way that they can ransom themselves.' Saladin said that he would take counsel, and he should come back the next day.

So Balian took leave and returned to the city. He went to the patriarch and called all the burgesses to tell them what he had achieved. When they had heard it they were very angry on account of the ordinary people of the city. So they discussed matters and it was said that there was a very great store of money belonging to the king of England at the Hospital. It would be a good idea if they could arrange to use this wealth to redeem some of the ordinary people. King Guy had taken the money that had been in the house of the Temple and had spent it on hiring the people that he took with him, and they had all been lost along with the Holy Cross. If they could get the money that was in the keeping of the Hospitallers, it would be put to better use than the money from the Temple. So the patriarch and the burgesses and Balian went and told the Hospitallers that they wanted to have the king of England's treasure that was in their house to ransom the ordinary people of the city provided that they could so arrange it with Saladin. The commander said that he would have to consult the brothers. The men of the city said that they should take care as to what conclusion they came to, for they could be absolutely sure that, unless they handed over this wealth to ransom the poor, it would be seized by Saladin, and as a result they would know no favour with God or with Christendom. The commander took counsel with the convent. The brothers said that it was good idea, and that, if the treasure had to be given up, they wanted it to be used to ransom the poor. So the commander went to the patriarch and the others and told them that the brothers of the house were happy that the king of England's treasure should be given over to them to ransom the poor people, and they all begged Balian to go to Saladin and make the best peace he could.[98]

So Balian went to the Saracen host and greeted Saladin. Saladin asked him what he wanted. He answered that he was entirely dependent on his mercy and on his promises for his request. Saladin said that he would seize whatever was at the convent, but that he would not touch what was not there: 'For the city and what is there is all mine.' Balian said to him, 'For the sake of God, sir, give reasonable terms for the poor people of the city, and I shall do what I can so that you will be paid, for only two in every hundred can pay this ransom.' So Saladin said that first for God and then for his own sake he would reduce the ransom so that they could

98   For King Henry II's stockpile of treasure, see above, para. 29.

benefit. Then it was agreed that a man should give ten bezants, a women five and child one, and thus was the sum fixed for those who could ransom themselves. Whatever goods they had, they could sell, mortgage or carry off safely, and no wrong would be done to them.

When they had agreed the ransom, Balian said to Saladin: 'Sire, we now have agreed the price for those who are able to pay. There are still more than 20,000 in the city who cannot pay a man's ransom. For the sake of God, make a reduction, and I shall take steps to get the patriarch, the Templars, the Hospitallers and the burgesses to pay the ransom for the poor.' Then Saladin replied that he would gladly make a reduction. He would let them all go for 100,000 bezants. But Balian answered, 'Sire, when all those who can ransom themselves have paid the ransom, there will not be enough to raise the total that you are demanding for the poor.' Saladin said that he would go no further. So Balian decided not to try to make a deal to ransom them all, but just some of them, thinking that if he could have some of them he would have God's help in getting a better deal for the rest. So he asked Saladin how much he would want for 7,000 men. Saladin said 50,000 bezants. Balian said to him, 'Sire, for God's sake, this cannot be done.' Saladin and Balian talked it over and agreed on 30,000 bezants for 7,000 men, with two women or ten children who were under age being counted as one man.

56   When it was all agreed, Saladin set a day for them to sell and mortgage their possessions and pay their ransom: the person and goods of anyone still there after 50 days would belong to the sultan; once they had come forth from the city, he would have them conducted in safety to Christian-held territory. Saladin told Balian to order that all the citizens who possessed arms and could carry them should keep them so that if any robbers or thieves came among them they could defend themselves; when they came to the defile, the army would guard the defile until the last had passed.[99] When the terms had been finalized, Balian took leave from Saladin and said, 'Sire, I shall go into the city and, if you are agreeable, I shall bring you the keys.'

So Balian went back to the city and came to the patriarch, and they called the Templars, the Hospitallers and the burgesses of the city to hear if the peace agreement that had been made was acceptable to them. They replied, 'Since there is nothing better to be had and we cannot do anything else, then yes.' After he had explained everything that he had agreed with the sultan, they took the keys of the gates and carried them out to him. When Saladin had the keys, he was very happy and rendered thanks to Our Lord and to his Mohammed. He sent knights and sergeants to guard

---

99   The defile is presumably the pass known as Le Puy du Connétable on the coast between Botron and Nephin. See below, para. 60.

the Tower of David and so prevent any Christian from leaving because of the ransom. It was there that the Saracens entered to buy the things that the Christians had to sell. The day that Jerusalem was surrendered to Saladin was a Friday, and it was the feast of Saint Leger which is the second day of October.

57   Once his men had occupied the Tower of David and were in control of the city gates, Saladin had it proclaimed in the city that the people should bring their ransoms to the Tower of David where he had appointed officials and scribes to collect them; they should not wait until the 50 days had passed, for he would then seize the person and property of anyone still there. The patriarch and Balian went to the Hospital and collected the 30,000 bezants which they then took to the Tower of David to ransom 7,000 poor Christians. After the money had been paid they called together the barons and burgesses and chose two of the worthiest men they knew from every street. They had them swear on the relics that they would show no favour to any man or woman, neither relatives nor friends, and would have them swear on the relics to declare what each owned; they were not to let them keep anything beyond what would be needed to reach the Christian-held lands. By this means they would be able to ransom more of the poor. They had the names of the poor people in each street put into writing so that they could make an exact list totalling 7,000. Then they escorted out of Jerusalem those that had been ransomed, but when they were outside the city, there seemed to be just as many left.

The patriarch and Balian had a discussion, and they called together the Templars, the Hospitallers and the burgesses and begged them for the sake of God to do something for the poor who were left in Jerusalem. They made some provision, but the Templars and Hospitallers did not give as much as they should, since, thanks to Saladin's assurances, they were not afraid that what they had would be seized by force. Had they thought that violence would be done them, they would have given more than they did. From the surplus taken from the poor who had already gone out, the burgesses of Jerusalem ransomed more of the poor people. But I cannot say how many.

I shall now tell you how Saladin had the city of Jerusalem protected so that the Saracens would do no harm to the Christians there. He placed two knights and ten sergeants in each street to guard the city, and they guarded it so well that I never heard of any wrong being done to a Christian. When the Christians came out of Jerusalem they camped less than a bow-shot away from the Saracen host. Saladin had his troops guard the Christians day and night so that no one could do them any harm and no robbers could fall on them.

After they had come forth from Jerusalem, there still remained those who had not been ransomed. Many of them - at least 40,000 - were poor.

So Saif al-Din, Saladin's brother, said, 'Sire, I have helped you conquer the land and the city of Jerusalem. I ask you to give me 1,000 slaves from among the poor people of Jerusalem.' Saladin asked what he would do with them and agreed to his request. He instructed his officers to give him 1,000 slaves, which at the sultan's command they did. Saif al-Din let them go for the sake of God. Afterwards the patriarch and Balian went and begged Saladin that for the sake of God he would grant them those people who could not ransom themselves. He handed 2,000 over to them, and he gave the Templars, the Hospitallers, the burgesses and other people at least another 10,000. He would have given even more, had not a misadventure occurred. Saladin told his people that he too wished to do an act of charity similar to those done by his brother and Balian and the patriarch. He ordered his officials in Jerusalem to have the postern near Saint Lazarus opened, and they placed sergeants at the gate and had it proclaimed throughout Jerusalem that the poor people should leave the city. He ordered his officials to have the sergeants who were near the David Gate check and if they found anyone who could ransom themselves take them back into custody. They placed the ordinary people and the young men and young women in the space between the two walls, and the old people were put outside the city. This enquiry lasted from sunrise to sunset and was held just outside the postern. This was the act of charity that Saladin did for countless poor people.

He would have let even more of the poor people who remained go had it not been for the misadventure of which I shall tell you. Among the poor there was a man carrying a gourd on his shoulders tied to a stick. There were certain Saracens there who are considered very devout and who are monks known as hadjis. These men regard wine as an abomination just as we regard lust. One of them thought that this gourd was full of wine and said, 'This pig can never leave with wine. It is because of wine that God has cleansed the city of them.' He grabbed the stick which held the gourd and broke it, and all the wealth that was in it spilled out. The Saracens were astonished, and they informed Saladin that the Christians were carrying away their money and would not redeem the poor. It was said that the man carrying this gourd was English. Then Saladin forbade them to let any others go unless they paid the ransom. Afterwards they counted those who were still in the city, and they found that there were still at least 11,000. When the patriarch and Balian realized that so many would be left in captivity, they said to Saladin, 'Sire, for the sake of God hold us in prison until we find the ransom, and let these poor people go.' To this Saladin replied that he could not hold two men for the 11,000 who remained, and he would not discuss it further. And so it was that the people who were left were Saladin's prisoners.

58   Now I shall tell you of a great act of courtesy that Saladin did for the ladies of Jerusalem. The women and daughters of the knights who had been killed or taken in the battle had fled to Jerusalem. After they had been ransomed and had left the city, they came before Saladin and craved mercy. When he saw them he enquired who they were and what it was they were asking. They told him that they were the wives and daughters of the knights who had been killed or taken in the battle. He asked what they wanted. They explained that he had their husbands and fathers in prison and that they had lost their lands, and they called on him for the sake of God to have mercy on them and give them counsel and aid. When Saladin saw them weeping, he had great pity on them and said that they would be informed as to which of their husbands were alive and he would have them all freed. They made enquiries and found some of them, and they freed all those who were in Saladin's custody. Then he ordered that the ladies and maidens whose fathers and lords had been killed in the battle should be provided for generously from his goods, more to some and less to others according to who they were. He gave them so much that they praised God and man for the kindness and honour Saladin had shown them.

When all the Christians had come forth from Jerusalem - all who should come out, both rich and poor - and they were assembled in front of the Saracen host, they were astonished at how many people there were. So they told Saladin that so many people had come out of the city that they could not travel in one body.

59   Saladin ordered that they should be split into three groups. The Templars would take one, the Hospitallers another and the patriarch and Balian the remainder. When they had organized their departure in this way, Saladin assigned 50 knights to each party to escort them in safety to Christian-held territory. Now I shall tell you how they escorted them. Twenty-five knights formed the vanguard and twenty-five the rearguard. During the day those who formed the vanguard would, after they had eaten, lay down to sleep and give provender to their horses. Later, when they had supped, they would get on their horses fully armed and would patrol all night around the Christians so that thieves could not come among them. Whenever those who made up the rearguard saw a man, woman or child who could no longer go on, they would have their squire get down and go on foot and carry the exhausted person as far as their camp. They themselves carried the children in front and behind on their horses. When they came to their camp and had supped, they lay down to sleep, and the next day those who had formed the vanguard provided the rearguard. On arriving at the defile where they had reason to be fearful, they had the Christians who had weapons arm themselves in order to guard the defile until all had passed by. Whenever they made camp the peasants of the land brought plentiful supplies of food, so that the Christians could buy what they needed. The party with the Templars went first and those with the Hospitallers next. Last came the patriarch and Balian who had hoped to win over Saladin by their prayers to free those who remained in the city. But he was not to be persuaded.

60 Thus did Saladin have the Christians escorted as far as the land of Tripoli. Just after they had passed Le Puy du Connétable and had entered the land of the lords of Botron and Nephin, Reynald, who was the lord of Nephin, stationed his sergeants in a defile in his land with orders to rob and despoil the people of Jerusalem as much as they could. So they seized what little Saladin had let the Jerusalemites keep.

Who could recount for you the tears and the sorrow of so great a misfortune as befell the holy city of Jerusalem? She who was named the mistress of other cities had become a slave and handmaid. She who should have ruled as sovereign was now under tribute.

Those who escaped the lord of Nephin's retinue passed on towards Tripoli and expected to be received there. But the count ordered the gates to be shut against them so that none might enter, and he sent his men to a defile that is called Saint William. There they seized the burgesses of Jerusalem, and they robbed them and handled them so foully that it would be shameful to tell of it. The people of Nephin and Tripoli treated them worse than the Saracens. For the Saracens, as you have already heard, escorted them to safety and provided them with food in plenty, but they robbed them and refused to let them find refuge. For the sins of these people Our Lord punished the lord of Nephin in his lifetime so that he lost his sight, and in their time his heirs lost their lordship and they and their descendants have remained disinherited ever since.[100] It was not only the family of the lords of Nephin but all who had been party to this evil who suffered loss. Most of the poor people went on to Antioch and the land of Romania.[101] Some remained outside Tripoli and later came to live there.

The people of Ascalon and Gaza and some of those of Jerusalem went to Alexandria, and they were better received in the land of the Saracens than the others who had gone to the land of Tripoli. When they arrived at Alexandria, the local governor received them kindly and had palisades put round them and had them guarded day and night. He protected them in this fashion throughout the winter, and there they remained until March when they boarded ships to go overseas to the land of the Christians.

---

100 Nephin, a lordship in the county of Tripoli, was a few miles south of Tripoli itself.
   The family was dispossessed in a civil war in about 1206.
101 The Byzantine lands.

61   Now I shall tell you what the Saracens of Alexandria did each day. The leading men of the city came out and gave great gifts of bread, wine and money to the Christians. The rich among the Christians invested their money in merchandise which they loaded on to the ships and gained great wealth from it when they crossed the sea.

Now I shall tell you another incident that happened. The Pisans, Venetians, Genoese and others had 38 ships wintering at the port of Alexandria, and in March there would be a lot of commercial activity because of them. When March came and they were back on their ships, the masters went to the governor of Alexandria and paid the tax that they owed and told him to let them have their steering oars for as soon as they were ready they would be leaving. The governor said that on no account would he let them have their steering oars until they had taken the poor people on board. To this they replied that they would not accept them, because they had not hired the ships and there were no supplies for them. So the governor said, 'What are you going to do then?' They replied, 'We shall leave them.' 'And how,' asked the governor, 'will you steer? Do you want them to remain behind to perish or become slaves of the Saracens, and break the safe-conduct that Saladin has given them? This cannot be. You must take them with you. I shall tell you what else I shall do to honour the sultan's safe-conduct. I shall give you enough bread and water, and you shall take them on your ships. Otherwise you cannot have your steering oars.'

When the masters of the ships saw that they had no choice, they agreed to let them on board. The governor, who was a wise man and who feared God, even though he was a Saracen, said to the masters and the navigators of the ships, 'Come forward and swear to me on your gospels that you will bring them properly and in good faith to a port of safety in Christendom, and, just because I have forced you to take them, be sure to convey them to the same place as you take the rich people and do not do them any evil or harm. If I find out at some time that you have treated them badly or shamefully, I shall seize the merchants of your land who come to this country.' And so it was that the Christians who had spent the winter in Alexandria went away in safety from the land of Egypt.

62   Now hear what Saladin did once he was in possession of Jerusalem. He had no wish to leave the city without worshipping at the Temple. He sent for his sister - the one whom Prince Reynald had captured - so that she could come to worship with him at the Temple to render thanks to God and Mohammed for the honour that God had done them. When she heard this summons, she had 20 camels loaded with rose water and set off for Jerusalem. Before either Saladin or his sister would enter the Temple, they had it cleansed in the same way that prelates have churches restored after they have been violated. For the Saracens say that no pig nor any man who eats pig should enter the Temple that Saladin dedicated to God.

Some Saracens climbed on the top of the building and threw down the cross that was on the pinnacle of the Temple. Then they dragged it as far as the David Gate. They made a great hue and cry around it in scorn of Christianity. Some say the cross was broken into fragments. Others say that after it was thrown down from the Temple it was transported to Kerak after its capture by Saladin. Saladin had the Temple washed with the rose water that had been brought from Damascus, and he entered the Temple and worshipped and gave thanks to God that He had entrusted him with mastery over His house.

Then he set out from Jerusalem in the direction of Tiberias and came to a castle belonging to the Hospitallers called Belvoir. They surrendered it to him. Then he came to the Templar castle of Safed, and the people there surrendered it too.[102] After he had taken all the cities and castles that are on this side of the River Jordan, he went off to besiege Kerak. He anticipated that it would be surrendered to him on his arrival. But there were good people within the castle who had no intention of bringing shame on themselves or doing harm to Christendom. They held out and defended themselves vigorously. They resisted for so long that they ate the dogs and cats and all the animals in the castle. Saladin had the siege continued in his absence because he wanted to besiege Tyre and he fully expected to take it. He also had Montreal which is 36 miles from Kerak besieged. Montreal is situated in Idumea and Kerak is in Moab. They endured the siege until they sold their wives and children to the Saracens to get bread. At Montreal the men went blind as the result of not having any salt. They did not want to make the mistake of handing the castle over unnecessarily but from day to day expected God to send them aid. Saladin repeatedly offered them plenty of money and a safe passage to Christian territory, but they would not accept.

Leaving the sieges of these castles in progress, Saladin departed and went to Damascus. There he prepared his siege engines and loaded them up and appeared before Tyre. He sent to Egypt and had his galleys come so that Tyre was under siege by both land and sea. He arranged for the marquis's father who was in his prison to be brought to the siege. He also had a large part of the people of Jerusalem who were passing before Tyre camp near a section of his host so that on seeing them the marquis and the Christians in Tyre would be fearful for them and so would surrender the city of Tyre all the sooner. The marquis was a wise man, and nothing that he saw caused him to fear or despair.

63 Saladin sent to the marquis saying that he should bear in mind how he had won Jerusalem and that he had his father in prison. If he would

---

102 The events are misplaced. Both castles surrendered after lengthy sieges, Safed in December 1188 and Belvoir in January 1189.

surrender the city, he would release his father and give him great wealth. The marquis replied that he could do his worst, for he would never, if it pleased God, surrender Tyre to him but would defend it against him with God's help. When Saladin had heard this, he ordered his fleet to blockade Tyre so closely that no one could enter or leave. He also commanded his men to get the petraries ready. They constructed at least 14 petraries or mangonels which operated day and night but did no damage to the people of the city. Not a day passed without the Christians making two or three sallies against the Saracens. They were led by a knight from Spain who was in the city of Tyre named Sancho Martin. He bore arms *vert*. When this knight issued forth, the Saracens all rushed up, more to see his fine bearing than for anything else. The Turks called him the Green Knight. He bore the antlers of a stag on his helmet, and this greatly befitted him. The marquis had boats covered in hides with windows made in them and put crossbowmen in them. They were so light that they could keep close to the land, and the crossbowmen did great damage to the Saracens whose galleys and other vessels could not approach them. They called these boats *barbotes*.

When the marquis saw that he was besieged by land and sea, he had a ship made ready, and it slipped out of Tyre under the cover of darkness. He sent it to the count of Tripoli, calling on him to assist him with men and supplies of which he had great need. When this message got through, the count of Tripoli equipped ten galleys and had knights and victuals placed in them and dispatched them to Tyre. But when they had come to within four miles of Tyre, God forbade them entry. He raised a wind and a storm which forced them all to return to Tripoli, though without suffering any damage. Once the marquis realized that he could have no help from anyone, he prayed to God that he would advise and help him to hold on to the city of Tyre. He did aid him as you will hear. It happened that there was a young Saracen, the son of an emir, who had quarrelled with his father and had fled the Saracen host and had come into the city. The marquis soon had him made a Christian. Now I shall tell you what the marquis did. When the young man who had become a Christian had been in Tyre for some time, he had him write letters to Saladin, sending him greetings as to his lord and telling him that he knew everything that was going on there: the Christians were all going to flee the city that night by sea; if he did not believe him, he should listen at the port and would hear the noise of the people who were to flee preparing the ships. When the letters had been written, the marquis had a sergeant of Tyre shoot them into the Saracen host.

64 When the Saracens found the arrow to which the letters were attached, they took it to Saladin. He had the letters read to him and so learned their contents. His emirs were informed, and he had his best men stationed on his galleys so as to attack the Christians. The marquis had the tower that is below the main gate made ready, and he placed a garrison below the main wall, so that, if the Saracens tried to make an assault, they would stop it. He ordered the men in this garrison to stay completely quiet so that no one would know what was going on. Then he had the gates of the barbicans shut. No one was allowed out; they all stayed in the city all day. When he had deployed his men in the tower and at the walls in this way, he went to the port and had the galleys made ready and ordered all who could bear arms to go to the port that night. There they made a great commotion, so that the Saracens would think that the letters the young man had sent were true.

The Saracens armed themselves and were in their galleys ready to attack the Christians. As dawn broke they came close to the port and found that the chain was down. They assumed that the Christians would sail out of the port at that hour and flee. The marquis had planned all this because he wanted the Saracen galleys to enter the city harbour, and he had the towers of the chain well provided with men who played their part very well that day. The Saracens saw that the chain was down and decided to enter the port. In fact five Saracen galleys came in. When the marquis saw that the galleys had entered the port, he ordered the chain to be raised. As soon as the chain was up, the Christians attacked the galleys and captured them, killing all the Saracens who were on board. Then the marquis armed the five Saracen galleys that he had taken together with two that he had found at Tyre. He stationed plenty of well-armed knights and men on board. At dawn the following day they sailed out silently and attacked the Saracen galleys. When the Saracens found that they could not withstand the Christian onslaught they made for land close to where their troops were. The Saracens who were on horseback came to the shore in great numbers and went into the sea to aid the men on the galleys, and because of it many men and their horses were killed or drowned. When they could no longer endure the fighting, they ran five of their galleys on to the shore, and two others went off to Beirut where they later did great damage to the Christians as you will hear in due course.[103]

---

103 In the account of the Christian recovery of Beirut in 1197, the Continuation of William of Tyre relates: 'It was found written at the castle that the galleys mentioned earlier that escaped from Tyre and came to Beirut had done harm to more than 14,000 men whom they captured and sent bound to the pagan lands, not counting those whom they killed. I shall tell you how. There is a mountain near Beirut that sticks out into the sea and at its foot the galleys were always armed. Above on the mountain there was a look-out who watched the sea constantly for ships coming from the land of Armenia, Antioch and Tripoli on their way to Tyre and Acre. For it was not possible to go from these lands to Tyre or Acre or back again without going past Beirut. When the look-out saw them, he would inform the galleys and they would attack those that were passing and they would seize and kill

65   Now I shall tell you what the Saracens did on land. They brought ladders and got inside the barbicans and so came as far as the main wall. There they attempted to set up their ladders, but the walls were so high that could not get up. Again they tried, but they could do no damage because of the defenders on the top. When they realized that they could not climb on to the walls, they had their miners come and dig beneath them. They managed to undermine enough that they only had to knock the facing-blocks over towards the Christians and they could enter fighting hand to hand. At this point God quickly brought aid. After the Christians had defeated the Saracens on the sea, they were told that they were assailing the walls of the city and that the barbicans were already overrun. When the marquis heard this report he returned and came to the city gate. The gate was opened and they all sallied forth together against the Saracens. When the Saracens saw the men of the city attacking them they fled leaving those who could to make their escape from the barbicans; those who could not get out were hurled down. The Christians pursued them as far as the Saracen host. More than 3,000 died at the barbicans and on the sea. Thus did God aid the city of Tyre. This defeat was inflicted on New Year's Day. The siege had begun on All Saints' Day and lasted until the first day of January in the year of the Incarnation of Jesus Christ 1188.[104]

66   Saladin saw that he had been defeated on both land and sea and ordered that there should be no more assaults on the city. At nightfall he had the galleys that had escaped and the petraries and mangonels set on fire and burnt. That night he departed and went and camped about two miles from Tyre. There was still a castle that he had not yet taken. It was called Beaufort and it belonged to the lord of Sidon. Saladin believed that if he could secure that castle he would greatly weaken Tyre and would be better able to capture it at a later date. He was well aware that Reynald of Sidon was there. After the marquis had driven him from Tyre he had gone to Tripoli, and then he had come back and gone to Beaufort.

67   When Saladin came before Beaufort, he realized that he could achieve nothing there by force. So he decided on trickery and a wicked deception. He commanded Reynald to come and speak with him under the promise of his safe-conduct. He refused to go on the grounds that one should not trust to the safe-conduct of an unbeliever. Saladin repeated this

---

as many people as they could. These two galleys harmed the Christians for as long as Beirut was in Saracen hands.' 'Eracles', p. 226 and variants pp. 227-8.
104   I.e. 1 Nov. - 1 Jan. Muslim sources, while agreeing that the defeats occurred at the very end of December, would have the siege start on about 12 Nov.

order several times, threatening that if he did not come and he were to take him by force he would have him burnt along with all the men in the castle. This struck fear into him. Then, after the summons had been repeated again, Reynald took counsel with his men as to whether or not to go. His men advised him not to go, for if he did Saladin would seize him and then take the castle. Reynald rejected his men's counsel and went to Saladin against their advice on the safe-conduct of an unbeliever. Before he set out from the castle he had all his men swear to guard and save the castle for Christendom and not surrender it to Saladin come what may. So it was that he left the castle and came to Saladin. Saladin gave the appearance of showing him goodwill and was very joyful at his coming.

68　　Once Saladin had Reynald of Sidon in his power he was sure he would gain the castle. So he ordered for him fine gifts and rich jewels and the sort of harness the Saracens knew appealed to Christians, and he placed guards around and about it. When Reynald became aware of the trickery that he was trying to perpetrate, he sent demanding leave to return in safety to his castle on his safe-conduct just as he had come. Once Saladin saw that Reynald had become aware of his stratagem, he gave him leave.

After Reynald had left Saladin and was near Beirut and Beaufort,[105] a scribe from Beaufort named Belheis who was Reynald's man came to Saladin and asked him why he had let the lord of Sidon go. Saladin said that he had come on his safe-conduct, and he had no wish to betray the guarantee of safety he had given. Belheis answered, 'If he enters the castle you will never have it. You have been free from the safe-conduct that you gave him from the time he left you.' Saladin said that under no circumstances would he have him taken. The scribe said to Saladin, 'Give me men who will obey my orders, and I shall go and take him, and that way you will have honoured your safe-conduct.' Saladin ordered some of his men to go with the scribe and follow his orders. They set off from the host, and the scribe ordered them to go quickly to take the lord of Sidon and his men before they reached the castle. The lord of Sidon's men said to him, 'Sire, large numbers of men are following us.' Reynald replied, 'I am sure that I have been betrayed. These people are coming to seize me. Arm yourselves and hold the castle as best you can. By the homage that you owe me, do not surrender it so long as you can hold it for the cause of Christendom, unless it is at my command in order to free me.' The knights went to the castle, but the Saracens came and took the lord of Sidon and brought him to Saladin.

---

105 Evidently a mistake since the two places are a long way apart.

69   After Saladin had had the lord of Sidon taken captive, he was sure he would get Beaufort. When he was led into his presence, Saladin told him to surrender the castle. Reynald replied, 'If it pleases God, sire, you are such a great man and, since God had done you such great honour, you will not breach your safe-conduct for that poor castle. For until now you have duly honoured your safe-conduct for everyone to whom you have given it.' Saladin replied to him, 'Reynald, my prophet Mohammed teaches me that I should take the enemy of God by the promise of God. On the other hand, I have sworn that I shall not let any city or castle remain that I shall not take by whatever means I can. I have no wish to be a perjurer.' Reynald replied, 'Sire, for the sake of God, allow me then to go to the castle, and I shall surrender it to you.' The unbeliever replied, 'Let your words stand. You must hand over the castle or I shall have you killed by a cruel death.' Reynald committed himself to God and said to him, 'My body is in your hands, and my soul is in the hands of God. You can do what you will to my body. For you cannot have the castle.'

70   Saladin was roused to great wrath against Reynald after these words and he had him brought near to the castle. There he began to have him beaten and cruelly tortured, and he hung him by the arms and feet in full view of his men in the castle, so that they would take pity on him. But when he was tortured there he cried, 'Hold fast! Do no evil deal because of me! Save the castle for the good of Christendom!' Saladin saw that Reynald endured the torture and would not let them surrender the castle, and so he increased the pain. When Reynald could no longer bear the torment and feared that he would die from the torture, and, perhaps because God wished that he should live and have heirs (as indeed he did later), he had them bring him to the castle where he asked pity from his men. 'I can no longer endure the pain. I release you from your oaths. Surrender the castle and set me free. I fear that if you will not free me I shall lose both body and soul.' They took counsel among themselves, and surrendered the castle to Saladin in return for the release of their lord.[106] And so the Saracens held it until the coming of the king of Navarre, as we shall tell you later.[107]

---

106 This account is at considerable variance from the more plausible story as given by the Muslim sources. Saladin first directed his attention to Beaufort in April 1189, but Reynald managed by a series of negotiating ploys to stave off attack for several months. Saladin then held Reynald in prison and the garrison capitulated in April 1190. Making this episode follow directly on the failure of the siege of Tyre is completely erroneous.

107 An allusion to the crusade of Thibaut, king of Navarre and count of Champagne who arrived in Acre in 1239. In 1240 he won important territorial concessions from the Muslims including Beaufort.

71   Saladin was delighted when he was able to take Beaufort, since Tyre was greatly weakened as a result. After he had taken possession, he told Reynald that because of the treachery he had shown him he would give him half of Sidon with its lands and no Saracen would ever take it back. Reynald held it for as long as he lived, and his son Balian had it after him until the truce that the emperor Frederick made with the ruler of Egypt, al-Kamil. Al-Kamil assigned Balian the other half of Sidon because he had negotiated the truce.[108] This Balian lord of Sidon was the son of Helvis who was the daughter of Balian of Ibelin and Queen Maria. Reynald married this maiden after the land was lost and after he had been delivered from Saladin's captivity. Saladin left Beaufort and went with his army to Damascus.

72   Now I shall leave off telling of Saladin and tell you about Archbishop Joscius of Tyre who went as an envoy to the pope at Rome and brought tidings of the great ill fortune that had befallen the Promised Land.[109] He boarded a galley whose sails were painted black. They had them painted like this so that whenever the galley came near to land the people who saw it would know that it brought bad tidings. It arrived in the land of King William who was lord of Sicily, Apulia and Calabria. This king had a daughter of King Henry of England named Joan as his wife. He was close by when the archbishop of Tyre arrived, and so the archbishop went and told him about the catastrophe that had befallen the land of Jerusalem. When King William heard about it, he was most distressed and accepted that he was partly to blame for the loss of the land, and I shall now explain why.

When Alexios had had his brother blinded and had himself made emperor, King William took counsel with his vassals and decided to send a large army to Constantinople to conquer the land for himself.[110] He hired as many men as he could, and prepared a great fleet of ships and galleys. He sent to the land of *Outremer* and all the lands nearby and recruited knights and sergeants and gave them pay in accordance with each

---

108 Balian of Sidon had been one of the negotiators of the truce between Frederick II and the Egyptian sultan, al-Kamil, in 1229. Sidon had been occupied by the German crusaders at the end of 1227 and so the treaty in effect sanctioned the status quo.

109 Joscius left the Holy Land in the autumn of 1187 and had made his way to Gisors on the frontier of Normandy by the following January.

110 Yet again the writer makes the mistake of believing that these events occurred after the blinding of Isaac II by his brother Alexios (actually in 1195). William II's invasion of the Byzantine empire had taken place in 1185, and the approach of his army had been a major factor in the fall of Andronicos Comnenos that year. The Normans captured both Dyrrachium and Thessalonika, but the events surrounding their final defeat bear little resemblance to the account given here. See Brand, *Byzantium Confronts the West*, pp. 160-75.

man's status. He also retained the pilgrims from other lands who were passing through his kingdom. So for two years he held up the passage so that no one could cross to the land of *Outremer*. Because no one was coming to the land of *Outremer*, the land was greatly weakened. When Guy was defeated he had very few men at his disposal. He took into battle everyone he could find, and so when Saladin came to the cities and the castles he encountered no opposition; with the exception of Tyre they all surrendered. That was why King William said that he was much to blame for the loss of the land.

73 I shall tell you now about what became of his fleet and then I shall tell you about the help he sent to the land of *Outremer*. King William did not himself go in his fleet, but stayed behind to forward supplies and reinforcements. He sent the greatest men of his land to lead and command his forces. When the ships and galleys were ready, they set off and came to Dyrrachium which they seized and garrisoned. Then they went to Thessalonika, conquering all the land that is between Dyrrachium and Thessalonika, and they took Thessalonika and garrisoned it too. Then they set off towards Constantinople. When the Greeks saw how much they had conquered, they were very sorrowful. They came to the leaders of the army and told them that it was good that they had come and that they were delighted by their arrival; they would be even more delighted if they could avenge the good man who had been blinded, who himself had avenged the malice of Andronicos. Then they told them that they would have to make a great detour to get to Constantinople but that they could go by land. They would go with them and guide them and arrange supplies in great plenty, for they had no love for the emperor. The Greeks begged the invaders to go with them and leave the fleet, and they led them to a place six days from Constantinople near a city named Philippi. There they camped in a valley. While the Greeks had been leading the invading force overland, they had let it be known everywhere that their forces should be ready to do battle with them near Philippi, and so they were. When the call to arms had come and they were all assembled, they made ready and at dawn the following day charged the invaders. They killed or captured them all, except for a few who escaped and got away to their ships. Thus was this army lost.

Now I shall tell you what aid King William sent to the land of *Outremer*. He sent 200 galleys[111] and 200 knights and the following August he sent another 300 knights to help and protect what land remained to the Christians. Then he had a large fleet of ships and galleys made ready on which he intended coming with the king of England, the brother of his wife. I do not say that he had taken the cross, for not long after he

111 Other versions put the figure for William's fleet at four galleys or 100 galleys.

had begun this fleet he died without heirs. The people of Apulia, Sicily and Calabria took his cousin who was named Tancred and made him king. This took place in the year of the incarnation of Jesus Christ 1188.[112]

74   We shall put off talking about Tancred until a more suitable time and tell you about Joscius, the archbishop of Tyre. King William gave him horses and money so that he could go to Rome. He found Pope Urban at Ferrara and recounted the great loss that had befallen the Christians in the land of Jerusalem and how the Saracens had conquered it. When he heard about it he was so upset and sorrowful that he died of grief. This was Urban III. It is a remarkable thing that it was an Eraclius who had brought the cross to Jerusalem and an Eraclius who had taken it forth from Jerusalem when it was lost; it had been in the time of Urban II that Jerusalem was conquered, and it was in the time of Urban III that it was lost to the Saracens. After Urban came Gregory VIII who lived for two months. Then came Clement III who sent his messengers throughout Christendom to spread the news that Joscius had brought from the Land of Promise. He sent to all the great men of Christendom - emperors, kings, counts and marquises - and to the knights and sergeants telling them that he would take upon himself and acquit before God all the sins of those who would bear the sign of the cross to go to recover the Promised Land provided that they had confessed and were truly penitent. He announced that he would grant the tithe to all who wished to have it so that they might do God's service.

When the great men of Christendom heard the news, the emperor, the kings, the archbishops, the bishops and all the other people took the cross. The first to take action and set off was Frederick, the emperor of Germany, and he travelled overland and got as far as Romania as you will hear later. This emperor had four sons. The eldest was named Henry, and he had married Constance, King William's aunt - she was the sister of his father. The second was Otto count of Burgundy. His wife was the daughter of Count Thibaut of Blois, and he died without heirs. The third was Philip who was provost of *Pavenberc* and who later, after the death of the his father and Frederick his brother, left the priesthood and became duke of Swabia. Frederick married the daughter of Isaac, the emperor of Constantinople, who had been the wife of King William the younger of Sicily, and he took her with him to the Land of Promise. He later died in the city of Acre.[113]

---

112 William II died in 1189. Tancred was the illegitimate son of William's uncle.

113 Frederick Barbarossa's eldest son was Henry who ruled the empire as Henry VI (1190-97) and was king of Sicily by virtue of his marriage to Constance. Frederick's second son was Frederick duke of Swabia who died at Acre in 1191. It was the youngest son, Philip duke of Swabia (d. 1208), who in 1197 married Irene, the

King Philip of France and King Henry of England had begun a great battle in the archbishopric of Bourges near a town known as Issoudun. The lines were already drawn up and the squadrons set in order to go into battle when the messengers from the Church of Rome turned up. They found the armies ready, but, by their holy preaching and their earnest entreaties, the grace of the Holy Spirit was shed over the two kings so that they abandoned the war they had begun and made peace and took the cross.[114] The knights and people of the two realms took the cross following the example of their lords. The two kings did not set off as soon as the emperor. I shall not tell you why there was war between these two kings until later, but instead I shall tell you about Saladin who had taken possession of the land.

75 The news reached Saladin that the emperor of Germany, the king of France and the king of England and all the high barons overseas had taken the cross to come against him. He was not at all pleased or confident. He had Acre strongly garrisoned, and he fortified it in every way necessary with siege engines, supplies and men. He had the city defended by men of the highest rank and by those in whom he had the greatest trust, for he knew that if he was not careful the Christians would be arriving outside the port of Acre. He commanded those to whom he had entrusted the city's defence that on no account should they sally forth against any people who came to besiege them, but that they should stay calm and quiet inside the city. If any Christians should lay siege to them, they should let him know and he would quickly come to their aid; if he was sitting down to eat he would not finish his meal but would get up and come to their rescue immediately, and whether the messenger came to him by day or by night, even if he was ill, he would have himself carried and go to their assistance. So Acre was put on a war-footing. Then he had the castles and the cities that he had conquered along the coast made ready. Afterwards he had his army summoned and went to besiege Tripoli.

Just as Saladin was coming to lay siege to Tripoli, King William's navy arrived at Tyre and with it 200 knights.[115] The marquis was getting his galleys made ready to go to the relief of Tripoli, and he ordered King

---

daughter of the emperor Isaac II Angelos. Irene had previously been married not to King William but to Roger duke of Apulia, son of King Tancred of Sicily. Philip had been provost of Aachen and had been nominated to the bishopric of Würzburg before forsaking his clerical career. There was also fifth brother named Conrad who was murdered in 1196.

114 In June 1187 there had been an unresolved military confrontation between the two monarchs at Châteauroux after Philip had occupied Issoudun and other places. The idea that the papal envoys found the battle lines drawn and the engagement about to start is fanciful.

115 Early summer 1188.

William's knights to go as well. Off they went, and the Green Knight was with them. After they had arrived and had rested a little, they made a sally against the Saracen host, and the Green Knight took the lead. When the Saracens saw the Green Knight and Saladin was told that he had come, he sent word to him begging him to come to visit him under the guarantee of his safe-conduct. He went, and Saladin had him presented with a horse and with gold and silver and made a great fuss of him, but he had no thought of seizing him; he told him that if he decided to remain he would give him extensive lands. He replied that he had not come to live with the Saracens but to do his best to destroy them and harm them as much as he could. He took his leave and went off to Tripoli. Saladin could see that he could do no damage there because of the great force that had come, and so he went off to a city named Tortosa which is situated on the coast.[116]

After his departure, Queen Sibylla, the wife of King Guy, who was in Tripoli, wrote to Saladin to say that he should abide by the agreements that he had made with her husband when he surrendered Ascalon to him, and that it was high time he released him. Saladin wrote back saying that he would do so gladly. He sent word to Damascus with instructions that they should send him the king and ten captive knights that he should choose. As you have heard, he had already chosen them.[117] Saladin also ordered that they should bring the marquis William and the others to him at his siege of Tortosa. On their arrival Saladin had the king and all the barons that had been freed swear that they would never bear arms against him, and then he let them go.[118] The king crossed on a galley as far as the island which is before the city of Tortosa and told Saladin's messengers who had gone with him that they should bear witness to the fact that they had passed over seas.[119] Then he came to Tripoli which was where the queen was and he was received with great joy.

Saladin had the marquis William sent to his son who was in Tyre. Then he went to Kerak, taking with him Humphrey whom he still held as his prisoner. When he was outside the castle he had Humphrey speak to the garrison. Humphrey said, 'Sirs, if you can maintain yourselves and the castle in the interests of Christendom, then stay as you are, but if you don't think you can hold out, I call on you to surrender it and free me.' The men of the castle who by now were in great discomfort agreed among themselves that if Saladin would give them a safe-conduct to go securely and safely with their wives, children and possessions to the Christian-held lands and would free their lord, they would surrender the castle. Saladin received this reply with pleasure and promised again that he would ransom

---

116 The siege of Tortosa was in the first half of July 1188.

117 Above, para. 49.

118 Guy was released in June 1188.

119 A second condition of Guy's release was that he should go overseas. See below, para. 87.

their wives and children for them wherever he could find them in the pagan lands. Assured of this agreement between Saladin and themselves, they surrendered the castle to him. From there Saladin went to Montreal. Since these castles had been held for two and half years after the land was lost and there was no prospect of them being relieved, it was understandable that they should be surrendered. He had Humphrey taken to his mother and escorted the people of the castle as far as the land of Antioch.[120]

He then went back to besiege Tortosa. When he had been there for a while and saw that he could do nothing, he went to another city five miles away named Valania. He took it and laid it waste. He did not want to put a garrison in it because of the castle on the mountain above.[121] Then he went to the land of Antioch and took two cities and garrisoned them. One was named Jabala and the other Latakia.[122] From there he came before Antioch and found that it was well defended. He remembered John Gale who was still in La Roche Guillaume.[123] He went to besiege it, but he could not take it. Then he turned back and went to Damascus so that he and his army could rest and recover. Nevertheless he was still angry at the Templars for having taken his nephew and for maintaining John Gale against him.

76 While Saladin was in the city of Damascus, he decided on an evil course of action and had all the Templars and the other people that he had captured in the battle put to death. He sent orders to his men that all who were holding prisoners should bring them to him. They immediately obeyed, and when the prisoners had come into his presence, he said, 'You are knights and men-at-arms; great profit can still come to you. You see that I have conquered all the Christian lands on this side of the sea, and I have captured the Cross and have killed or taken the king and most of the barons. I have had pity on you because you are knights and fine people and there are great advantages that can come your way in the pagan world. If you will do my command you will live, and I shall give you wives, fiefs, silver and gold, and I shall grant you lands that I have conquered just like the lands I have granted my own men.' They asked what he wanted them to do. He told them that they should renounce their law and the cross and the faith of Jesus Christ and turn to the law of

---

120 Kerak surrendered in November 1188 and Montreal in April or May or 1189. The idea that Saladin left the siege of Tortosa with Humphrey, secured the surrender of these fortresses and then resumed the siege is totally wrong.

121 Valania fell in mid-July 1188. It is overlooked by the great Hospitaller castle of Marqab.

122 Jabala and Latakia fell to Saladin on the 15 and 21 July respectively.

123 Above para. 45.

Mohammed. They replied together in one voice that if it pleased God they would never forsake the law of Jesus Christ, He whom the Jews had crucified in Jerusalem. 'And just as He suffered death for us on the cross, we wish to suffer death for Him at your hands. For we know well that the law of Mohammed is false and deceitful.'

77   When Saladin heard this answer he was outraged. He immediately ordered the Templars to be killed. As soon as he had given the order, the slaughter began. Great was the sorrow, and great was the massacre and the shedding of blood. He considered that he would be doing a great service to God by having the Christians killed. As Our Lord said to His disciples in the gospel: 'The time will yet come when they who kill you will think they are doing me a great service.'[124] After Saladin had given this order, an old Saracen called Caracois, who had seen Godfrey of Bouillon and the first barons at the time of the conquest, said to him, 'Sire, you have not been well advised in that you have had the Templars killed. Do you imagine that you will have put an end to your war? I must tell you that the Templars are born with their beards already. Moreover, let me tell you that their friends and relatives will not let their deaths go unheeded, but will want to avenge them and take their recompense.' So it would prove when James of Avesnes arrived at the siege of Acre with his cogs, as you will hear later in this account.[125] The news reached Pope Clement III. He was greatly angered by it and sent his messengers to hasten the crusaders.

78   In the year of the incarnation 1189, after Saladin had conquered the kingdom of Jerusalem and had freed King Guy from prison, he held the kingdom in peace for two years or more. As soon as the news of the tragedy that had occurred in the kingdom of Jerusalem became known in the lands overseas, Geoffrey of Lusignan, who was the brother of King Guy and who was wise and brave, hurried to cross the sea without waiting for the kings of France or England to depart, bent on helping the king. With him crossed a nobleman named Andrew of Brienne, his companion in arms. They and other knights with them hastened to make the journey before the others and arrived at Tyre. There Geoffrey had news of his brother and the kingdom of Jerusalem. He was told how Saladin had defeated and captured the king, and how he had been freed. When Geoffrey heard this news, he was very sad and was appalled at the shame his brother had suffered. Then he asked where he could find the king and was told that he had gone to Antioch.

---

124   John 16 v. 2.
125   Below, para. 84.

79 He immediately left Tyre and went to Tripoli. There he was received with great honour, and the people rejoiced when they heard of his coming. After they had rested, the count of Tripoli escorted them to Antioch.[126] There he found his brother who received him joyfully. On Geoffrey's arrival the king, the master of the Templars and Aimery the constable, who was the king's brother, assembled the knights who had escaped the defeat. There were at least 600 of them. They set off to go to the kingdom of Jerusalem. When they arrived before Tyre, the king and queen expected to enter the city as they considered it to be theirs. The marquis of Montferrat, who had defended it against Saladin at the time he had taken Jerusalem and captured the king, refused to let them enter because the people of the city had received him as their lord while Guy was in Saladin's prison.[127]

80 Once the king had witnessed the marquis's insulting effrontery towards him in refusing to allow him to enter the city and realized that in all the kingdom there was not a village or a house where he could lodge, he had great sorrow in his heart. He preferred to die honourably than live in shame. He took counsel with Geoffrey and the master of the Temple and the other barons who were with him. They said that he knew the land better than they did, and in any case he was the lord and king and they were foreigners. It was up to him - they would do his will and his command. Geoffrey, his brother, told him that the emperor of Germany and the kings of France and England and plenty of other barons had taken the cross and would soon be arriving. 'It is much better that they should find that you have besieged a city than that you have been idle.' Then the king asked them if they would follow him wherever he would go. They replied that because they had come from overseas they would obey his commands even unto death.

81 When King Guy heard the reply that these lords gave, he rejoiced at their goodwill towards him and knew that Our Lord would not 'beat the Christians with two sticks'. He took his courage in his hands, committed his designs to God and set off and established his camp on a small hill outside Acre.[128] Great was the faith of God's people in that so few dared to undertake so great a deed as laying siege to Acre, for there were so many Saracens within the city that there was scarcely one Christian for

---

126 The count of Tripoli by now was Bohemond, son of Bohemond III of Antioch. He was later to hold both Tripoli and Antioch (as Bohemond IV, 1201-33). See below, doc. 5a.

127 Guy's rebuff at Tyre was in the summer of 1189.

128 August 1189.

every ten of them. They placed themselves between the hammer and the anvil. If the men of the city had so desired, they could have devoured the Christians and taken them just as a sparrowhawk takes a small bird.

82 Saladin thereupon sent throughout his kingdom of Egypt and Damascus and all the other parts of the pagan world commanding his men to come to him. They were to capture the remaining Christians who had escaped the battle and who had foolishly rushed in and had had the temerity to place Acre under siege. On hearing this order the Saracens came to Saladin.

83 When Saladin had assembled his people and mustered his army, he camped on a small hill which is situated a league from the city of Acre and which, as it was there that he lodged, is now called the Toron de Saladin. There was a huge number of Saracens there surrounding our people with the result that those who had come to lay siege to Acre were themselves besieged. On many occasions the Saracens and their emirs said to Saladin, 'Let us go and take them and then we can relax for we will never again encounter anyone who will come against us to make war.' Saladin said that he wanted to wait for Saif al-Din his brother whom he had sent to the caliph at Baghdad and with whom he wanted to share the victory and the celebration. When the Christians saw the Saracen forces and how they held them in scorn, they were very frightened, and this was not to be wondered at. They prayed the King of Mercy that just as they had gone and placed themselves at His service so as to avenge His shame, He would send them His Counsellor[129] - that Counsellor who knows our needs both militarily and bodily - and would not permit the enemies of the cross ever again to have power over the Christians such as they did. Our Lord visited them with His Counsellor and His Comforter, for they had made their request with a pure heart and true mind.

84 After Saladin had mustered his forces, you must know that Our Lord visited His people with His grace and sent them a nobleman from overseas named James of Avesnes with a fleet of at least 50 cogs.[130] No one should doubt that it was God who sent this aid and comfort to those who trusted in His mercy. Saladin rode out with an emir of his named Caracois. When he saw the cogs arriving, Saladin said, 'By God, it seems to me that the Franks have gone mad and built their towers on the sea.' 'Sire,' said Caracois, 'this is the aid that has come to the Franks. I told you when you

---

129 Paraphrasing John 14 v. 16.
130 September 1189.

ordered the Templars to be killed that they are already born with beards.'
When he heard these words Saladin was angry and cast down, and he
ordered Caracois to go to the city of Acre and be its lord and governor on
his behalf. The same day that Caracois entered Acre the cogs arrived
before the city. This was in the third month since Guy had begun the
siege. When the cogs arrived, the Saracens tried hard to prevent them
landing the people and goods that were in them. But Our Lord aided His
people, and their goods were landed and brought to safety. The knights of
Jesus Christ were assured of the providence of God.

James of Avesnes camped on the sand before Acre. The Frisians,
Germans and Bretons who had come with him strengthened the siege.
They dug a ditch between them and made palisades and barriers out of the
masts and timbers of the cogs, and then they managed to divert the river
that flowed past the city through the sand towards their camp so that the
Saracens who were in the city had a shortage of fresh water. There was
scarcely any fresh water in Acre except in the rain-water cisterns. Saladin
watched the Christians grow in strength, and he ordered his men to attack
them often and fiercely without sparing themselves. He also ordered his
men who were in the city to assail them savagely, allowing them no
respite so that the Christians had to defend themselves on two fronts. The
siege continued in the manner that we have described until the coming of
the kings of France and England. One way or another the time was fully
occupied with fighting. The barons from overseas who had taken the cross
made their journey with great difficulty and played their part in taking the
city of Acre.

85   While King Guy and the barons from the kingdom of France and the
other kingdoms who had come to the siege were before the city, Saladin
and all his forces were encamped over against our people. He had them
surrounded so tightly that they could get no supplies from any direction
with the result that their food ran out. Hunger so afflicted the common
people in the army that they could no longer bear their sufferings. The
king and the great lords of the army took counsel as to what to do, and
they decided to go and destroy the Saracen camp. They issued forth and
attacked Saladin's base. The master of the Temple, Brother Gerard of
Ridefort, led the vanguard, and Andrew of Brienne the rearguard. King
Guy and his brother Geoffrey of Lusignan guarded the encampment
against the Saracens of the city. As soon as Saladin saw them coming, he
had his men abandon the camp and withdraw. The Christians entered the
Saracen camp all starving. They ate their fill and loaded up the goods they
found. They then turned back in good order. But by an ill chance for the
Christians, a horse belonging to a pilgrim ran off. As they were trying to
capture it, they began to break ranks and got bunched together, and the
formations in which they were arranged began to break up and move in a

less disciplined fashion than they should. Saladin saw their disorder from his vantage point and asked a renegade who was with him how it was that the Franks could get into such a muddle all by themselves. 'Sire, it is because they have no leader. If you attack them at once, you will have all the spoils.' When Saladin had seen the pilgrims come forth and enter his camp, he had no hope of ever stopping them because of the great numbers that had come out against him, but now he attacked and thoroughly defeated them. The Saracens killed so many that the river ran with blood. On learning that the Saracens were causing so much havoc, a large force of Christians under King Guy, the master of the Temple and Andrew of Brienne went out to their rescue.

86 When the Saracens who were in the city of Acre saw that the camp had been emptied as everyone had gone with the king to save the Christians, they sallied forth in great strength. They would have taken the whole camp had not God by His grace sent aid through Geoffrey of Lusignan. With the small number of people that the king had left under his command, he defended it stoutly, as the valiant and brave knight that he was, and so the Saracens could not gain control of the camp. He drove them back at the point of the sword through the gate of Saint Nicholas. That day he had the praise of everyone in the camp, for he had done more by his own hand than all the others put together.

The king, the master of the Temple and Andrew with their forces defended and rescued the common people who had been in Saladin's camp as best they could. But in the descent from the Toron de Saladin the Saracens charged so ferociously at the king and his men that it might easily have come to pass that few would have escaped. The master of the Temple and Andrew formed the rearguard and held out until the people were brought to safety. In the descent from the Toron they were attacked so heavily that both the master of the Temple and Andrew were killed. There was great distress and sadness in the camp over the deaths of these important figures.[131] Afterwards the Templars elected a man of high birth who was in their house named Brother Robert of Sablé as their master.

87 After this defeat, Saladin sent word to King Guy accusing him of failing to abide by his oath and the undertakings he had made when he had released him from prison; he ought not to have borne arms against him, and in addition he had promised he would go overseas. The king replied that he had indeed kept his oath, for he had crossed the sea in the presence of his messengers; nor could he ever say that he had borne arms against him, though it was true that his horse carried a sword on its saddle bow

---

131 October 1189. For another account of this engagements, see below, doc. 6b.

and he wore a hauberjon on his back so that darts would not harm him. Thus did the King Guy make his excuses to Saladin concerning the oath that he had sworn.[132]

88 While the siege of Acre was in progress, Frederick the great emperor was making his preparations to come overland, and he brought with him many knights from Germany and great wealth and riches as befits the imperial crown. He crossed Hungary and entered Romania. The emperor of Constantinople did his best to prevent the emperor from passing through his land. So Frederick, the great emperor, sent him his envoy, Hermann bishop of Münster, with other well-born men. When the envoys arrived in Constantinople they told the emperor to make ready the road along which their lord the emperor of Germany and all his people would pass so as to restore the land of Jerusalem. The Greek emperor replied that they would not pass through his land. Then he seized the envoys and put them in prison. That is not something to be surprised at, for the Greeks have always hated the Church of Rome and Latin Christians.

When the emperor Frederick learned of the imprisonment of his envoys he was greatly angered. He had to spend the whole of that winter in Romania, and he made war on the emperor of Constantinople until he had seized the greater part of his land. When the emperor saw that Frederick had occupied most of his empire, he feared that he would lose the rest. He took counsel and humbled himself, and wise men on both sides made peace and concord between the two. The envoys and the other wise men - Bishop Hermann of Münster and the others - were freed. Then the emperor of Constantinople arranged transport via Negroponte for those who wanted to go by sea, and to those who wanted to go by land he gave great wealth and provided much aid and assistance so that they might come to succour the land of Jerusalem.[133]

89 When the sultan of Iconium[134] heard that the two emperors had made peace and that the emperor of Germany would pass through his land, he was very worried and was determined to prevent him. He assembled all his people and organized the defence of the passes and the roads along which he would have to go. Had he been able, he would gladly have stopped him from passing through his land. When the emperor heard that he wanted to bar his way, he abandoned his road and set off on another,

---

132 Above, para. 75.
133 Frederick had set out in May 1189. He was not able to cross into Asia until the following March.
134 Qilij Arslan II (1155-92).

for he had found some peasants who could show him the way. The Saracens did not think that any Christian would go the way the emperor went; it was a matter of great surprise since the roads were rough and hard going, what with the rocks and the mountains, and it took him right away from the true road. After he had crossed that desert where he had been afflicted by hunger and thirst and his knights and men had suffered much harm, he came to a plain which he found rich and well supplied. From there he made to go towards Iconium where he expected to find a better road that was clear of obstacles. But although he expected to find a good road, he came upon a swamp and a marsh through which no one whether on foot or on horseback could go. Her ordered his men to lay down their shields and hauberks to make a road for the people and to kill their horses to make bridges for those who would cross. His orders were obeyed, and so he passed through that perilous place with God's help and came near to Iconium.

The sultan of Iconium came out against them with all his forces, expecting to bar the emperor's progress. When the good emperor saw that the Saracen forces were so strong and numerous, he set his divisions and squadrons in order. His son, the duke of Swabia, who was also named Frederick and who was devout, honest and of good renown, led the rear-guard. The emperor took the vanguard. Thanks to his good organization and the grace God gave him, they defeated the sultan of Iconium and took the city. Those who could fled with their wives and children, and the city was abandoned to the emperor. Thus did he occupy Iconium on his arrival.[135]

90   After the emperor Frederick had taken the city of Iconium, the sultan made a truce with him promising that he would be at his command and would give him good hostages to keep the peace; he would provide food and horses for sale and a reasonable market for whatever the host needed; and he would become his man and would hold Iconium from him. When the emperor heard the sultan's words he was well pleased, for he was intent on making for the kingdom of Jerusalem. He agreed a truce with the sultan on the basis that he should have 24 hostages from him from among the best men of his realm and that he would arrange a market as he had promised. The sultan and the emperor for his part swore to abide by the truce just as was normal for lords to do. As soon as the agreements were confirmed on both sides the emperor came forth from the city of Iconium with all his people and set up camp outside. The sultan provided him with a market as stipulated so that our people could replenish their food supplies and their mounts and whatever was needful. This occurred in the month of July.

---

135 May 1190.

91   Now hear how the Germans behaved in Turkey after the emperor had made the truce with the sultan and had taken hostages. There was no rhyme or reason for what they did once they had the upper hand. When they were up against it they conducted themselves in a seemly fashion, and all their people were good comrades. But because they had gained the advantage over them, they began to commit outrages against the Saracens of Turkey, as was their wont. They seized the food and the horses and the other things that they found in the markets without paying, and, if anyone demanded payment for what they took, they killed them. So the sultan came to hear how the Germans were ill-treating his subjects. He sent his messenger to inform the emperor, and the emperor had some of them make amends, but by no means all those who had wronged the Saracens did so. When the outcry began to grow and the Germans' behaviour deteriorated, the sultan feared that worse was to come. So he ordered his men to get ready with their horses and arms to follow the host and avenge the evil that the Germans had done to his people.

The emperor set off along the road towards Armenia with all the 24 hostages that he had taken from the sultan, securely confident in the truce that he had made. But the truce was worthless, and the sultan attacked him without prior warning and with no formal defiance. It is usual among the Saracens that when they see that it is to their advantage they break a truce at will and with little excuse. As the emperor was travelling towards Armenia, the sultan reneged on the truce that he had promised on oath to uphold. He had undertaken that neither he nor any of his people would harm the host, but instead he assembled his whole army and began to violate the truce he had sworn. Each day he attacked the emperor's host, so that his troops suffered much damage and loss. When the emperor saw that the Saracens were multiplying and growing daily, he organized his column wisely and vigorously. He led the rearguard and his son led the vanguard, and together they successfully protected his people. The Saracens repeatedly confronted the emperor's troops and challenged them to combat, but the emperor forbade his men to respond and they were never allowed to be drawn into conflict. Maintaining this discipline, the emperor shepherded along both his foot soldiers and the mounted men so that night or day they had no rest. Thus it was with difficulty that they entered the land of Armenia. There they were safe.

92   When the emperor saw that the sultan kept neither faith nor trust and had no concern for the hostages but went on attacking his troops, he had the hostages executed at various camping places. In the army there was a respected figure who was a count and bishop of Würzburg, a man of good repute and wisdom as well as being a fine speaker and well educated.[136]

---

136 Godfrey, bishop of Würzburg (1184-90) and count of Helfenstein.

He was the emperor's chancellor and bore his seal. This good man often inspired the Christians by his holy preaching and pious exhortations, and he comforted them by telling them that the affliction they suffered was for the sake of God and in remission of their sins.

93   At the time that the emperor arrived in Armenia, the lord of that land was called baron Leo of the Mountain. He was later crowned as king of the Armenians as you will hear.[137] On the news of the emperor's approach, the Saracens abandoned the castle of Baghras which Saladin had taken after the fall of the kingdom of Jerusalem. Fulk of Bouillon, Leo's cousin, heard that the Saracens had evacuated this fortress, and so he occupied it and held it for 20 years. In consequence Leo made war on Prince Bohemond after the death of his father. It was all to do with Rupen, Bohemond's son.[138] The Templars demanded this castle because it had been theirs, and they besieged it on one occasion at the command of Pope Innocent. In due course Leo did a deal with the Templars under which he would surrender the castle to them when he had gained possession of Antioch for his nephew Rupen. Thus the castle by God's grace remained in Christian hands, and, as I shall describe later, Leo gave it to the Templars who had owned it previously.[139]

94   In the summer when the sun is at its hottest and people are most oppressed by the heat of the day, the emperor Frederick came with his whole army into Armenia. There they were safer than previously because the sultan of Iconium had left them and had returned to his own land. The emperor camped on the borders of Armenia by a river which is near the castle of Selefke.

The lord of Armenia travelled through his land to welcome him, but he could not get to him so great was the congestion in the army. This congestion had come about because it was necessary to cross by a bridge. Finding that they could not pass, he sent two nobles of his land, the brothers Constans and Baldwin of Camardeis. These two came to the marshal

---

137 Leo II had become ruler of Cilician Armenia in 1187. He was crowned as the first king in January 1198 and died in 1219. See para. 185.

138 War between the Armenians and the princes of Antioch over the succession to Antioch began in 1201 on the death of Prince Bohemond III. Bohemond was succeeded by his second son, Bohemond IV (1201-33), but the Armenians advanced the claims of Rupen (often known as Raymond-Rupen) who was the son of Bohemond III's deceased eldest son and Leo's niece. The war lasted until the early 1220s. The chronicler errs in describing Rupen as the son of Bohemond.

139 In 1211 the Templars were involved in a campaign against Armenia sanctioned by Pope Innocent III. They eventually recovered Baghras in 1216. The cross reference in the text is to the events of 1211. 'Eracles', pp. 317-18.

of Germany and told him that they were there on behalf of Leo, their lord; they had been sent to the emperor to guide him and show him the roads and the ways into Armenia. The marshal brought them before the emperor. When they came into his presence they bowed down to him and gave their message. The emperor received with favour what Leo had to tell him. He asked if they knew of any nearby road, other than the one leading to the bridge, along which they could travel without hindrance. In reply they said there was a way if he would ford the river. 'For the river has a good ford and is hardly swift.' He mounted his horse since he wished to cross the river, and his son Frederick, duke of Swabia, went with him. They said to him, 'Sire, we shall cross the river ahead of you and show you the way by which you can cross in the greatest safety.' The emperor told them to go across. They crossed over before him and then came back. He ordered them to cross with his son. They returned again, and the emperor set off to cross the river following the two knights and with a large number of other people in front and behind. When he came to the middle, the horse on which he was sitting stumbled and he fell into the water. As a result of the heat that he had endured and of the coldness of the water into which he fell, he lost his strength and could do nothing to help himself. The veins of his body opened, and he drowned. His men were scattered around and were not able to do anything to save their lord.

95   The death of such a great and powerful lord who was coming so honourably and devoutly to aid the Holy Land of Jerusalem was a great loss for Christendom. Who could recount and recall the sorrow and the tears of the barons who were in his company, and the sadness of the knights and the other people who had lost their leader so suddenly? For in him was fulfilled what is written in the Book of Solomon: 'They have made you captain. Be also as one of them.' He who was such a great emperor had become so humble before the knighthood of Christendom that he even called the poor people his brothers. So great was his humbleness of heart and nobility of spirit that if the wheel of a cart was broken on his route and he was present, he would not pass on until the damage had been mended. Christendom suffered much harm by his death. It occurred in the year of the incarnation of Jesus Christ 1190 on Sunday 5 August.[140] His body was dragged from the river and wrapped and embalmed as becomes an emperor and was carried to the city of Antioch where it was honourably interred in the church of Saint Peter on the right of the choir near the tomb of Gobert who had been bishop of Le Puy. On the left is the place where the lance with which Longinus pierced Our Lord Jesus Christ on the Mount of Calvary was found.[141]

---

140 Frederick died on Sunday 10 June 1190.
141 Gobert is clearly an error for Adhemar, the bishop of Le Puy who accompanied the

96   Now I shall tell you the reason why the emperor came by land. While he was in Germany an astronomer came to make himself known to him. The emperor was highly educated, and because of this he was keen to acquaint himself with good clerks and would frequently engage them in learned discussion. When he found one who pleased him, he would keep him by him and reward him and so have him enter his service. One day he asked his astronomer what death he would die. The astronomer asked for time to reply to his question, and the emperor gave him as long as he needed. Later the astronomer returned to the emperor and said, 'Sire, it will come about that you will die in water.' The emperor took the word to heart and never forgot it. When he took the cross he remembered the words of the astronomer, and so he avoided the sea and came by land. It was a great marvel that of all those who crossed the river with him not one fell or stumbled except the emperor. Having avoided the peril of the sea, the same peril befell him in this river.

Saladin was so frightened at the coming of the emperor that he had the walls of Latakia, Jabala, Jubail, Beirut and all the other cities along the coast destroyed so that the Christians could have no protection there. He was afraid that as the emperor made his way down he would fortify the cities and castles and, if he found them intact, he would occupy them and have them garrisoned and thus damage the Saracen cause. For this reason Saladin had the cities and castles of the coast laid waste.

97   The emperor's great army remained leaderless after his death. The troops scattered in different directions like sheep without a shepherd. Frederick, duke of Swabia, the emperor's son, was severely weakened by illness when he arrived in the plain of Cilicia, and he could not climb up into the mountains, so weak was he from the sickness that afflicted him. For the Cilician plain is hot and disease-ridden in summer, while the mountains are fresh and healthy. Accordingly the inhabitants of the land have their dwellings in the mountains, and because of the heat they live there from the beginning of June until the middle of September; then they come down to the plain because the land is cooler and less unhealthy. The duke had himself carried to Antioch ill though he was, and a large part of the host went with him. After the great hardships and difficulties that they had suffered, they found Antioch a land of plenty and they set themselves to drink, eat and relax. But they were afflicted by a great plague that resulted in death, and so the knighthood of Germany began to diminish. Those who survived the sickness accompanied the duke to Acre, but the duke himself died of it later after the capture of the city, and he was

---

First Crusade and who died at Antioch in 1098. The discovery of the Holy Lance had occurred shortly after the capture of Antioch that same year.

buried in the house of the Germans.[142]

At that time the German Order could not cater for the sick because they did not yet have a hospital. For the Hospitallers of Saint John said that they had a privilege from Rome that no one should have a hospital in the city of Acre unless they were subject to them. It used to happen that when a great man died in Acre, particularly if he died in the house of the Germans, they would go and seize him and bury him in their cemetery. It was for that reason that at his end the duke ordered the Germans not to do him any honour when he was dead but bury him in a poor grave among the poor people. For they knew that the Hospitallers of Saint John would want to take him by force, and he would rather be buried in this poor house than anywhere else. As soon as he had died the Hospitallers went looking for him, but they did not find him and they could not know that he would be among the poor.

At that time the German Hospital did not have such great power as it does now. The device that they wore on their mantles was a wheel with a half cross in black. The brother knights had mantles of Stamford cloth. They did not dare wear white mantles because of the Templars. But since the Damietta campaign[143] they have had their white mantles with the cross without the wheel. The Hospital of Saint John demanded authority over them so that when the master died their master and brothers would choose the new master. Sometimes the Order of Saint John has insisted on this right over the Germans, but the Germans reply that under no circumstances will they allow anyone else authority over the election of their master. The dispute between them still continues.[144]

98 The Germans buried the duke in their house, and much wealth came their way thanks to this burial. He was widely regarded as a man of outstanding qualities considering how young he was.

Once the people in Germany heard the news of the death of the emperor Frederick, they had his eldest son Henry, who was already king of Germany, crowned emperor by Pope Celestine who at that time governed the Apostolic See in Rome. He was crowned the day after Celestine had been anointed pope.[145] Henry had married Constance, the aunt of the noble King William (II) of Sicily. She was the rightful heir to that kingdom after the death of her nephew, the son of King William (I)

---

142 Frederick of Swabia died on 20 Jan. 1191, before (and not after) the fall of Acre.

143 An allusion to the Fifth Crusade of 1217-21.

144 For the protracted efforts of the Hospitallers to assert their jurisdiction over the Teutonic Order, see J. Riley-Smith, *The Knights of Saint John in Jerusalem and Cyprus c.1050-1310* (London, 1967), pp. 397-8. The disputes continued until at least the middle of the thirteenth century.

145 Celestine III was anointed pope on 14 April 1191 and crowned Henry emperor on 15 April.

her brother, because he had died without children. She bore Henry a son named Frederick who was later emperor and king of Sicily.[146]

Now let us return to our subject and tell you about the kings of France and England. The war between the two kings was over Richard, who was then count of Poitou. King Henry had four sons and three daughters by Queen Eleanor, who formerly had been the wife of King Louis of France. The eldest son was named Henry. He had married the sister of King Philip of France, whose mother was the queen of Spain.[147] The second was called Richard. He had been given the county of Poitiers. The third was Geoffrey, and he was count of Brittany. The fourth was known as John Lackland. Of his three daughters, one he gave to King Alphonso of Castile to whom was born Queen Blanche;[148] the second was given to the duke of Saxony,[149] and the third married William (II) king of Sicily.[150] It was said that John, who was later king of England, had the children of his brother Geoffrey drowned.

99   After the death of Henry the son of King Henry, at whose behest Saint Thomas was martyred,[151] the king wanted to crown John, his youngest son, king. When Richard heard this news he was furious. He went to King Philip, and said, 'Sire, I tell you that my father wants to disinherit me and do a great wrong. For he wishes to have my brother crowned who is younger than I. As you know, I am your vassal. I pray you that you help me have my rights.' The king replied that he would gladly assist him. He soon had his host assembled and entered the land that King Henry held on that side of the Channel. He took Le Mans, Tours and Chinon, and delivered them to Richard. When King Henry heard that King Philip had seized the lands that he held in France, he mustered his army and crossed the Channel and came to where King Philip was. They were all set to do battle when messengers from the pope brought them letters with the news that the land of Jerusalem had been lost.[152] The power at King Henry's disposal did not measure up to that

---

146 Further details of Henry's rights in Sicily are given below at para. 168. Henry's son, Frederick II, was crowned emperor in 1220 and died in 1250.

147 The younger Henry married Margaret, Louis VII's daughter by his second wife, Constance of Castile.

148 Henry II's daughter Eleanor married Alphonso VIII of Castile. Their daughter was Blanche, wife of King Louis VIII of France (1223-26) and famous as the mother of Saint Louis.

149 Matilda married Henry the Lion, duke of Saxony (died 1195).

150 Joan, whose fortunes were to be closely involved with Richard's crusade. See below, paras. 107, 110-12, 142.

151 The younger Henry died in 1183. For the martyrdom of Saint Thomas of Canterbury in 1170, see above, para. 29.

152 See above, para. 74. For the disputes between Henry II and Philip at the end of

possessed by King Philip, and he let the king of France have the Auvergne and decided against crowning his son John. He set out for England but, because of his grief at losing so rich a land as the Auvergne, he died.[153] Richard his son came to the king of France and did homage to him for the land he held on that side of the sea and swore that he would take his sister to be his wife after he had been crowned king in the city of London.[154]

100 Richard and Philip parted on good terms, and they named a day on which they would set off to go to rescue the kingdom of Jerusalem. King Philip decided on the forthcoming feast of Saint John (24 June) in the year of the Incarnation of Jesus Christ 1190. Richard went to London where he was crowned.[155] When he had taken possession of his kingdom, he made his preparations and came to King Philip in France. He brought a request to the king, saying, 'Sire, I must tell you that I am a young man and newly crowned king, and as you know I have undertaken the same road as you to go overseas. If it is your pleasure, I would ask that you should put off the marriage until I come back. I shall be bound to you by oath to marry your sister within 40 days of my return.' The king decided that he ought to agree, and so he received the request favourably and allowed the postponement. Then they made ready their departure.

101 King Philip of France had his fleet made ready at Genoa, while the king of England had his prepared at Marseilles. On the feast of Saint John the French king went to Saint Denis to take his leave. There he took the staff and scrip, and he and King Richard swore to one another that they would be good companions and would act in good faith towards each other. Then Philip set off for Genoa, and Richard went to Marseilles. Many of the great men of France accompanied their king on this expedition. Among them were Count Philip of Flanders; Count Henry of Champagne; Count Thibaut of Blois; Count Stephen of Sancerre; Hugh, duke of Burgundy; Philip, bishop of Beauvais and William of Barres, together with many other knights and plenty of gentlemen. King Philip and Queen Isabella, the daughter of the count of Hainault, had a son named Louis. Philip left him in France to guard his kingdom with his uncle, Archbishop William of Reims, and Count Reynald of Ponthieu.[156]

Henry's reign, see W.L. Warren, *Henry II* (London, 1973), pp. 608-26.

153 Henry II died at Chinon in July 1189.

154 Richard had done homage to Philip in November 1188. The idea that he should marry Philip's sister Alice had been first suggested as far back as in 1168. Their betrothal was confirmed directly after the death of Henry.

155 3 Sept. 1189.

156 Philip's son, the future Louis VIII, as born in 1187. The regents during the king's absence were the queen-mother, Adela of Champagne, and her brother, the arch-

When he arrived in Genoa he had his ships and vessels loaded, while King Richard had his loaded at Marseilles. The king of France set sail from Genoa only to run into bad weather and he had to put in to Messina. His supplies and ships had suffered much because of the storms. When King Tancred heard that the king of France had arrived in his land, he went to him and received him with great honour. Then, placing the whole of the kingdom of Sicily at his disposal, he begged him to winter in his land. Philip could see that his supplies and ships had been damaged and that Tancred's advice was good, and so he wintered in the island of Sicily.

King Richard sailed forth from Marseilles. When he was near the island of Sicily he decided to go and see his sister, Queen Joan, who had been King William's wife, and enquire whether the king of France had arrived there. As soon as he was close to land, he sought news as to whether he had turned up. They told him that he had and that he was lodging in the city of Palermo. This is the chief city of the kingdom of Sicily, and one of the richest and most luxurious palaces in the world is there. In that city the king of Sicily is crowned. The king of France was staying in the palace, for King Tancred had vacated it in his honour.[157]

102 When King Richard of England learned that the king of France was lodged at Palermo, he was delighted, and he ordered his men to land near where the king was so that he could spend the winter with him. They soon landed the knights, their mounts and the equipment they needed. When the king of France heard that the king of England had arrived he rejoiced and came to meet him, and both kings were very pleased to see each other. There was great love between the king of England and the king of France on the journey, as they had sworn together to be loyal companions and keep good faith with one another. I do not know why they went to war, but much harm was done during the conflict between them. Before they came overseas to the Promised Land they were both good friends and addressed each other as 'my lord'. Had their love lasted, they would have been honoured for all time, and Christendom would have been exalted. You will find it recounted later how war began between the two kings.[158]

After the king of England had greeted the king of France, King Tancred of Sicily came to Richard and made him welcome and invited him to go and stay in the palace at Palermo where the king of France was lodging. The palace was so large and so delightful that the two kings could easily have stayed there together. When the king of England heard

---

bishop of Reims. The count of Ponthieu, whose name was John (and not Reynald), had joined the crusade and died at Acre.

157 The episode in Sicily was played out at Messina and not at Palermo as stated here. Richard had arrived at Messina on 14 Sept. and Philip on 16 Sept.

158 Below, paras. 138, 145-6.

that the king of France was living in the royal palace, he thanked King Tancred greatly and said that he would not impose upon the king of France but would lodge elsewhere. The king of France was staying in the palace as we have said, and the king of England took up residence at the top of the town on the other side. Because he knew that the French are proud and the English tetchy, he resided well away from the king of France so that there could be no brawling.

After they had set up their camp, the English heard what the local people had to say. As a result there was a violent quarrel between the king of England's men and those of King Tancred, and it reached the stage of open war. So the king had a castle built in no time at all and called it 'Mate Griffon', so that if the need arose and the local people chose to take up arms against him he would have a refuge. When King Tancred saw that he had built this castle, he placed himself at Richard's mercy and brought the people who had done the king wrong to be at his mercy so that nothing worse should happen. The king received them favourably. An agreement was made and peace restored. They stayed there until March.

103 King Richard went to see his sister Queen Joan who was overjoyed at the arrival of her brother.

The siege before the city of Acre had been going on for a year. Count Henry, Count Thibaut, Count Stephen of Sancerre and Philip, bishop of Beauvais, had crossed to Acre before the coming of the two kings and had brought some of the king of France's supplies and siege engines with them.[159] Count Henry was in command. He took the supplies, and he had the engines set up before the city of Acre and used them to bombard the city walls before the French king's arrival.

There was a great dearth in the host so that a *muid* of corn sold for 30 bezants; a chicken sold for 60 sous; beef and mutton were not to be found; an egg sold for 12 deniers. The best meat that the people of the host could eat was horse meat or the meat of mules or donkeys. The hardship was so great that when the poor people could find a dead animal they ate it as a great dainty. So it came to pass that, after the arrival of the count of Champagne, the sergeants in the host began to murmur against the barons and the great men who were at the siege because of the shortages, and they reproached them and said many derogatory things because they would not go to fight against Saladin. The nobles contended that they would not fight against Saladin while Acre remained in Saracen hands. Matters in the host got to the point where no knight would dare go into the field of combat unless taunted and shamed into going. The sergeants adopted such a haughty attitude towards the knights that they regarded themselves as being of greater worth than they were and

159 Henry of Champagne and the others arrived at Acre in the summer of 1190.

imagined that they could easily fight against Saladin without their help. On many occasions the sergeants asked the king and the barons to let them mount an attack. When they realized that they were not to be dissuaded, they told them that they could go at their own risk. If they did well there would be great joy, and if ill befell them they would find no one to help them. The sergeants sallied forth. As soon as Saladin saw that they were coming out against him, he abandoned his camp. Once the sergeants saw that the camp was empty, they rushed up as fast as they could go. Saladin let them take their ease and eat, knowing full well that no knights had come out with them. Then he charged at them in the camp and killed so many that the number of the dead amounted to more than 16,000. It was said that almost all were killed and only 100 sergeants escaped.

Thus did Our Lord allow the haughtiness of the sergeants towards the knights to be avenged. Saladin commanded his men to drag out the corpses and throw them in the river. The river flowed with blood, dead bodies and grease for more than eight days so that the people of the host could not drink the water. There was great illness in both the Christian and the Saracen camps that year because of the corpses, and there were so many flies that no one in either camp could endure them. This occurred on the feast of Saint James which is 25 July.[160]

At about that time Queen Sibylla and her two daughters, Alice and Maria, died.[161] The kingdom then passed by inheritance to Isabella, the wife of Humphrey of Toron and daughter of King Amaury and Queen Maria.

104 With the death of Queen Sibylla, the marquis Conrad, who held the city of Tyre, realized that there was no other heir to the throne apart from Isabella. So ambitious was he to have the kingdom of Jerusalem for himself, that he persuaded Isabella's mother, Queen Maria, to challenge the validity of her daughter's marriage to Humphrey and to get her daughter to agree to a separation. The queen told her daughter to comply and leave Humphrey in order to marry the marquis. But she did not want to, because she loved her husband. This angered her mother, and she remonstrated with her repeatedly and explained that she could not become lady of the kingdom unless she left Humphrey. She reminded her of the evil deed that he had done, for when the count of Tripoli and the other barons who were at Nablus wanted to crown him king and her queen, he had fled to Jerusalem and, begging forgiveness, had done homage to Queen Sibylla, telling her that they had wanted to make him king against

---

160 The archbishop of Canterbury's chaplain alludes to this incident, putting the deathtoll at 4,000. See below, doc. 6c.

161 Late summer or early autumn 1190.

his wishes.[162] So long as Isabella was his wife, she could have neither honour nor her father's kingdom. Moreover, they told her that when she married she was still under age and for that reason the validity of the marriage could be challenged. So Isabella consented to her mother's wishes.

What Maria wanted was that the marquis should have Isabella as his wife. Maria herself hated Humphrey for another reason. For when Humphrey married Isabella, he began to hate his mother-in-law and wanted to prevent her from seeing her daughter. He was acting on the advice of his own mother, Stephany, the lady of Kerak.[163]

Then the marquis came from Tyre to the siege of Acre and persuaded Philip, bishop of Beauvais, and Hubert, archbishop of Pisa, who was the legate of the Church of Rome,[164] to help him so that he could have this marriage. It was said that he corrupted many people in the host by his gifts and promises, especially those who were in the circle of the legate and the bishop. So when the queen challenged the marriage, it was very easily dissolved. As Queen Maria told the legate, the marriage was invalid because her daughter was only eight years old when she was married and so she was too young.[165]

Humphrey was summoned to hear this allegation and give reason, if he could, why the lady should stay with him. As the lady had not herself been called, Humphrey claimed that she had consented to the marriage. Among others the butler of Senlis got up and gave the lie to Humphrey and tendered his gage saying that the lady had never consented to the marriage and that everything King Baldwin had done had been against the wishes of the lady and her mother; if he wanted to assert the contrary he would have to prove it against his body. Humphrey, who was cowardly and effeminate, drew back and dared not take up the gage. Those who had been corrupted by the marquis's gifts advised him to let the marriage go, even though he had never asked them for their advice, and they told him that he would not be able to govern the kingdom and that it would be pain and grief. He took their advice and gave up.[166]

---

105 The legate, who was a Pisan, readily separated the couple. Had he so wished, the marriage could have remained in being, for there was no

---

162 Above, para. 19.
163 Stephany of Milly, the heiress to the lordship of Outrejourdain, had been married in turn to Humphrey III of Toron, Miles of Plancy and Reynald of Châtillon.
164 Philip of Dreux, bishop of Beauvais (1175-1217), was a cousin of King Philip. The legate was Ubaldo, archbishop of Pisa (1174-1209).
165 William of Tyre informs us that the couple had been betrothed in 1180 when Isabella was just eight years old. The marriage took place in 1183. WT, pp. 1012, 1055-6 (B/K, 2, pp. 451, 499).
166 For other versions of what happened, see below, doc. 6e.

particular reason why it had to be annulled. But the legate supported the marquis's cause, because the Pisans had brought him from Constantinople to the city of Tyre and they had given him their support.[167] If he had lived longer, they would have expected to gain greater rights and properties in the kingdom of Jerusalem.

106 No great deed can begin by falsehood and come to a good end. After the hearing before the legate, Queen Maria brought her daughter to hear the sentence in her case. He decreed that she could marry whoever she wished. God knows if this sentence was in accord with the law, for the lady was not in the power of her husband but was in the power and control of the marquis who married her as soon as the sentence had been given.

Isabella immediately claimed the kingdom and called on the barons who were there to do homage. They treated her as the rightful heir. After she had taken possession, she stated in the presence of the barons of the kingdom that, since she had been separated from her first husband by force, it was not her wish that he or his heirs should be disinherited, and said, 'I render to him all those things that he gave my brother when he married me. That is to say, Toron and Châteauneuf and all their appurtenances and all the properties that belonged to his father and grandfather.' After these words, the marquis arranged the wedding for himself and Isabella. It was said that he married her twice. The first marriage was in private and the second was in church. If the lady had been in the power of Humphrey her husband, quite likely she would never have agreed to their separation. Nevertheless the marquis had scarcely any joy of it. One might yet question whether the kingdom of Jerusalem was not put on a dangerous and dwindling course because of this deed.

107 King Philip of France and King Richard of England wintered in Sicily. From the moment he arrived, King Richard, who was very devious and greedy, never stopped begging his sister to sell her dower and go with him on his pilgrimage. He promised that as soon as he returned to England he would repay her all that he had received from her for her dower and would marry her to an appropriately powerful and rich husband.[168] When the lady heard this promise she took counsel and agreed to her brother's wish that she should sell her dower and let him have the proceeds. The king was delighted that his sister had agreed to sell her dower, for he had already come to an agreement with King Tancred over its sale. On the advice of his men, Tancred had struck a bargain with

---

167 Above, para. 47.
168 In 1196 Joan married Count Raymond VI of Toulouse.

Richard that he would buy the dower for over 100,000 marks.[169] By the time Richard had received Tancred's payment, the March sailing was approaching, and so the king was having his navy made ready for the crossing. Tancred gave both him and the king of France plenty of supplies. The two kings then left to come to the siege of Acre. Joan, the queen of Sicily, could not travel with King Richard, her brother, because she had some business to complete in the kingdom and wished if possible to proceed at greater leisure.

After the two kings had left Messina, King Philip of France came straight to Syria with his whole company and arrived at the port of Acre which was still under siege.[170] The nobles who were there had long been expecting his arrival and were looking forward to it. As soon as he arrived, he was given an honourable and magnificent reception, as is appropriate for a man as exalted as the king of France. The people of the host were greatly emboldened and gladdened by his coming. He brought with him a great fleet of ships loaded with food and many other supplies, and he had in his company plenty of barons and knights as befits the crown of France, including Count Philip of Flanders, Hugh, duke of Burgundy and William of Barres, a Poitevin over whom the two kings quarrelled for a time.

108   Directly after his arrival he mounted a horse and went right through the host and around the city of Acre so as to see from which side he could most easily gain possession of the city. When he had seen it, he said, 'Considering how many noblemen have been at this siege, it is extraordinary how slow they have been to take it.' Then he ordered screens covered in iron that had been tinned so that they shone like silver to be erected around the city. He ordered his crossbowmen and archers to shoot continuously so that no one could show a finger above the walls of the city. When the people in the city found themselves so fiercely assailed, they arranged their signal on the church of Saint Lawrence which they used as a mosque. They had a basket set up on high which they raised and lowered as a signal, and banners which they displayed as a sign to the Saracen host calling for aid and assistance. After they had displayed the banners and basket for a long time, they pulled them down in recognition that they could no longer hold out.

Thus did the king of France invest those who were inside the city of Acre until the arrival of the king of England, and he set miners to undermine the wall which abutted the Maudite Tower. The Pisans made an engine which they called the cat and they brought it up to the wall where

---

169   The transaction was a matter of indemnification rather than sale, since Tancred had withheld Joan's dower after her husband's death.

170   Philip sailed from Messina on 30 March 1191 and arrived at Acre on 20 April.

the miners were working. The Saracens set fire to it and threw down the hams, oil and fish that they found in the city so that they burnt the cat and the people who were in it. The miners dug under the wall and shored it up; then they set it on fire and the wall fell. The marshal of France and a great company of knights with him entered the city through the breach in the wall, but the Saracens prevented their entry and drove them back. In this incident the marshal and many of the knights with him were killed. This greatly angered the king of France and the other barons who were there.

109 The king of France could easily have taken the city had he wished. But he was awaiting the arrival of King Richard of England because they had travelled together and had made an agreement after they had left their lands concerning all the conquests they should make. So he waited for him, as he wanted him to share in the joy and conquest of the city.

110 Before King Richard left England to come to the aid of the kingdom of Jerusalem, he had sworn an oath and promised King Philip's sister that he would marry her on the fortieth day after his return. When Eleanor his mother, who had been queen of France and was queen of England, heard that her son was bound to marry the French king's sister on his return, she was very angry. She hated the heirs of King Louis of France, her former husband, and she had no desire for her heirs to wed his offspring. So she decided that she would prevent the marriage to which her son had committed himself. She made enquiries as to where she could find him a wife and was told that the king of Navarre had two sisters.[171] If she would take enough trouble over it, she could have one of them for her son. She immediately sent word to the king of Navarre and asked him to send one of his sisters to marry her son and become queen of England. The king was thrilled by this proposition, and he had the elder sister whose name was Berengaria fitted out richly and honourably in the appropriate fashion and sent her to Poitou where Eleanor was waiting. The queen had great joy at her coming.

She immediately made arrangements for her journey and set off to catch up with her son before he left Sicily so that she could secure this marriage. On her arrival in Sicily from Poitou, she sought news of him. King Richard and the king of France had already set off, but her daughter Joan, the queen of Sicily, had sold her dower and had gone to Messina where she was making ready her passage to follow her brother to Syria. Eleanor had great joy at this news and was very pleased. She hurried to find her daughter so that she could send the maiden with her and so have a

---

171 King Sancho VI (1150-94). Berengaria was his daughter, not his sister.

better chance of achieving her desire. That way she would go with greater honour, and so it was more likely that the marriage would take place all the sooner and her ambitions would be fulfilled.[172]

111 Queen Eleanor made great haste to come to Messina. As soon as she arrived in the city she found her daughter, who received her with great honour, and the people of the land gave her good cheer. As soon as she was lodged, she discovered that her daughter was just about to set out on the journey she had undertaken. She entrusted the maiden to her and told her to take her with her and tell Richard her son to marry her and on no account to delay. They then bade farewell to each other and parted.

Queen Eleanor returned to Poitou and Queen Joan set off for Syria. As they voyaged they found themselves in the waters off Cyprus. When they saw land, the queen said to the mariners and the others who were with them that she was keen to find out if the king had passed by. They replied that that would be a good idea and they were ready to do her bidding. So the queen ordered them to come near to land. They furled the sails and approached the shore. Isaac,[173] the lord of Cyprus, had assembled his men and had stationed them to guard the coast because he feared that the kings of France and England might seize his island on their arrival. When he saw the ships coming towards the land, he sent some men in a small galley to discover who were there and where they were going. They came out to meet the ships and were told that they carried the queen of Sicily, King Richard's sister, who was on her way to Syria following her brother on his pilgrimage. The people on the ships asked those in the galley if they knew whether the kings had passed by. They replied that they did not know.

112 The men in the galley went back and told Isaac, the lord of Cyprus, that it was the queen of Sicily, sister of King Richard, who was going to Syria. Isaac, who was malicious and hated the Latins, decided on trickery and falsehood, and he sent to the lady, begging her if it was her wish to come and stay and take her ease in his land until she should hear news of her brother. He sent the small galley out to her. The messengers came to the queen and invited her on their lord's behalf to come to stay, if she so

---

172 For a discussion of the circumstances surrounding the marriage of Richard and Berengaria, see J. Gillingham, 'Richard I and Berengaria of Navarre' in *Richard Coeur de Lion: Kingship, Chivalry and War*, pp. 119-31. Gillingham tacitly rejects the account of the events leading to marriage as given here.

173 Cyprus was a province of the Byzantine empire, but Isaac Ducas Comnenos (mentioned above, para. 13) had rebelled against the government in Constantinople in the mid-1180s and had been ruling independently since then.

wished, and take her repose on land and replenish her water and food; she could wait there where she would be comfortable until she had news of the king. She took counsel with her men as to what to do. They advised her not to go. She told the messengers to thank their lord profusely and say that she dared not come to land without the permission of her brother the king. The messengers went back to their lord and reported what the queen had said to them: that she thanked him for the offer he had made but she did not dare come to land without the king's permission, although she would allow her men to replenish their water.

On receiving this report, Isaac ordered all his men to prevent the people on the ships from obtaining water. He made this prohibition because he did not want anyone to become familiar with the coast of Cyprus. He immediately had his galleys go against the ships to take them by force. As soon as the people in the ships became aware of Isaac's deception and that his galleys were being prepared to attack them, they raised their anchors and set sail for the high seas. On the next day they encountered King Richard's fleet and rejoiced greatly because of it.

113 At that time of which we are speaking three ships full of pilgrims had been on their way to aid Jerusalem. They encountered storms and ill fortune at sea and were wrecked on the island of Cyprus. The pilgrims who had escaped the perils of the sea expected to be safe there, but instead they found themselves in a greater peril. The Greeks of Cyprus arrested them and held them most cruelly. They brought them to Isaac who was very spiteful towards Latin Christians and was always looking out for the opportunity to do them some evil. He was related by marriage to Thoros of the Mountain[174] who had been the lord of Armenia and who had given his daughter to be Isaac's wife. By her he had a daughter whom King Richard captured and took overseas after he had conquered the island of Cyprus, as you will find later in this account.[175] When the pilgrims were brought before him he immediately ordered them all to be decapitated. Such was his cruelty that he gave this vile order to kill them even though they had done nothing wrong and had not come against him but rather had come for the sake of God to avenge the dishonour that the Saracens had done to Jesus Christ. They encountered greater cruelty among those who called themselves Christians than they would have found with the unbelieving Saracens.

114 He had given this wicked command to his evil Greeks, and they would willingly have obeyed. They took the pilgrims to the place where

---

174 Thoros II was the ruler of Cilician Armenia 1148-68 and uncle of Leo of Mountain.
175 Below, paras 117, 119, 144.

they were to be slaughtered. But a knight, who had been born in Normandy and who was in Isaac's pay, was moved to great pity, and he had a great sadness in his heart because they had taken the foreign pilgrims to be put to a wretched and cruel death though they had committed no crime and there was no reason for it. He commended his soul to God and surrendered his body to death in the name of his creator. He preferred to die alone rather than let all these people perish without having done any wrong. He hurried off and mounted his horse and came as fast as he could to where the pilgrims were to be slain, and in Isaac's name he ordered those who had to do this cruel deed not to kill the pilgrims. He was believed, for he was one of Isaac's companions, and they imagined that he had indeed come from their lord. So they were stopped from executing the pilgrims. The knight, who was anxious to do what he could to save them from death, spoke to them in French and advised them to take refuge in the island until God should aid them. He begged them to pray to God for him and for his soul, for he knew well that he would be put to death for having rescued them. Not long afterwards God came to them and avenged them through King Richard as we shall now tell you.

115 When Isaac found out that the knight had acted against his orders and had prevented the execution of the pilgrims, he immediately ordered his head to be cut off. This order was carried out promptly and willingly. For the Greeks regard the Franks as heretics and reckon killing a Latin to be very pleasing in the sight of God.

116 After this episode Isaac greatly feared the coming of King Richard and was fearful because of the great wrongs he had done the Christians in Cyprus. He at once came to Limassol and garrisoned it with men-at-arms, both horse and foot. He gave orders for watchmen to be stationed along the coast and instructed his men that as soon as they saw the fleet of ships they should mobilize the troops and assemble them there. All these precautions were in place when King Richard arrived with his forces and ships at the port of Limassol.[176] There he came to hear the tales about Isaac. Some of his men went ashore to get fresh water and supplies for the king's use. The Greeks who were guarding the coast refused to let them land and told them that they could have neither water nor food from the island. When news of this reached the king he was extremely angry. He immediately ordered his men and the crews of the ships to make ready to force a landing.[177] They readily obeyed his command. They filled their

---

176 6 May 1191.

177 For an alternative version of Richard's conquest of Cyprus, beginning from this point, see below, doc. 7a.

galleys and boats with knights, sergeants and crossbowmen, and the king himself came to land with them. When Isaac saw the king's forces coming to land, his men drew back, and as soon as King Richard saw that they were in retreat he ordered his troops to storm ashore. They made their landing with the king himself joining in the fray. They immediately advanced on foot against the Greek forces, and with God's help the king defeated the Cypriots at the city of Limassol.

117   After this battle in which Isaac was put to flight and abandoned his land, the king ordered his horses to be brought ashore. As soon as they were landed, he rode rapidly after the Greeks and caught up with them on the plain before they could get to the mountains. On the plain near Limassol they beat them again. So for a second time King Richard defeated Isaac, on this occasion near a village called Kolossi. Isaac fled to the mountains, and there was nowhere in the whole island that he could find protection or live securely for fear of the king. He brought together all his forces - Greeks and Armenians and other people that he had in the island - so as to engage King Richard in battle once more in an attempt to do him damage and expel him from the island by force. But the King of Glory, who had brought King Richard thus far and who wanted to plant here the good seed on the island, that is to say establish the Holy Church and Roman Christianity and to eradicate the evil root of the wicked Greeks, sent His good counsel to King Richard that he should hasten and go speedily to the castle of Kyrenia. He captured this castle on his arrival, and inside the king found Isaac's daughter, together with great riches and much gear which he seized. The king could be well satisfied, for he had found a base for himself and his navy and great wealth and rich treasure which he gave generously to his men.

118   After that Isaac assembled all the men he could raise from his domain, and stationed himself between Nicosia and Famagusta. There he waited for King Richard in the hope of defeating him. But the providence and aid of the King of Glory, who does not forsake His own, gave strength and victory to the king'so that once again he defeated Isaac the Greek and all his men. This was the third victory in battle that King Richard won over Isaac on the island of Cyprus. Isaac saw that he was defeated and had lost his army, and realizing that he lacked the power in Cyprus to resist the king, took refuge in a very strong castle named Buffavento. The king then besieged this castle and captured it, taking Isaac prisoner. Thus, with the help of God, the king subdued the whole lordship of Cyprus to his power and brought it within the realm of Latin

Christendom. Alan, who had been the archdeacon of Saint George of Ramla, was made archbishop of Nicosia.[178]

119 After King Richard had defeated Isaac and had conquered and occupied the whole island of Cyprus and had delivered it from the power of the Greeks, he ordered his ships and galleys to be made ready at Limassol to come to the siege of Acre. He was very keen to get there for he was much needed. He himself then came to Limassol where his sister and the maiden he was to marry were waiting. As soon as he arrived he married the maiden whom his mother had sent, in a chapel dedicated to Saint George.[179] Then, taking with him Isaac and his daughter, he put to sea and joined the army outside Acre.[180]

The king of France and all those who were before Acre had great joy at his coming, but the Saracens had sorrow and grief. He was received with great enthusiasm and great honour by the nobles who were there. When King Richard's wife came ashore, the king of France behaved with great courtesy and went to meet them on the shore. He himself embraced Richard's wife and took her to dry land, and he was careful not to betray his feelings or show any sign of outrage at what King Richard had done to him. For Richard had reneged on the marriage to his sister in order to marry Berengaria, the sister of the king of Navarre. But he showed his outrage clearly when he got back to France.

120 Just as he arrived at the city of Acre, Saladin had a great ship called a dromond come from Egypt. It was full of men, arms, Greek fire and supplies intended to sustain the Saracens and afflict the Christians. On board there were large numbers of venomous snakes that were to be let loose in the Christian host. When King Richard learnt that this ship was approaching the city of Acre and was bringing help to the Saracen port, he immediately sent orders for his galleys to be got ready and armed to go out and engage it in battle. The galleys were prepared with all speed with Raymond of Bone Done in command. They mounted the attack bravely, and the people in the ship defended themselves vigorously as best they could. But Jesus Christ, who does not forsake His own, gave victory to the king of England, and his galleys overwhelmed the ship and sank it on the high seas. So everything on board was lost, and the hearts and wills of the Saracens who were inside the city of Acre were weakened as a result.

---

178 The Latin ecclesiastical hierarchy on Cyprus was not set up until 1196. The first archbishop of Nicosia was Alan, the former archdeacon of Lydda.

179 Richard and Berengaria were married on 12 May.

180 Richard arrived at Acre on 8 June.

121 While King Richard was at the siege of Acre he camped on the side of the city that was towards Casal Imbert, and the king of France camped on the other side.[181] The noble king of France had the people of the city bombarded relentlessly from his side, and the king of England also made severe assaults on the besieged so that the city walls were broken into fragments by the stones thrown by the petraries. When the people of the city saw how violently they were being assailed and that Saladin could not help them, they took counsel among themselves and decided to surrender the city to the Christians for they realized they could no longer hold it. The king of France's siege-engines had broken down the walls of the city so much that it was possible to get through and engage in hand to hand fighting, while the renown of the king of England and his deeds so terrified them that they despaired of their lives. The Saracen commanders in the city completely gave up hope of getting any help or aid from Saladin, for the Christians had totally invested the city and ringed it tightly. So they sent to the king of France, praying and requesting that he should pause his assaults and give them a safe-conduct to come and speak with him. He sought advice and agreed to let them have safe-conducts for this purpose. The Saracen envoys came out to speak with the king in his tent, and they told him that they would surrender the city to him on condition that they could go safe and sound to the Muslim lands, together with their wives, children and possessions. The king would not agree: the city was his and all that was within, but if they would surrender to his mercy he would spare their lives.

122 While they were speaking with the king of France, the king of England, so as to get his own back on the king of France because he would not keep him informed of what was going on, had the assault on the city stepped up. When the Saracens who were with the king of France saw that they were attacking the city, they were greatly angered. They said to the king of France, 'Sire, we have come on your safe-conduct, and we assumed that your safe-conduct would hold good for us and for the people in the city until we should return. We now see that the king of England is severely harming those who are inside. So we ask you to give us leave to go since you lack the authority to forbid the assault.'

When the king of France discovered that the king of England was attacking the city despite the safe-conduct that he had given, he was furious. He gave leave to the Saracens and had them escorted to the city, telling them to defend themselves. The king was so angry that he even ordered his men to arm themselves to go and attack the king of England. He had already put on his own leg armour, when the wise men in the host intervened and calmed him down. There would have been great harm done

---

181 Casal Imbert was near the coast to the north of Acre.

that day for Christendom. The Saracens returned the city and defended themselves so stoutly against King Richard that he gained no honour at all that day and lost many of his men.

123   After this the king of France and the king of England made peace with one another and they ordered the city to be assaulted vigorously and without cease. When the Saracens saw that they could do no more, they sent to Saladin calling on him to rescue them and raise the siege of the city in accordance with his oath.[182] Saladin replied saying that he could not rescue them and that they should do the best they could. On receiving this response, Caracois, the commander in the city, sent to the kings asking for a safe-conduct to go to speak with them. They granted it reluctantly. He came out to the king of France's tent, which was where the king of England and the other barons were assembled. Caracois told them that he would voluntarily surrender the city on condition that their lives were spared and on the understanding that Saladin would return the Holy Cross, lost by the Christians at the Horns of Hattin when King Guy was defeated and taken, and would release all the prisoners he held. 'If it turns out that Saladin does not do what I have said, we shall remain at your mercy to be treated as your slaves.' The two kings agreed these terms with Caracois, and then the Saracens surrendered the city of Acre to the Christians. This was on the eleventh day of June in the year of the incarnation of Our Lord Jesus Christ 1191.[183]

124   The Christians entered the city amid great rejoicing, giving thanks to God that by His mercy He had delivered Acre from the hands of the Saracens. After Acre had been surrendered to the Christians, the kings of France and England spoke to the men of the host and ordered them to reside in the city. The king of France then entered the city and lodged in the castle while the king of England went to stay in the house of the Temple. Other knights took up residence in the houses in the town that belonged to the burgesses, but the burgesses had been expecting to reoccupy them themselves. Those who were ensconced turned them away and told them that they could not have them because they held them by right of conquest. So the burgesses went to the king of France and begged him not to allow them to be deprived of their properties. 'The Saracens took them by force, and you have come to liberate the kingdom of Jerusalem. It is not right or lawful that we should be disinherited. On the other hand, the knights who are lodged in our houses say that they have

---

182   Above, para. 75.
183   Acre surrendered to the Christians on 12 July 1191. It looks as if a copyist has confused 'juing' and 'juignet'.

conquered them from the Saracens, and so we beg you not to allow us to be dispossessed.'

The king of France sent word to the king of England and to the other barons asking them to confer with him over the governing of the city. When they were assembled at the castle at Acre where the king of France was residing, he himself began the discussion. He set forth the views of the burgesses of Acre, explaining that they had asked him to take counsel so that they should not be deprived of their properties. For they had not sold or mortgaged them, but the Saracens had taken them by force. 'And I say that we have not come seeking wealth or property nor to seize the houses of others. We have come for the sake of God and for the salvation of our souls to conquer the kingdom of Jerusalem that the Saracens have taken from the Christians, and we should restore it to them and put it in Christian hands. It seems to me that, since God has enabled us to conquer this city, it would not be right that those who have properties here should lose them. This is my view and I hope you will concur.'

The king of England and the other barons agreed with the opinion that the king of France had expressed and said that the properties should be handed back to anyone who could show by warranty or by privilege that they were theirs. Then they decided that the knights who were lodged in the houses that they had taken should hand them over to their owners, but that they should let the knights stay put for as long as they wished to remain in the land.

125 When Acre was surrendered, Saladin, who was encamped at Saffran, had promised the kings of France and England that he would hand the Holy Cross back to the Christians and would release one Christian that he held in prison for every Saracen they had captured in the city. They agreed to this, for they were keen for the Christians to be released from Saracen captivity. Saladin fixed a day to fulfil the undertaking he had promised. It was said that he arranged for most of the prisoners that he had in his realm to be brought along together with the crosses that he had seized from the churches of the kingdom, and he was all set to hand over the Christians and receive the Saracens. But on the day that he had promised he did not come. He sent word requesting another day, saying that he had a good reason why he had been unable to come on the date he had promised. The kings had a great desire to recover the Holy Cross. They took counsel and agreed another day. That day came, and the kings and the knighthood of Christendom and all the men-at-arms were made ready in serried ranks. The priests and the clerks and the men of religion were vested, and they came forth from the city of Acre barefoot and in great devotion to the place that Saladin had specified. They had come expecting Saladin to bring them the Holy Cross, but he withdrew and reneged on the agreement and the promise that he had made. So the kings of France and England found themselves deceived, and there was great sorrow among the Christians; many tears were shed on that day, and all the men of the host were greatly troubled.

126 When King Richard saw the people weeping and lamenting because Saladin had deceived them, he had great pity and wanted to calm those who were in such great distress. He ordered that the Saracens whom he had captured in his sector be brought before him. He then had them taken between the Christian and Saracen hosts, near enough to the Saracens that they could see them well. The king boldly ordered that their heads should be immediately struck off. They took hold of them - there were 16,000 in all - and killed them there in the sight of the Saracens. When Saladin saw that the Saracens who had been captured in the city of Acre were being killed before his eyes, he was afraid that the Christians would succeed in wresting the kingdom of Jerusalem from him. He went off to Ascalon and had it destroyed, since it was a strong city on the coast. He feared that the kings of France and England would go and besiege this city and that if they were to capture it he would have to go to Egypt by some route other than the road through Gaza - the simplest and most direct way of getting from Syria to Egypt.[184]

127 After this episode Count Philip of Flanders fell seriously ill and died.[185] During his illness he asked the king of France to come and talk with him since he had a great desire to speak to him before he died. The king came to where the count was lying ill. When they had spoken together the count said to the king that he should be on his guard for there were people in the host who had sworn to kill him. But he would not say who they were. The king took his words to heart, and he became so worried and angry that he fell seriously ill of a double tertiary fever. The illness afflicted him so grievously that he nearly died. While he was stricken with this illness, King Richard conceived a great crime whereby he would kill the king of France without touching him. Once someone is held culpable towards another, all the reproach follows him around. King Richard was accused of many ill deeds against the king of France. For example, he had been betrothed and promised to his sister but then he changed his mind and married Berengaria the sister of the king of Navarre. Another wrong he perpetrated at the siege of Acre was when he

---

184 Richard himself put the number of Muslim prisoners killed at 2,600. See below, doc. 7c. The slaughter occurred on 20 Aug. 1191; the fortifications of Ascalon were destroyed in September.
185 Philip of Flanders died on 1 June, before the surrender of Acre.

took the king of France's men into his service by means of gifts and promises.

128 While the king of France was lying ill, King Richard went to call on him. As soon as he arrived he enquired after his illness and how he was. The king replied that he was at God's mercy and felt himself severely afflicted by his illness. Then King Richard said to him, 'As for Louis your son, how are you to be comforted?' The king of France asked him, 'What about Louis my son that I should be comforted?' 'It is for this,' said the king of England, 'that I have come to comfort you, for he is dead.'

129 Then King Philip said, 'Now I do need to be comforted. For if I die in this land, the kingdom of France will be left without an heir.' Immediately the illness lessened and the fever left him. King Richard took his leave and departed. He thought he had achieved his wish, but evil cannot prosper in opposition to the grace of God. It was a horrible crime that Richard tried to commit against the king of France, but he had little joy of it, and the reproach stayed with him and his heirs.

After he had gone, Philip called the duke of Burgundy and William of Barres and the other members of his privy counsel and demanded of them on oath and on the undertakings that they had made to him that they should tell him if they had news of the death of his son Louis. The duke of Burgundy replied, 'Since your arrival at the siege of Acre no vessel has come from overseas that could bring such news. The king of England has told it to you out of wickedness and malice, for he thought to cause you so much distress while you are ill that you would never get up again.'

130 The king of France, aware of the English king's intention, did nothing of the kind. He sought out doctors and gave them fine jewels and begged them to comfort him and advise him as to how he could be quickly healed of his illness. The doctors offered their advice and God gave him grace to recover from his illness. He immediately ordered his galleys to be made ready so that he could pass overseas. Then he called the duke of Burgundy and all the French knights and placed them under the duke's command. He gave him a large part of his treasure and ordered him to act in his stead.

The king then boarded his galleys and set sail. When he was in the Gulf of Satalia a great storm took hold of them for a day and a night.[186] While it was night in this storm the king asked what hour it was. They told him that it could well be midnight. Then the king said, 'Have no fear now, for

---

186 Philip left from Tyre on 3 Aug.

the men of religion of France are awake. They are praying to God for us. We do not fear danger any more.' Immediately the sea calmed. They continued their journey until they arrived at Brindisi. The king went on from there to Rome and spoke with the pope, explaining the condition of the army that was in the land of Jerusalem. It was said that he hastened to go so as to prevent anyone taking the county of Flanders, for Count Philip of Flanders had died and the county had escheated to him.

131 Now we shall leave off telling of the king of France and tell you about the king of England and the barons who remained behind. The king of England was informed that the Saracens had evacuated the city of Jerusalem and that he could easily take possession of it without the need for an assault. He told the duke of Burgundy and the barons of the host about it, and they took counsel and agreed they would go and leave Acre well garrisoned. They had their ships loaded with supplies and sent them to Jaffa. Then they ordered their march, deciding who should be in the vanguard and who should be in the rearguard. King Richard and Count Aimery[187] commanded the vanguard with the duke of Burgundy and James of Avesnes leading the rearguard. But Saladin heard that the Christians were setting off in this direction, and he assembled all his forces in an attempt to prevent them getting to Jaffa. He followed them from behind and to right and left, attacking them vigorously with his skirmishers. He greatly harassed them from one side or the other, and the engagements were very heavy until they passed the Destreit river. After they had crossed this river, the rearguard came under heavy attack from the Saracens. The king then ordered his banner to be displayed and drew up his units and squadrons near a village called *Des Bufles*. There by the aid of God they defeated Saladin; many Saracens were killed as were a number of Christians. Among them was James of Avesnes, whose loss was a big blow to the Christians of the host, and several other knights suffered a cruel death in the battle that day. Nevertheless, thanks to the aid of Jesus Christ, on that occasion the victory belonged to Christendom.[188]

132 Saladin and those Saracens who were able to escape from the battle withdrew to Jerusalem. Our men followed them and camped at a town named Beit Nuba which is between Jaffa and Jerusalem.[189] They could easily have taken Jerusalem and the rest of the land that Saladin had

---

187 Presumably Aimery of Lusignan, later count of Jaffa.
188 The march south had begun on 22 Aug. The battle took place on 7 Sept. near Arsur.
189 After occupying Jaffa and consolidating his position in the surrounding area, Richard did not arrive at Beit Nuba until December.

occupied had not discord arisen among them. When they had spoken together they ordered their march - who should be in the van and who in rear - intending to take the holy city of Jerusalem. The king was to lead the vanguard and the duke the rearguard. When that had been formally agreed each went to his tent.

This set the duke of Burgundy thinking, and when he had pondered the matter he sent for the leading men from France and told them what was in his mind: 'Sirs, you know well that our lord the king of France has gone away, but the whole flower of his knighthood has remained. By comparison the king of England has only a few men. If we go to Jerusalem and take it, it will not be said that the French have taken it. Rather it will be said that the king of England has taken it. Great shame will it be to the king of France and great reproach to the whole kingdom, and they will say that the king of France had fled and the king of England has won Jerusalem, and never again will France be without reproach. What advice,' said the duke, 'do you give?' There were some who agreed with his point of view and some who did not. So the duke said that he would go no further: let them follow him who so wished. When the morning came the king knew nothing of this discussion. He armed himself and his men and set off towards Jerusalem, and he would easily have taken Jerusalem and the rest of the kingdom were it not for the discord fostered by the duke of Burgundy.

The king proceeded until he came to Saint Samuel which is also known as Montjoie and is two leagues distant from Jerusalem. The king dismounted to say his prayers for he had seen the holy city. It is the custom for all pilgrims who are going to Jerusalem to worship there, since the Templum Domini and the Holy Sepulchre now come into view. After the king had said his prayers, lo and behold a messenger came to him from one of his friends in the army telling him that the duke of Burgundy and the greater part of the French were returning to Acre. When the king learned that the duke had gone back, he was extremely angry and upset. He immediately turned round and came to Jaffa. The duke of Burgundy did not live long after his return to Acre but died and was buried in the cemetery of Saint Nicholas. Great harm was done to Christendom by his counsel. But for his disagreement over the march on Jerusalem and his departure from the king of England's side, the Christians would have won the whole kingdom. The king of England had Jaffa occupied, and then, when he had seen to it that it was well provided with men, arms and supplies, he left to come to Acre.[190]

---

190 The writer has conflated the two advances Richard made in the direction of Jerusalem (December 1191-January 1192 and June-July 1192). The duke of Burgundy died in August 1192.

133 Now I shall leave off talking about the land of Jerusalem and tell you about the island of Cyprus. Richard sold it to the Templars for 100,000 Saracen bezants, and when they had taken possession they thought they could govern the people of the island in the same way they treated the rural population in the land of Jerusalem. They thought they could ill-treat, beat and misuse them and imagined they could control the island of Cyprus with a force of 20 brothers. The Greeks hated their rule and were oppressed by it, and they still remembered the riches and the luxury to which they had been accustomed. When they saw how badly treated they were, they could not bear the indignities the Templars inflicted on them. They rose in rebellion and came to besiege them in the castle of Nicosia. When the Templars saw such a multitude of people coming to besiege them, they were greatly taken aback. They told them that they were Christians just as they were, that they had not come there by their own strength, and that, if they would let them quit the island of Cyprus, they would go willingly. When the Greeks saw the Templars abase themselves before them, they grew bold and were filled with great pride and said that they would not let them go but would take vengeance on them for the relatives and friends whom the Latins had tortured and killed.

When Brother Reynald Bochart who was their commander and the other brothers realized that the Greeks would have no mercy, they commended themselves to God and were confessed and absolved. Then they armed themselves and went out against the Greeks and fought with them. God by His providence gave the victory to the Templars, and many Greeks were killed or taken.[191] They immediately came to Acre and explained what had happened to the master and the convent. They took counsel among themselves and agreed that they would no longer hold the island as their property but, as they had no need of that purchase, they would return it to King Richard in exchange for the security that they had given him.

134 The master, Brother Robert of Sablé, and the convent came to the king and asked him to return the property they had given him and take back the island for it was not something they could hold. It clearly showed their great poverty of resolve that they could not nor dared not keep the island of Cyprus in their domain. When the king heard their wish he took the island back. But when they asked for the security that they had given him, he replied that he would not return it. For he had taken their security at three or four times its value.

After King Richard had taken the island of Cyprus back from the Templars and was holding it in his own possession, King Guy, who was

---

191 April 1192.

left without land and without a kingdom, came to him and said, 'Sire, you know that I am dispossessed and without a realm. If it should be your pleasure, I should like to ask you to sell me the island of Cyprus on the same terms as you sold it to the Templars.' The king agreed and said that it suited him well that he should have it on these terms. King Guy was delighted, and he immediately spoke to his chancellor, a man named Peter of Angoulême who was bishop of Tripoli. He told him how he had bought the island of Cyprus and that he now had need of friends as he was trying to find ways of borrowing the money. He asked, 'How long have you got to raise this sum?' He told him he had two months. The bishop replied that within two months God would have given him good counsel. He immediately took a galley and went to Tripoli. There he borrowed 60,000 bezants from Saïs, a burgess of Tripoli, from John de la Moneie and from other leading citizens,[192] and before the month was out he brought this wealth to King Guy who paid King Richard as had been agreed. Then he went to receive the island of Cyprus and take formal possession. King Richard asked King Guy for the 40,000 bezants that he still owed, and Guy requested a postponement until he was in possession of the island. After he had taken possession, King Richard again sent to him demanding the 40,000 bezants. Guy wrote back asking that he should be freed from this debt because he was poor and disinherited and before he had become a king he had been his vassal; accordingly he ought to excuse him the payment. Richard was courteous about it and did not ask again.

135 After King Guy had paid the 60,000 bezants to the king of England, he went to Cyprus, taking with him some of the knights who had been disinherited in the kingdom. As soon as he had taken seisin of the island, he sent messengers to Saladin asking advice about how he could maintain his rule there. Saladin replied that he had no great love for Guy, but since he had asked his advice he would give it the best he knew how. For once you have asked advice of someone, whether he be friend or enemy, he ought to give it in good faith. So he said to the messengers, 'I advise King Guy that if he wants the island to be secure he should give it all away.' At this the messengers departed and came to Cyprus and gave this reply to the king who followed Saladin's advice closely.

136 Now I shall tell you what King Guy did when he had taken seisin of the island of Cyprus. He sent messengers to Armenia, to Antioch, to Acre and through all the land saying that to all those who wished to come and

---

192 Saïs and John de la Moneie (or 'of the Mint') were prominent residents of Tripoli who between 1179 and 1199 are frequently found together witnessing the counts' charters and other legal instruments.

dwell in Cyprus he would give generously so that they might live. The knights, sergeants and burgesses whom the Saracens had dispossessed heard the word of King Guy. They set off and came to him, as did great numbers of young women and orphans whose husbands and fathers were killed and lost in Syria. He gave rich fiefs both to the Greeks and the knights he had brought with him and to shoemakers, masons and Arabic scribes so that (may God be merciful!) they became knights and great vavassors in the island of Cyprus. He had them marry the women on their arrival as befitted their station, and he provided for them out of his wealth so that those that married them would be well satisfied. He granted so much land away to those who would take it that he enfeoffed 300 knights and 200 mounted sergeants, not to mention the burgesses who lived in the cities to whom he gave substantial lands and allowances. When he had finished this distribution, he had not kept enough for himself to support 20 knights. Thus did King Guy people the island of Cyprus, and I will tell you that if the emperor Baldwin had peopled Constantinople in the manner in which Guy had peopled the island of Cyprus, he would never have lost it. For he died because he wanted to retain too much of the empire in his domain, and because of this he lost it all.[193] As the saying goes in reproof: 'Who covets all, loses all.'

137 Now we shall leave off speaking of the island of Cyprus to which we shall return in due course, and tell you about the land of *Outremer*. It happened one day that a merchant ship from the Saracen lands belonging to the lord of the Assassins arrived at Tyre. The marquis who had need of wealth sent his men to the ship and had them seize it. When the lord of the Assassins heard that the marquis had taken his men and his property he sent word telling him to return them. He refused. Again the lord of the Assassins told the marquis that he should watch out for if he did not return them he would have him killed. The marquis replied that he would not return them. So the lord of the Assassins went and ordered two of his men to go to Tyre and kill the marquis. When they got there, they became Christians. One of them stayed around the marquis and the other around Balian, whose wife was Queen Maria and who was living in Tyre.

Now it happened one day that the marquise Isabella, the marquis's wife, was at the baths. The marquis did not want to eat before she was finished, but he was then told that she was staying longer. He was hungry, and so he mounted his horse together with two knights and went to the house of the bishop of Beauvais intending to eat with him if he had not

---

193 The allusion is to Count Baldwin of Flanders who became the first Latin emperor of Constantinople in 1204. The Continuation of William of Tyre later tells how he failed to honour his promises of grants of land in the territory he conquered. 'Eracles', p. 278.

eaten already. When he arrived he found that the bishop had eaten, so he said to the bishop, 'Sir bishop, I would have joined you for your meal, but since you have already eaten I shall return home.' The bishop said that if he would like to wait he would be happy to give him something to eat. The marquis replied that he would rather go back. When he came outside the gate of the archbishopric at Tyre that is near the exchange and was half way down the street where it is narrow, the two men were sitting one on either side of the road. As he came between them they rose up to meet him. One of them came and showed him a letter, and the marquis held out his hand to take it. The man drew a knife and plunged it into his body. The other man who was on the other side jumped onto the horse's rear and stabbed him in the side, and he fell dead. He was buried in the house of the Hospital of Saint John. This took place in the year of the incarnation of our Lord Jesus Christ 1192.[194]

138 The king of England, who had spent some time at Jaffa, had news from overseas that King Philip of France had arrived safe and sound in his kingdom and had launched an invasion and taken Gisors and wanted to seize and occupy all the land.[195] So he left Jaffa and came to Acre. The news then arrived that the marquis had been killed by the Assassins, and the king was widely held responsible. It was said that he had arranged for the Assassins to kill him. It was even said that he had persuaded the lord of the Assassins to send men to kill the king of France. Whether that was true or not, the king of France was told. After he had heard this report he had himself guarded, and for a long time no unknown man was allowed to approach him. Others blamed King Guy, because of the way Conrad had humiliated him when he and Queen Sibylla came from Tripoli and wanted to enter the city of Tyre and he prevented them.

As soon as the king of England knew for certain that the marquis was dead, he went to Tyre, and on the advice of the barons of the kingdom of Jerusalem he took Count Henry with him. It was his intention to arrange for him to marry Isabella, the marquis's wife. The king spoke to the count and told him that he wanted to give him this lady, but he explained that she was pregnant by the marquis and if she bore a male heir he would inherit the kingdom. To this the count replied, 'And I shall be stuck with the woman. You will know why I cannot then go to Champagne.' The king said, 'I shall give you more than you would ever get by going back to Champagne. I promise you that if God grants that I can go to England, I shall come back here to you with such a great armed force that I shall conquer your whole kingdom for you and much of pagan lands as well. I

---

194 Conrad died on 28 April 1192.
195 Gisors, a major fortress on the Norman frontier, was actually surrendered to Philip on 12 April 1193, during Richard's captivity in Germany.

expect to have such great power that on my arrival I shall conquer the empire of Constantinople whereby you will have great aid. I shall give you the island of Cyprus which I have conquered, since King Guy has not paid me the whole price but still owes 40,000 bezants. I shall seek him out, and he will not depart from my presence until he has restored the island to me.'

Because of this Count Henry agreed to the marriage, and he married the lady on these assurances. It was said that most of the people of the kingdom including the leading figures swore to Count Henry that they would make his heirs lords and kings of Jerusalem. But those who swore to Count Henry were in no way bound to the marquis or to his heirs. If they acted otherwise, it is well known.[196]

139 The Pisans who were at Tyre and who had lent their wealth to the marquis feared that they would not be paid back. So they tried to come to an agreement with King Guy. They let him know through a secret messenger that if he came to the kingdom they would turn the city of Tyre over to him. King Richard had caught them unawares, for the marquis was killed on a Monday and on the Thursday Isabella married Count Henry.[197] Richard had immediately sent his messenger to seek out King Guy, with the result that both messengers arrived together. Nevertheless the plot could not be concealed.

Saladin, who was by no means slow to take advantage of a situation, knew that King Richard had left Jaffa and had come to Acre. So he assembled all his forces and went to besiege Jaffa. He directed so many engines, petraries and mangonels against the castle there that those inside could have no rest day or night. They immediately sent messages to tell the king of England that Saladin was vigorously besieging the castle that he had garrisoned, and that if he did not come to rescue it immediately it could be lost. On hearing this news, King Richard was extremely troubled and angry. He straight away sought out the nobles who were in Acre. He showed them the letters that had come to him telling him how Saladin had besieged the castle of Jaffa and asked for their views as he wished to know whether they would aid him in relieving Jaffa. They all with one accord replied that they would go with him for the good of Christendom. It was decided that the king should go by sea and the knights by land. They appointed commanders for the vanguard and the rearguard: Hugh of Tiberias and Baldwin of Bethsan were to lead the vanguard, and Balian of Ibelin and William of Tiberias the rearguard. The Saracens heard tell that

---

196 On Isabella's death in 1205, she was in fact succeeded by Maria, her child by Conrad.

197 A slight exaggeration: Conrad had died on 28 April, a Tuesday, and the marriage took place eight days later on 5 May.

King Richard was coming to relieve Jaffa. They redoubled their efforts and assaulted the castle more intensely. When the people in the castle saw that they were getting the worst of it, they asked for a safe-conduct so that they could send envoys to Saladin to arrange to surrender the castle in exchange for their lives. These envoys were Randolf bishop of Bethlehem and a good man named Aubrey of Reins.

King Richard set off from Acre with all his ships at vespers and arrived at Jaffa at daybreak.[198] The Saracen spies came to Saladin and told him that relief was about to come to Jaffa and that the king was coming by sea. Saladin ordered his men to storm the castle and take it as quickly as they could. The Saracens did what he commanded. They attacked the castle and seized it. No sooner had they taken it and the people were celebrating, than lo and behold King Richard arrived at the harbour at Jaffa and heard the shouting. He asked a man who was under the wall of the city what all the noise was about. He told him that the Saracens had taken the castle and were rounding up the Christians as prisoners. He swore that by God's calves they would never take them captive. He armed himself with his hauberk, hung his shield at his neck and took a Danish axe in his hand. He jumped into the sea followed by his men. Then he climbed up to the castle and rescued the Christians so that none were taken prisoner. Thus did the king keep his oath.

140 The king ordered the men from the galleys to make palisades and barriers out of trees and the yardarms of the ships in front of the castle as a defence against the Saracen assault. His orders were quickly carried out and the palisades were put in place. The Saracens launched a great attack that day against the king and his men, and they got into hand to hand fighting with our men inside the palisades. The king and the men who had come with him defended themselves like lions so that when the Saracens came in through one entrance they forced them out through another. For his part the king conducted himself most nobly. The haft of his axe broke, and he defended himself with his hand and the sleeve of his hauberk - whenever he struck out he threw everyone to the ground.

Some of the Saracens returned to their camp. Saladin demanded to know why they had returned without capturing the castle. They told him that the king of England had come and had relieved it. Saif al-Din, Saladin's brother, asked where the king was. They pointed him out on a small hill with his men. Saif al-Din was concerned with good and honour, and he sent one of his mamluks with a restive horse for him which was in great pain in the mouth. He charged him to say to the king that it was totally unacceptable that a king should be fighting against the Saracens on foot. The king, who was well aware of Saracen malice, realized that the

198 1 Aug. 1192.

horse was in pain and told the messenger to ride the horse at a gallop. Once he had done so he could see that it was restive. He said to him, 'Thank your lord. Take him his horse and say to him that it is not out of any love between us that he has sent me a restive horse so as to take me.' The mamluk returned and took it to his lord and told him that Richard had realized that the horse was restive. Saif al-Din was shamed and ordered the same mamluk to take him another one, more amenable than the first. The king ordered the smith to pull out the horse's canines and incisors. This was done immediately and when the man had extracted them he had a bridle put on it and had someone ride it. The horse was now easy to handle. The king mounted and did many feats of arms. The following day the host with the knights came to Jaffa. Saladin had the bishop of Bethlehem and Aubrey of Reins tortured and beaten and made them suffer so much that they died in prison.

141　After the army had arrived and the king had retaken Jaffa, a major dispute arose between Saladin and his emirs. Our people were not aware of it until after the Saracens had left their base near Jaffa and had gone to camp between Lydda and Ramla. The king and the army went to camp at the Castle of the Plains.[199] Saladin heard that the king was coming after him. He feared his brother Saif al-Din and the other emirs. So not daring to wait, he broke camp and went off with a small force towards Syria Sobal to garrison Kerak and Montreal which he had recently conquered.[200] The king and the army set up camp near a Templar castle called Toron des Chevaliers.[201]

Some bedouins made contact with the king and received a safe conduct from him. They swore that they would serve him loyally and act as spies and would keep him informed of Saladin's movements and the affairs of the whole Muslim world. The mamluks of the emirs learned of the king's largesse and gifts, and any who had angered his lord fled and came to the king of England. Sometimes the king had at least 300 mamluks, and he took 120 with him overseas when he left this land.

The bedouins espied a rich company that was coming from Egypt to Damascus. They came to the king and told him that the richest caravan for seven years was about to pass, secure in the knowledge that the king of France and the French had left and King Richard had so few men that he would let it pass through the mountains. They were well aware of the disputes among the Saracens and the position of King Richard. Saladin had sent them 1,000 men-at-arms to escort them as far as Gor.[202] King

---

199　Yazur, near Jaffa.
200　See para. 75 and note.
201　Latrun, between Ramla and Jerusalem.
202　North of the Sea of Galilee.

Richard told the bedouins who brought him the news to reconnoitre the land to see where he could come upon them most easily. They answered that they would see to it that he would know their goodwill and would take the caravan. The king was not miserly but generously gave them silver in abundance. They departed and went showing the gifts that the king had given them so that the others tried all the harder to spy out news of the caravan and other affairs in the Muslim lands and inform the king. So nothing happened in the Saracen lands without him knowing.

The bedouins tracked the caravan until it was a day's journey away from the king's camp, and once they had brought him that news he rewarded them lavishly. He now knew definitely that the caravan was nearby. He and his knights and sergeants went lightly armed. At that time hardly anyone had a bacinet, shoulder pieces, pointed coif, grieves or a helm with a visor unless he were a king, a count or a great lord. Because they were lightly armed, if by some chance a knight or sergeant lost his horse he could manage on foot, may God be merciful! But now their armour is so tight and heavy that if a knight falls from his horse he can do nothing to help himself. The king and his army set off at the first hour of the night and rode through the night so that at daybreak they were at Cisterne Rouge. There they found the people of the caravan encamped. They ran to arms and put up a defence, but it was no good for the king defeated them and captured the whole caravan. It was said that at least 1,200 Saracens were killed. The king brought the caravan to Jaffa, and he and his men came back safe and sound. The Christians lost at least 60 men, but never again did they make such a fine haul. The king distributed the booty from this caravan to the knights and sergeants and there was still plenty for himself.[203]

He left Jaffa and went to fortify Ascalon. He then fortified Gaza which he handed over to the Templars, and then he fortified Daron.[204] Saladin saw that King Richard was prospering, and so he assembled his army and came to besiege Daron. The king mustered all the men he could and went to its relief. He himself had a great desire to encounter Saladin face to face on the field of battle. If it came to pass that he could find him with a substantial force and defeat him in pitched battle, he might expect to gain the whole kingdom thanks to such a victory.

King Richard's renown terrified the Saracens so much that when their children cried their mothers would scare them with the king of England and say, 'Be quiet for the king of England!' When a Saracen was riding and his mount stumbled at a shadow, he would say to him, 'Do you think the king of England is in that bush?', and if he brought his horse to water

---

203 23 June 1192. Cisterne Rouge is well to the south of the routes linking Jaffa and Jerusalem.
204 These activities had occupied Richard in the first months of 1192.

and it would not drink, he would say to it, 'Do you reckon the king of England is in the water?'

142 Not long afterwards Saladin wrote to the king saying that, if he wanted to go to his own lands, he would make a truce with him and restore part of the kingdom he had won from the Christians. Saladin did this because he was afraid of his brother Saif al-Din. Richard had promised Saif al-Din that if he would become a Christian he would give him his sister - the one who had been queen of Sicily - to be his wife, and Saladin feared that if this marriage were to take place he would lose everything he had won. He would gladly have given him half the kingdom or more. When the king heard Saladin's message he answered that he wanted to have the whole of the kingdom of Jerusalem including what Nur al-Din had taken in the time of King Amaury; if he was not prepared to hand over what he was demanding, he should set up camp in Egypt because that was where he was going and so he would have to defend himself there.[205]

Meanwhile King Guy had come to Acre on the king of England's orders. When he arrived and did not find him there, he wanted to return to Cyprus. Count Henry, who knew why he had come, told him to wait for the king. Guy had good reason to fear that if he were to tell the count he would not wait, he would get angry and would arrest him. He disingenuously let Count Henry know that he would go to Jaffa, which was where the king was, so that he might hear his orders and act upon them. Guy said this to deceive the count, because he had already realized why he had summoned him. He told him to send two or three knights to go with him in his galley, but this was all part of his ploy to escape the count's clutches. He took with him three of Henry's most trusted knights. King Guy let the Pisans know that he was promising them many properties and privileges in Cyprus. He told them not to do him any service or other favours except to tell Aubert Marie, the commander of the galley, to follow his instructions when they were at sea. The Pisans spoke privately to Aubert Marie and gave him his orders and had him swear to obey the king once they were out of Acre. Guy and the knights who were with him in his galley set off from Acre on the count's orders. When they were near Haifa they found a small boat. They hailed the people in it, and they came alongside. He suavely had the count's knights put in the boat and told them to greet Count Henry for him and tell him that he could not go to Jaffa. The knights went to Acre, and King Guy went to Cyprus. There is no need to ask whether Count Henry was angry at how King Guy had tricked him.

---

205 Nur al-Din's principal conquest at the expense of King Amaury had been Banyas. For Richard's plans to invade Egypt, see below, doc. 7d.

143 In this sailing[206] there came messengers and letters to King Richard telling him that the king of France was seizing all his lands, and, moreover, that his brother John was in England and was getting the cities and castles and the whole kingdom to swear allegiance to himself. When he heard this news he was very worried. He tried to get Saladin to revive the offer he had previously made, but he could not. When he sent messengers asking for the truce on the terms he had proposed earlier, Saladin replied that he would not grant it because when it had been on offer he had turned it down. The messenger that the king sent was Balian of Ibelin. The king had ordered him to do the best he could, but he could get no truce from Saladin unless the king would have Ascalon, Gaza, Daron and Jaffa laid waste, for his spies had already told him the news that the king had received from overseas. Balian came back to the king and reported Saladin's demands - how that he wanted him to destroy all he had achieved. This weighed heavily on the king since he knew how weak a position the people of the kingdom would be in if he went off without making a truce. He ordered Balian to go a second time and arrange things so that at least Jaffa would not have to be destroyed. He went and proposed that Ascalon, Gaza and Daron should be wasted on condition that the Saracens would never live in Ascalon, that Jaffa should remain intact and that the Christians should possess it, and that Arsur, Caesarea and Haifa should be covered by the truce. Saladin agreed to these terms. The king had Ascalon and the other cities reduced to ruins.

Richard sent for Count Henry and had him swear to abide by the truce for ten years.[207] Then he told the count not to be dismayed that Ascalon was to be razed because he was having to go. 'If God grants me life, I shall come and bring so many men that I shall recover Ascalon and your whole realm, and you will be crowned in Jerusalem.' Henry had Jaffa supplied with food, men and arms and went off to Acre with the king.

144 Now we shall leave speaking about the kingdom of Jerusalem and tell you about the departure of the king of England. When he came to Acre he had his galleys equipped and his ships loaded, and he put his wife and sister and the daughter of the duke of Cyprus in the ships. He asked the master of the Temple, brother Robert of Sablé, to give him ten brother knights and four brother sergeants to be his companions and to be at his command, and he requested that this be done secretly. 'For I fear that the king of France will have made a deal with some people to take me captive. I have heard that he is lying in wait for me along the way.'

---

206 I.e. the fleet that would have arrived in the late spring or early summer of 1192.
207 The truce was agreed on 2 Sept. 1192. It was to last for three years and three months.

The master had the brothers and sergeants who the king had named and in whom he had the greatest trust made ready, and they came on board the ships and galleys. There were spies in the king's company. As soon as they had left the port of Acre and were on the high seas, the king decided that he would secretly transfer from one ship to another. But he was unable to maintain secrecy for he had a spy with him in his galley. He ordered the rest of the fleet to go to Marseilles.[208]

The king and Templars sailed the high seas until they came to Aquileia. This is one of the chief cities of Germany and is at the head of the Greek Sea.[209] After their arrival they bought horses and set off on their road. They travelled until they came to the duchy of Austria. The duke was in one of his castles nearby. The spy went to the castle and told the duke that the king had arrived at his castle. 'Now you can take him if you wish, for he is in your power.' The duke had great joy as he could now avenge himself for the great dishonour that the king had done him at Acre. He ordered the gates of the castle to be shut and had his men armed and go with the spy to where the king was lodged. When Richard's men heard the noise and clamour of those who were coming to take the king, they were dismayed and surprised. They did not know what to do. However, the king had an idea. He went to the kitchen, took off his robe and put on the clothes of a scullion. Then he sat down and took a spit on which there were some capons and started to roast them. The spy came into the building and searched until he found him. He said, 'Get up, good master, you are too fine to be a cook. The duke wants to speak with you.' Then he said to the duke's men, 'See, here is the king. Seize him.'

145 Thanks to the spy, the duke's men were able to identify the king, and they seized him and took him to the duke. The duke ordered him to be guarded closely but with suitable honour in a tower until he had informed the emperor. When the emperor Henry knew of it, he was delighted. He ordered the duke to bring him to him, and he immediately obeyed. The emperor held him in prison for a good while until he ransomed himself.[210]

I shall tell you about the hatred between the king of England and the duke of Austria. When the city of Acre was recovered from Saladin and the Saracens, the duke of Austria and Walram, duke of Limburg, had taken lodgings in the city. The king of England's marshal forced them to

---

208 Richard left Acre on 9 Oct. 1192.

209 I.e. the Adriatic.

210 The story of Richard's arrest has clearly been romanticized. Richard was apprehended in Vienna in December 1192. Leopold of Austria had him imprisoned in the castle at Dürnstein and handed him over to the emperor the following February. See J. Gillingham, *Richard the Lionheart* (2nd edn, London, 1989), chap. 11.

give up these lodgings and threw them out so shamefully that they were extremely angry. When they got the chance they took their revenge. By such deeds arise great wars and great hatreds as a result of which many kingdoms have been wasted and destroyed.[211]

When the king of France heard that the king of England had crossed into Germany, he had the roads guarded. He assembled his forces and entered the king of England's lands. He began to take the cities and castles and burn whatever he could until he captured the earl of Leicester whom the king had left in charge of Normandy and all the land that the king held on this side of the Channel.[212] He remained a prisoner for a long time. This was in the year 1194.

146 When the king of England had been in the emperor's prison for a while, he arranged to speak with him and told him that it would do him no good to hold him in prison; after all, he had done him no wrong and he had not been taken in war. But it made no difference. He was held to ransom all the same. The affair dragged on until the king's ransom was fixed at 200,000 silver marks. The king sent to England and had money, pledges and hostages brought for him to hand over to the emperor until he could complete the payment. He swore to him that he would deliver the money by a date that he would set. Once this was guaranteed by the pledges that he had, he let the king go. The king was not slow, and his friends and vassals aided him very well. It was said that he had horses organized in relays so that he reached his own lands extremely quickly, and it was claimed that he did four days' journeys in one. The king of France could not guard the roads properly and prevent him reaching his land.

As soon as he was in England he raised the money to pay off his ransom. He sent it to the emperor so as to release the pledges and hostages he had provided and more especially to free himself from the oath that he had made.[213] Allegedly there was not a single chalice or censer left in any church in England as they were all taken as part of the ransom. It was said

---

211 The more commonly accepted story is that Richard's men had thrown down Leopold's banner from the walls of Acre after its capture in 1191. The duke of Limburg was named Henry; his son, Walram, was prominent in the German crusade of 1197.

212 Earl Robert III of Leicester had been a companion of Richard during the crusade. He had returned to Normandy in time to lead the defence of Rouen against King Philip in 1193.

213 The ransom was fixed at 100,000 marks. In addition Richard was to pay Leopold 50,000 marks as dowry for his niece to marry Leopold's son. The hostages included Richard's brother-in-law, the son of the king of Navarre, and the two sons of Henry's arch rival, Henry the Lion duke of Saxony. Richard was released in February 1194 and was in England by 13 March.

that the emperor had most of this ransom, the duke had a share and so did the king of France because he had allowed the money to pass through his lands. King Richard did not remain idle but was quick and artful. He assembled his armies, crossed the sea and recovered the lands that Philip had taken from him while he had been in prison. He made his nephew, Otto, who was the son of the duke of Saxony, count of Poitiers, and he made war on the king of France most vigorously.

147 After the departure of the king of England, Count Henry learned that the Pisans had called on King Guy to come and take Tyre, and he was extremely angry at this. At that time the Pisans had greater power in Syria than the Genoese. Therefore there was then no talk of anyone apart from the Pisans, just as now there is no talk of anyone but the Genoese. The Pisans had equipped corsairs, and they had come to engage in piracy in Syrian waters. Count Henry knew that they had come and were harming ships going to and from his land. He told the Pisans who were in the city of Acre that they should prevent them from harming the people of the kingdom. But they would not comply with this order. So the people who came to the kingdom suffered harm, and their complaints came daily before Count Henry. The count summoned the Pisans and told them that it was not good that men from Pisa should come to the seas near Acre and rob the people as they came and went. Aimery of Lusignan, who was the constable of the kingdom of Jerusalem and brother of King Guy, tried to exculpate the Acre Pisans for it was not they who were to blame, and the Pisans themselves denied responsibility. The count would not listen to this defence. He grew angry and drove the Pisans away, and he told them that they should leave his land: if he found any of them in his lordship he would hang them by the neck.

Aimery the constable wanted to help the Pisans, and he told Count Henry that it was not a good idea to expel such fine people and so large a community as the Pisans of Acre. Then Count Henry grew angry and said to the constable, 'You want to support them against me because they want to hand Tyre over to your brother Guy. And don't think I don't know. You will not be free to go until your brother has surrendered Cyprus to me.' The Constable replied, 'It is not right that you should arrest me because of my brother. I ought to be your vassal, and I am the constable of the kingdom of Jerusalem.' Count Henry said, 'I don't know that you should be constable. For he who gave you that office scarcely had the right.'[214] Then he had him arrested, and he held him in the castle for one day. The masters of the Temple and the Hospital and the barons of the kingdom went to the count and upbraided him for having arrested the constable who was one of the greatest men of the realm and was his

_____

214 A bizarre assertion since Aimery owed his appointment to Baldwin IV.

vassal. He defended his action and said that he had not received him as his vassal and did not accept him as constable. The barons and the liege men gave him their opinion and advised him to let him go, for if he held him any longer it would lead to shame and harm. The count accepted their advice and released him that same day.

The third day afterwards Aimery came before the court and surrendered the office of constable to Count Henry and went off to Cyprus. King Guy, his brother, now gave him the county of Jaffa. Guy did not survive much longer and died leaving the realm of Cyprus to his brother Geoffrey.[215] He was summoned but did not want to come, so the people of the island of Cyprus chose Aimery.

Count Henry gave the office of constable to John of Ibelin, the brother of Queen Isabella,[216] and he then came to an agreement with the Pisans. They returned to Acre, and he gave them a bath and an oven after they had had their tower shored up. All this occurred in the year 1194.[217]

148 During the time Count Henry held the lordship of Acre, Eraclius, who had been the patriarch of Jerusalem, died.[218] The canons of the Sepulchre postulated Monachus, the archbishop of Caesarea, to be patriarch.[219] They had made this postulation without telling Count Henry, and he was extremely angry when he found out because he had been given to believe that when a patriarch dies, as we have told you previously, the canons elect and then submit their choice to the king. If the election takes place at the hour of prime and they inform the king of it, he has until vespers to reply. So it is said that the canons are the apostles and the king is the lot.[220] It was for that reason that he was angered. He had the canons seized and treated them shamefully, and he threatened to drown them in the sea because they had tried to usurp the power which belonged to the kings of Jerusalem and which they were accustomed to have in patriarchal elections. He put them in prison, and this caused a great scandal. Arch-

---

215 Guy of Lusignan seems to have died towards the end of 1194. His brother Geoffrey (see paras. 78-80, 85-6) had been given the county of Jaffa and Ascalon but returned to the West, probably in 1192.

216 John was Isabella's half-brother, the elder son of Maria Comnena and Balian of Ibelin. He was later famous as lord of Beirut and died in 1236.

217 Henry's grant of a bath and oven to the Pisans is dated January 1195. His policy seems to have been to rescind the generous grants of privileges awarded during the years 1187-92. Riley-Smith, *Feudal Nobility*, pp. 68, 153-4.

218 Eraclius had died at the siege of Acre, almost certainly in 1190. Earlier attempts to replace him had failed. See Edbury and Rowe, 'William of Tyre and the Patriarchal Election', pp. 14-15.

219 The writer or a copyist has confused the name Monachus with the word for monk. He had become archbishop of Caesarea in succession to Eraclius in 1180.

220 Above, para. 37.

bishop Joscius and the other leading men rebuked the count for his wrong-doing in laying hands on the canons of the Sepulchre and treating them shamefully. They pointed out that, were it to be known in Rome, there would more trouble. 'And it can do you a lot of damage. For if the man who has been postulated become patriarch, he will be opposed to our deeds.' So they advised him to let the canons go in peace to their house, and to go and make peace with the patriarch-elect so that he would be on good terms with him and forget what had happened. The count followed their advice, and he went to the archbishop of Caesarea and made an agreement with him and gave the archbishop's nephew, who was called Gratian, a village named Quafarbole, which was in the territory of Acre, and 500 bezants for the service of his body and made him a knight.

The canons went to Rome and presented the postulation they had made of the archbishop of Caesarea and received the pallium and confirmation. Pope Celestine was told how badly the count had treated the canons of the Sepulchre. So the pope reproved Count Henry and made the decretal which began with the words, 'Since the land which is raised up and called the heritage and portion of God ...'[221] Since then the king of Jerusalem has no longer been the lot, but on the other hand the canons are still the electors.

No one should be surprised if the canons of the Sepulchre should have had this right in Jerusalem. For from the conquest of the land until now there have been few periods when there has not been schism in the church of Rome. When Godfrey and the other barons set off to come to conquer Jerusalem, there was a schism between Pope Urban and King Henry. Then there was Gelasius, and afterwards Innocent II, and then Pope Alexander and the emperor Frederick, the grandfather of the present one, which lasted for 18 years. Frederick made three popes, all of whom perished miserably. Accordingly he ought not to hold it by custom, and so Pope Celestine forbade it as is described above.[222]

149 At the time Aimery of Lusignan was crowned king of the island of Cyprus, there was an evil-doer named Canaqui who since the time of the

---

221 For the decretal which in fact belongs to 1191, see Edbury and Rowe, 'William of Tyre and the Patriarchal Election', pp. 15-17. The Latin text reads, 'Cum terra, quae funiculus hereditatis domini censabatur ...'

222 The Florentine *Eracles* perhaps makes better sense of this last paragraph by substituting 'king' for 'canons of the Sepulchre' in the opening sentence. The repeated schisms would then have made the royal intrusion into the election process possible. The allusions are to the schisms of 1080-1100 involving the anti-pope Clement III, the schism of 1118-21 in the time of Gelasius II involving the anti-pope Gregory VIII, the schism of 1130 involving Innocent II and the anti-pope Anacletus II, and finally the schism of 1159 and the imperially backed opponents of Pope Alexander III.

Greeks had done much harm to the Christians there. When King Aimery came to hear about him, he ordered that he should be captured and offered 1,000 bezants to whoever should bring him to him that he might do justice. When he learned that the king was seeking him, he fled from Cyprus and went to Cilicia to a Greek named Isaac who was the lord of the Antioch that is on the coast and which used to be called Pissidian Antioch. This evil-doer found a great protector in that lord Isaac. He received him very readily because he knew he was much hated by the Christians, for he himself was too. Canaqui asked Isaac to equip a small galley for him so as to make war on the people of Cyprus. Isaac readily agreed as this was something he wanted. In accord with his orders, he began to engage in piracy around the island of Cyprus. He found a boat in which were some people he knew, and he asked them for news of the king and of the land of Cyprus. They told him that the queen and her children had come to stay near the sea in a village named Paradhisi.[223] The queen had been ill, and, because she had had a change of air from the kingdom of Jerusalem, she had come there to rest and recuperate. As soon as Canaqui knew where she was, he landed with some of his companions. He was familiar with the lie of the land, and he came at dawn to the village where he surprised the people who were with her, captured the queen and her children, and took them off in his galley.

150 After he had absconded with the queen, the hue and cry arose in the land and the news came to the king who was greatly angered. He set off after them and hoped to catch them before they put to sea, but he could not. The king and queen's relations and everyone else were very sorrowful at this shameful event that had taken place in the kingdom of Cyprus. Canaqui came in great triumph to his lord bearing his rich prize. When Leo of the Mountain, who was lord of Armenia, came to hear of the outrage that had befallen King Aimery and his lady, he was deeply saddened because of the love that he had both for King Aimery who was his friend and for Baldwin of Ibelin whose daughter she had been. He immediately sent messengers to Isaac to say that if he valued his life, he should have the lady and her children brought to Gorhigos the moment he had read his letters. As soon as Isaac heard this order from the lord of Armenia, he accepted that he would have to do as he was told. He sent them to Gorhigos in fitting style, and when Leo heard of their arrival he went to meet them and, receiving them with appropriate honour, did much to please them.

---

223 The queen was Eschiva, daughter of Baldwin of Ibelin. Paradhisi is near the east coast of Cyprus just to the north of the ancient site of Salamis.

151 As soon as the lady had arrived in Gorhigos, he sent messengers to King Aimery telling him not to be angry or troubled for he had freed his wife and children from the power of their enemies. When the king heard this news he was delighted at the great service and act of kindness he had done them. He had galleys made ready and went to Armenia, accompanied by the best of his men. There he was received most honourably, and he was overjoyed to find his wife and children safe and sound. Thus did Leo of the Mountain win the love of King Aimery and the lady's family thanks to the service he had rendered them.

When they were ready to return to Cyprus, the lord of Armenia came with them from Gorhigos and invited the king and all his men to eat with him. They willingly accepted. When the food was made ready and they were about to eat, Raymond of Bone Done, who was the commander of the galleys, said to King Aimery, 'Sire, if you don't leave Armenia now, you will stay here longer than you would wish.' The king asked why, and he replied that the weather was changing. The king believed him and had the queen and their children and the people get up. He himself rose. The king of Armenia was very cross because he could do no more to please them, but when he saw that the king and his men could not eat with him he had the food loaded on the galleys still in its cauldrons. They straightway left Gorhigos and came to Kyrenia. As soon as they had anchored a great wind got up and there was a storm at sea. Had they been caught in it far from land, they all would have perished.

152 Earlier, when Bohemond prince of Antioch had gone to see his cousins the kings of France and England at the siege of Acre,[224] Sibylla, his wife, who was an evil woman, got to know Leo of the Mountain, the lord of Armenia, and discussed with him how he might take her husband captive. She did so because the prince had had another wife and was poor and in debt and had married Sibylla illegally. Leo promised her that he would marry her and that he would hold the prince in prison until he gave Antioch to her son William and made him his heir and disinherited his own heirs.[225]

---

224 Bohemond III was only distantly related to the kings of France and England.

225 Sibylla was Bohemond III's third wife. According to William of Tyre she 'had the reputation of practising evil arts'. The couple had married in 1180, when Bohemond had put aside his second wife, Theodora Comnena who may have been the sister of Queen Maria. Bohemond's relationship with Sibylla had brought disapproval from the church and led to disaffection among the Antiochene nobles. See WT, pp. 1012-16 (B/K, 2, pp. 452-7). Leo had married Sibylla's niece in 1188 or 1189. Sibylla was evidently attempting to displace Raymond and Bohemond, Bohemond's sons by his first marriage, in the interests of her own child. For an Armenian account of these events, see *La Chronique attribuée au connétable Smbat*, trans. G. Dédéyan (Paris, 1980), pp. 65, 68.

When the prince came to Antioch, Leo invited him to eat with him at the Springs of Baghras.[226] The prince, who had no idea that there was any trickery, agreed on Princess Sibylla's advice to accept the invitation. The prince and princess went to the Springs of Baghras in great estate and bringing many members of the Antiochene baronage with them, including the constable, Ralph of Mons, Bartholomew the marshal, Oliver the chamberlain, Richier of Lerminet and so many other vavassors that it would take too long to list them. No man of any consequence remained in Antioch except Aimery the patriarch and Raymond, the prince's eldest son. When the prince was at the Springs of Baghras, Leo saw that there was no way of doing what he had planned, and so he invited him to go to the castle of Baghras to see the place and take his ease as he had food made ready there. The prince agreed and went with him to the castle. When the prince had eaten and had rested, he ordered that his horses be saddled for the return to Antioch. One of his men told him that they had been impounded.

153 At this Leo, who had put heavily armed soldiers in the castle, came to the prince. He, seeing his treachery, said, 'What is this, Leo? Am I taken?' He replied, 'Yes you are, for I want to have Antioch which you have promised me many times. You have had much wealth from me. In particular I would remind you how you seized my brother Rupen when you invited him to eat with you and come with you into Antioch; you arrested him, put him in prison, took a great deal of wealth from him and would not let him go until he had handed over to you the land which lies between the River Jeyhan and the borders of Baghras.[227] It is for this reason that I want you to surrender Antioch to me and the wealth that you had from my brother. Otherwise you cannot escape me.'

154 On hearing these words the prince replied, 'Who will surrender Antioch while I am held? Let me go, and I shall hand it over to you.' Leo said, 'I shall not allow that. But send some of your men who are here with you, and they can deliver the city into the hands of my envoys. After that I shall let you go.' The prince agreed and ordered Richier of Lerminet and Bartholomew the marshal to go to Antioch and hand over the city at Leo's command. Leo sent a nobleman from Upper Armenia named Hethoum of Sasoun who was the husband of his niece, the daughter of Rupen. This

---

226 According to Smbat (see previous note) these events took place in 1193.

227 Bohemond had captured Rupen, Leo's elder brother and predecessor (1175-87), in the mid-1180s. The Jeyhan is the classical Pyramos. The cession of territory, which would have meant the surrender of the eastern portion of the plain of Cilicia, was never effective.

lady later married Raymond, the eldest son of the Prince Bohemond, by whom she had Rupen who became prince in the city of Antioch.[228]

155 When these knights came to Antioch to turn the city over to him, Hethoum told the marshal and Richier to go into the city and he would lodge at Saint Julian until they had placed the gates, the castle and the other strong points under his command; only when they had done that would he enter Antioch. After they had gone into the city, they occupied the Bridge Gate and came to the palace. When they were within the court, a eunuch whom Hethoum had sent to take possession looked around and saw a chapel that Prince Raymond had built in honour of Saint Hilaire of Poitiers. On seeing it, this eunuch asked the people in the court what it was, and, on being told that it was the chapel of Saint Hilaire, said, 'We do not know how to say Saint Hilaire. But we will have it baptized and known as Saint Sarquis.'[229]

156 Immediately the eunuch had finished speaking, the prince's men who were there were extremely angered by this outrageous comment and because of the sorrow that they felt for their lord the prince. Then a serving man who happened to be present cried out, 'Sirs, how can you suffer this shame and disgrace? To think that Antioch should be taken from the power of the prince and his heirs and handed over to such vile people as the Armenians!' He thereupon picked up some stones and threw them at the eunuch and struck him such a blow to his back that he fell to the ground. The others shouted out, 'To arms!' and all the people of the city with one accord and with one voice rushed together to the Bridge Gate and occupied it, seizing all the Armenians Leo had sent to take possession of Antioch.

157 They quickly assembled in the cathedral church of Antioch, and the Patriarch Aimery was there with them. They came to some decisions and formed a commune, something they had never had before. It has lasted from then until our own day.[230] They went to Raymond, the prince's eldest son, and told them that they would have him as their lord in place of his father until his father should be freed.

---

228 Sasoun is in the mountains south-west of Lake Van and far to the east of Cilician Armenia. Hethoum died later in 1193, and his widow, Alice, married Raymond of Antioch. Their child, usually known to historians as Raymond-Rupen, controlled Antioch 1216-19, interrupting the reign of Bohemond III's son, Bohemond IV.
229 Prince Raymond (1136-49) was himself from Poitiers.
230 For the commune of Antioch, see Prawer, *Crusader Institutions*, pp. 68-76.

When Hethoum who was waiting at Saint Julian heard the news that the people of Antioch had rebelled against the prince's orders and had arrested Leo's men, he feared that he too would be arrested and that they would seize him there and then. He made off as fast as he could towards Baghras where Leo was waiting for him.

158 As soon as Hethoum came to Baghras and recounted the news to Leo, the prince and those who were with him were immediately taken away and put in prison in the castle at Sis. There they were held honourably as befitted them until Count Henry came to free them.

159 In the year of the Incarnation 1194 Patriarch Aimery of Antioch, and Raymond and Bohemond, the prince's sons, sent a request to Count Henry that he would come and liberate their father from Leo's prison. Count Henry was happy to oblige since he was his cousin.[231] He set out from Acre, and when he had journeyed as far as Tortosa, the lord of the Assassins sent messengers to him asking him to come through his land for he had a great desire to get acquainted with him and accept him as his lord and friend. This invitation pleased Count Henry and he went there willingly.

After he had left Tortosa, the lord of the Assassins came out to meet him and received him most honourably. He took him through his land and showed him his castles. When they came before the castle of al-Kahf which is the strongest of all his castles, he asked the count, 'Do your men obey you as well as mine obey me?' The count replied that they did. The lord of the Assassins said, 'They won't obey your orders as well as my men will obey mine, as I shall show you.' He held a towel in his hand and gave a signal with it, and those who were on the top of the castle began to let themselves fall into the valley beneath and break their necks. When Count Henry saw this he begged him that it should go on no longer. He made a sign and they stopped. Then they entered the castle which had a piece of iron sharpened like a dart at the entrance. He said to the count, 'Again I shall show you how they do my orders.' He threw down the cloth that he held in his hand whereupon three or four of his men who were outside the gate impaled themselves on the iron spike and died. Count Henry begged him that he should have it done no more.

160 Count Henry stayed there and the lord of the Assassins gave him fine jewels and riches. More importantly, he pledged himself and all his men to him and he pledged to him all the friends that he had both beyond the sea and on this side of the sea. Henry departed and came to Antioch

---

231 Their kinship was more tenuous than indicated here.

where he was received with great honour. There he and the patriarch took counsel with the prince's sons concerning the release of their father. After these discussions the count left Antioch and went to Armenia. Leo came to meet him and received him honourably and brought him to the city of Sis. There they entered into negotiations, and the count arranged that Leo should free the prince from prison and that his niece, Rupen's daughter, should marry Raymond, the prince's eldest son.[232]

161 In the year of the incarnation of Jesus Christ 1195 King Guy died. The people of the kingdom of Cyprus sent to tell Geoffrey of Lusignan, his brother, of his death, and how that he had left him the kingdom of Cyprus; if he would come to receive it, they would accept him as lord and would crown him king. But he did not want to come, so the people of Cyprus, out of necessity, had Aimery crowned as king of Cyprus in his brother's place.[233]

In that same year Saladin died,[234] and Saif al-Din his brother took charge and deprived Saladin's children, his nephews, of the kingdom. He poisoned one of these nephews named Nur al-Din, who was the lord of Damascus.[235]

162 After Saladin's death, Saif al-Din came to Damascus to install his nephew as ruler. Just as the patriarch crowns the king of Jerusalem with a golden crown and anoints him, in the same way among the Saracens the greatest man in that lordship carries a saddle-cloth before him who is to become sultan, and displaying it says to the people, 'Behold your lord.' This is what Saif al-Din did for his nephew: he carried the saddle-cloth before him, displaying it and saying to the people, 'Behold the sultan of Damascus.'[236]

This Saif al-Din was very evil and ambitious, and he had a great desire to acquire the kingdom for himself and deprive his nephews of it. After he had honoured and served his nephew as he should, he returned to his castle and asked his nephew to get some apples for him to eat. After the apples had been brought in, Saif al-Din took in his hand a small knife that he carried on his belt. On its point he had put some poison. He peeled an apple and cut a piece with the middle of his knife and ate it. Then he cut

---

232 This last sentence is in the Florentine *Eracles* only.

233 Largely repeating information from para. 147.

234 Saladin died in April 1193.

235 For Nur al-Din (al-Afdal), see above, para. 25. For Saladin's prophecy that his brother would supplant his children, see para. 52.

236 The word here translated as 'saddle-cloth' is 'housse'. This is a reference to the *ghashiya*, the ornamental saddle-cloth that formed part of the royal regalia in Ayyubid and Mamluk times.

another piece from the same apple, stuck it on the end of the knife and as a courtesy offered it to his nephew. His nephew took the apple and ate it, and as soon as he had eaten it he felt the poison at work in his body. He sent for the doctors to help him recover and told them how his uncle had poisoned him. They were able to help him get over the poisoning.

163 As soon as Saif al-Din saw that his nephew had eaten the apple that had been poisoned, he left him and fled from Damascus as fast as he could and went off towards the land of the Medes, in other words to Mosul and Tekrit. For in that land there lived the Kurds.[237] There he assembled a great number of Kurds, mamluks and other people and returned to Damascus. As soon he arrived outside Damascus, the city surrendered to him. When he entered and came to the castle where his nephew was, some of the emirs that Saladin had appointed seized the son of their lord and divested him of the sword with which he was girded, so signifying that they had taken away his authority. Then they girded Saif al-Din to show that they had made him their lord.[238]

164 With Saif al-Din installed in power in Damascus, his nephew who had been the lord there went off to his elder brother, al-Malik al-Aziz, the ruler of Cairo. This man of whom we have spoken was called Nur al-Din Amir Ali, and his official name as king was al-Malik al-Afdal. Now that Saif al-Din was holding Damascus, the sultan of Aleppo, who was called al-Malik az-Zahir and who was a son of Saladin, got to hear what his uncle had done to his brother. He was very angry and upset about it. He ordered his constable to assemble his host to go to Damascus and avenge himself on his uncle for the outrage he had committed against his brother. He set off from Aleppo with a large army and came to besiege Damascus and his uncle who was within. Nur al-Din himself, who had been the lord there, came from the other direction with the men that his brother, the ruler of Cairo, had given him to help recover his lordship.

When they had besieged and worn down the city so that they were about to take it, Saif al-Din, a man who was wise in the things of this world, secretly sent men to the emirs in the nephews' armies with gifts and great promises and by such means won over to his side most of the best men of their host. The people of Damascus were so ground down that they expected to be taken by force. They said to Saif al-Din that he should

---

237 Saladin's family, the Ayyubids, were themselves Kurds.
238 Saif al-Din (al-Adil) began by supporting al-Afdal (Nur al-Din) in Damascus against his brothers who were ruling in Egypt and Aleppo. Al-Afdal was driven out of Damascus in mid-1196, whereupon Saif al-Din became the effective ruler there.

surrender the city in return for their lives, but Saif al-Din replied, 'Sirs, make yourselves ready, for I intend to go and take Cairo.'

165 It was not long before the sultan of Aleppo, who had besieged Damascus, discovered that his emirs had defected to his uncle. Realizing the trickery and deception that his uncle had perpetrated, he had the city attacked ferociously. During this assault, those who had accepted his uncle's gifts forsook him and entered Damascus. When the lord of Aleppo saw that his men had abandoned him, he departed and went to Aleppo. His brother went off to Cairo because he could no longer maintain the siege. Saif al-Din set off from Damascus after him, chasing him from camp to camp and came almost as far as Egypt.

When he reached Bilbeis, his nephew al-Malik al-Aziz, the lord of Cairo, had gone off hunting. While he was out, his horse stumbled, and he fell and broke his neck. Saif al-Din took the lordship of Cairo and held it, expelling his nephew, the former lord of Damascus of whom we have spoken. Thus did Saif al-Din, who afterwards was known as al-Malik al-Adil, conquer the kingdom. His heirs held it after him until the present.[239]

166 We have told you how Count Henry went to free Prince Bohemond, the son of the Poitevin,[240] from Leo of the Mountain's prison and arrange the marriage between Rupen's daughter, Leo's niece, and Raymond, the prince of Antioch's son. He then set off to return to Acre. He was advised to go via Cyprus, as the barons of the kingdom of Jerusalem who were with him had persuaded him to make peace with King Aimery. For while King Aimery was constable of the kingdom of Jerusalem, he and Count Henry had quarrelled over the constableship and various other things. So for example it was said that Count Henry had supported Aymar who had been elected patriarch with the result that King Aimery had left the kingdom without the count's good grace.[241] The barons of the kingdom saw that this ill will was doing the kingdom of Jerusalem no good at all whereas good relations between the two would be much to their advantage. In particular it was the Bethsans who worked hard to achieve peace between the king and the count.[242]

---

239 Al-Aziz the ruler of Egypt died in November 1198. It was only then that al-Afdal and az-Zahir besieged Damascus. Al-Adil entered Cairo in February 1200 and was proclaimed sultan there the following August. He and his heirs controlled Damascus, Egypt and most of Saladin's other lands until 1250, leaving Saladin's own descendants ruling in Aleppo.

240 I.e. Raymond of Poitiers.

241 The writer is confused here. Aimery had backed the patriarch-elect, whose name was Monachus, in the face of opposition from Count Henry. See above, para. 148.

242 Members of the family of the former lords of Bethsan were prominent among the

167 Count Henry could see the force of these arguments. He sailed from Armenia and came to Cyprus. As soon as King Aimery knew that he had arrived, he went to meet him and received him with due honour. They thereupon made peace and were good friends from then on. Then the barons of the kingdom of Jerusalem and the kingdom of Cyprus came to an agreement for the king of Cyprus's children to marry the daughters born to Count Henry and Isabella (who was later queen of Jerusalem). The arrangements for the dower were that King Aimery would pay the count all his daughters' dowries, and Count Henry, with the agreement and support of Isabella his wife, would make a gift and sale to his daughter of the county of Jaffa to be her dower and inheritance. Afterwards it came to pass that two of King Aimery's sons, Guiotin and Johanin, died before they came of age, with the result that the kingdom passed to Huet, later King Hugh, who married Count Henry's daughter Alice.[243]

168 In the year of the incarnation of Our Lord 1196 Pope Clement III died and Celestine III succeeded him.[244] We have already described how the emperor Frederick drowned in the Saleph on his journey. He had had his eldest son, Henry, crowned as king of Germany, and he had given him Constance, the aunt of King William of Sicily, to be his wife. This William died without heirs, and the kingdom of Sicily passed to her. His brother named Tancred seized the kingdom and had himself crowned as king, but it was said that he no right for he was born out of wedlock.[245] After Tancred's death, his children held the kingdom. King Henry pacified Germany and the whole of Lombardy and the lordships that belonged to him and the empire. Then he came with a large army and entered Sicily and took Palermo and the palace and Tancred's children who were there, and he immediately had them put to death. Tancred had two daughters who escaped; one of them was married to Count Walter of Brienne and the other to the count of Gravina. This King Henry destroyed many of the people of Apulia and Sicily.[246]

During this time the duke of Austria took King Richard of England captive and made a present of him to King Henry of Germany. He was

---

nobles of both Cyprus and Jerusalem at this period.

243 Aimery's sons by Eschiva of Ibelin and Henry's daughters by Isabella were all young at the time - hence the use of the diminutive forms of Aimery's sons' names. King Hugh I of Cyprus (1205-18) married Alice of Champagne (d. 1246) in 1210. The reconciliation of Henry and Aimery took place in 1197.

244 This should read 1191.

245 See above, paras. 73, 94, 98.

246 Henry completed his assumption of power in Sicily in 1195. Walter's activities in Sicily are described later in the Continuations of William of Tyre. 'Eracles', pp. 234-8.

held to ransom for 200,000 marks.[247] With the wealth that he had acquired from this ransom and the wealth that he had taken from Apulia and Sicily, Henry came to Rome and had himself crowned as emperor. He used the wealth to reach an accord with the Romans so that he could be crowned in peace. For it is said, and it has often been seen, that on the day that the emperor receives the imperial crown in Rome he has to pay a very great sum to the Romans, and if he cannot pay in gold he will have to pay in blood. At many imperial coronations it has come to pass that when the Romans cannot be paid in gold they are paid in so much blood that it flows in streams through the streets. Sometimes it has happened at the coronation of an emperor that the church of Saint Peter is full of blood. But it is said that this King Henry was crowned the day after the consecration of Pope Celestine.[248]

169 Frederick, the emperor of whom we have spoken, had so much power in the empire in his own lifetime that he had men swear that the empire would pass to his third heir. As a result they have been bound to him until the present. May God by His grace grant us someone better than the last![249]

170 After peace had been made between King Aimery and Count Henry as we have described, the count made ready to come to Acre. He had been told that al-Adil, who had deprived his nephews of the kingdom of Cairo, had already broken the truce that King Richard had made. He hurried to Limassol, and from there he sailed to Acre. The Saracens rode through the land and did much damage.

171 After the emperor Henry had taken Salerno and Palermo and the whole of the kingdom of Sicily as we have told you previously, he had great compassion for the kingdom of Jerusalem and made extensive preparations, calling to mind the good work that the emperor Frederick had begun but had not been able to finish. He would gladly have accomplished them himself, had not God required of him his life. Henry entreated and commanded the princes of Germany to take the cross and go to liberate the kingdom of Jerusalem.[250] They replied they had not left their lands in a fit state to make such a voyage or begin so great a deed but needed time to return to Germany to prepare their crossing. He agreed, and they went

---

247 Above, paras. 144-6.
248 Above, para. 98.
249 The allusion is to Barbarossa's grandson, Frederick II.
250 Henry himself took the cross at Easter 1195.

back to Germany and made ready for the journey in a manner that befitted them. The emperor himself made arrangements for plenty of ships and supplies to be held in readiness in Apulia.

172 As part of his preparations, Henry sent envoys to Alexios, the emperor of Constantinople, instructing him to make ready his roads and the ports to which his people and ships would have recourse and organize whatever they would need.[251] They were also to say that he himself should send his people to the kingdom of Jerusalem to free it from the hands of the enemies of the cross; if he would not act in accordance with this order, he should know for certain that Henry would come and visit him. Thus did he challenge him in advance.

173 When the emperor's envoys came to Constantinople, the emperor Alexios received them honourably out the love that he had for their lord. He wanted to show off his glory and riches to them, and so when he summoned them to deliver their message he had his palace decked out with sumptuous hangings of gold, silk, pearls and precious stones and had rich tapestries of gold and silk displayed. Only then did he have the envoys summoned. When they came before him, he received them honourably and with good cheer. Then he enquired after the German emperor, and the circumstances and wealth of their lord, whether he was as rich as he was and if he had such rich and fine jewels as he had. The envoys who were wise and well briefed had no trouble in making a good reply. They told him that their lord was ten times richer than he was and had more than all the riches they had seen in the empire of Constantinople. Then he said to them, 'Does he have such rich hangings as I have?' 'Sire,' they replied, 'Yes he does. He has the finer and richer ones than these.' 'In what way are they finer?' said the emperor. 'Firstly, he has the affection of his men. Secondly, he has the whole of his empire at his command - Rome, Tuscany, Lombardy, Germany, Burgundy, Apulia and Sicily. And so he is telling you through us that you should make ready for his ships and passage and whatever his men may need, and that you yourself should get ready to travel with him to the kingdom of Jerusalem. If you will not obey the orders that we have brought, he will come and pay you a visit in your empire. Then you will be able to see his hangings of which we have told you.'

174 When the emperor Alexios of Constantinople heard the envoys' speech, he was extremely angry and outraged. Nevertheless he managed to

---

251 The leader of this embassy was the imperial marshal, Henry of Kalden.

restrain himself and said, 'Sirs, I have heard clearly what you have said to me on behalf of your lord. Go to your lodging, and I shall take counsel and reply to you as I should.'

As soon as the envoys had gone, he ordered all the senior figures and nobles in Constantinople to come before him. When they were assembled, he related what the German emperor's envoys had been sent to say. His own reaction was a desire to try his power against that of the German empire and also to humiliate the envoys who had brought such a message into his empire. 'That is why I have assembled you all here, and I want your advice. Each of you shall tell me his opinion.' Some of the young men there fully agreed that the envoys ought to be humiliated.

175 But among the others whom the emperor had asked to give him advice there was an elderly Greek from the time of the emperor Manuel. 'Sire,' he said, 'do you want me to tell you what you want to hear, or shall I speak the truth?' 'I want you,' said the emperor, 'to tell me what is best.' 'Sire, let me tell you that King William, who was your neighbour, sent asking the emperor Manuel to give him his daughter to be his wife. He agreed and then changed his mind. Because of this rebuff King William made war on him so aggressively that he occupied a good third of the empire, and if he had not then died he would have taken the rest. It was not recovered subsequently until your brother became emperor and was wise enough to be able to do so.[252] You yourself have seen that the emperor Frederick, the father of the present emperor, while on his journey to the kingdom of Jerusalem, could easily have taken another third of the empire of Constantinople when your brother, the then emperor, refused to receive or obey him.[253] Frederick did not have as much power as this emperor does. For he has all that he had plus the kingdom of Sicily. So I advise you to give the envoys a good reply. God will give you his counsel when the emperor begins his campaign. It is said that the Germans are presumptuous and the Greeks are reasonable. So I advise you not to take action or do anything harmful to the envoys. They have only said what their lord instructed them.'

The emperor could see that this nobleman had given good and sincere counsel and accepted his advice. He had the German emperor's envoys called before him and told them to tell their lord who had sent them that he too loved the kingdom of Jerusalem and the furtherance of Christendom; in particular he would rejoice greatly at the recovery of the holy

---

252 Manuel Comnenos had promised William II his own daughter in 1172 but then reneged on his undertaking. William died in 1189, four years after the collapse of his invasion. Isaac Angelos, Alexios's brother, recovered Dyrrachium, the last Norman-held town on the Balkan mainland, in 1186.

253 Above, para. 88.

city, and he was glad that God had put it into the heart of so great a man as the emperor of Germany and king of Sicily to go to win back Jerusalem and avenge the shame done to Jesus Christ. He, if it pleased God, would, like his ancestors such the emperor Manuel, take pains to aid the recovery of the Holy Land. 'By the time the emperor travels through here I shall have made preparations for what he and his people need.' After that he gave the envoys fine and rich gifts. They took their leave and came to Sicily where they found their lord, the German emperor. They gave him the reply that the emperor of Constantinople had made.

176 When the envoys returned from Constantinople and had reported to their lord, the German emperor immediately instructed the princes and the other barons in Germany to come and embark on their journey to the kingdom of Jerusalem. To all those who would go to help in the conquest of the land of Jerusalem he gave sufficient supplies and shipping so that it would cost them nothing. This was the second time the people of Germany had set off to recover Jerusalem.

177 The emperor sent to the pope with the request that he should send a legate to Germany to preach the cross. He told the pope that he would give supplies and shipping to all those who wanted to help in the conquest of the kingdom of Jerusalem so that it would cost them nothing, and that he himself would never leave the Regno[254] until the kingdom of Jerusalem had been conquered. Many knights and barons took the cross in response to his command and in response to the preaching. They came to Apulia where the emperor was waiting for them and had ships and supplies ready for their journey. He appointed the chancellor of Germany as their commander.[255] They accepted his authority very willingly since the greater part of the knights were in the pay of the empire. Henry had them all swear that they would be at the chancellor's command, and he himself swore to them that he would not leave Apulia while they were in the land of *Outremer* and would aid them with men and supplies for as long as they remained in the service of Jesus Christ.

The shipping was made ready and the men assembled. They set off and came to Acre.[256] The participants included 4,000 knights, but the number of the foot soldiers and sergeants cannot be estimated. Present in this army were the legate of the Church of Rome, Archbishop Conrad of Mainz;[257]

---

254 I.e. the kingdom of Sicily.
255 Bishop Conrad of Hildesheim (1194-98), later bishop of Würzburg (1198-1202).
256 The main body of the crusaders arrived in Acre in September 1197.
257 Archbishop of Mainz, 1183-1200.

Conrad, chancellor of the imperial palace; Henry, the count palatine;[258] Henry, duke of Brabant[259] and very many others whose names would take too long to recount.

178 Some of the Germans who voyaged to the East came to Cyprus, and the others went on to Acre. Among those who visited Cyprus was the German chancellor. When Aimery found out, he went to meet him and did him great honour and said that, since he was representing the emperor, he would ask him to crown him for he wished to hold his land from the emperor. The chancellor was only too pleased and replied that he would do as requested. He took his knights with him and went to Nicosia and crowned him. After the coronation he went off to his ships and, leaving Cyprus, he arrived in Acre after the others.[260]

After they had arrived in Acre, they made Henry, the count palatine, the marshal of the host and the duke of Brabant the master justiciar, for it was said that he was wise and honest and a good judge. While they were in the city of Acre they ill-treated the local inhabitants, throwing them out of their lodgings and, worse still, when the knights of the land were off on raid, going into their houses, expelling their women and taking up residence. This greatly angered the people of the land and Count Henry was informed. On hearing about this outrage, the count took counsel with the people of the kingdom as to what to do. Sir Hugh of Tiberias said that this violence could not be allowed and that he knew all about people like these Germans: unless one made a show of force there would be no end to it. 'Let us put our wives and children in the Temple and the Hospital, and then, with the rest of the people, launch an attack on them. That way they will back down in this business.' But Our Lord did not wish that such an disaster should come about between Christians, and, just as his idea was being put in hand, a certain wise man from among the Germans who had got to hear of it, advised them to go out and camp on the sand and thus avoid any evil. They accepted this advice and made camp outside the city.

179 While they were encamped on the sand, al-Adil (Saif al-Din), who had seized the kingdoms of Egypt and Damascus from his nephews, Saladin's sons, mustered the whole army from his entire realm and entered the land of Acre. As soon as he appeared, Count Henry sent word to the duke of Brabant to say that the Saracens were near Acre and had

---

258 Henry of Brunswick, count Palatine of Rhine (1195-1227).
259 Duke of Brabant, 1190-1235.
260 This first paragraph is in the Florentine *Eracles* only. For Aimery's coronation and the inception of the Cypriot monarchy, see P.W. Edbury, *The Kingdom of Cyprus and the Crusades, 1191-1374* (Cambridge, 1991), pp. 31-2.

come against them armed and on horseback. Then Hugh of Tiberias said, 'Sirs, behold the kingdom of Jerusalem and the kingdom of Damascus. The pagan world is all before you. Now we shall see who the true knights are!'

When the Germans saw that the Saracen forces were so great, they were dismayed. It was said that al-Adil had 70,000 men-at-arms. There were many engagements that day between them. Eventually most of the men of the kingdom and the Germans who were leading the raid advised that they should return to Acre and leave the lesser men to the mercy of God. But when Hugh of Tiberias heard that the men from both the German empire and the kingdom of Jerusalem were proposing to leave the Christians in such a dishonourable and shameful way, he said to Count Henry, 'What? Are you going to stain your lineage and the kingdom of Jerusalem with this disgrace? If it pleases God, you will not commit this cowardice today.' 'What then do you advise me to do, Sir Hugh? You see that these lords have been worsted.' 'I advise you to call on your *arrière ban*, so that all the men that here are will come to your aid.'

Henry came to Acre and raised the men of religion, the communes and the other people. At the time there were many Pisans and Florentines there, and they willingly came at this time of need and were of great value to the Christian cause. As they were going out in response to Count Henry's orders at this moment of crisis, someone said to Escarlate, 'And you - are you not going to rescue your lord?' 'As for me,' he said, 'I shall do neither more nor less.'[261] When the reinforcements reached the host, Hugh of Tiberias said to the count, 'The Saracens have seen that we have aid. They will now make a great attack on us to try to see if they can make any gains at our expense. If they cannot harm us, they will withdraw and go away. Deploy your squadrons of knights and sergeants well, and order them not to break ranks come what may. For they will concentrate all their efforts on this next charge.'

180 The count agreed with Hugh of Tiberias and immediately ordered the squadrons to be deployed. The Pisans and Florentines who were well armed in the manner of their land, were placed in front of the knights, and there were plenty of other sergeants. The count ordered that on no account should they break ranks or make a move. When he had set his squadrons in order, the Saracens made a great show of charging towards our people. Hugh of Tiberias then said to the count: 'Let us make a show of charging at them.' The count replied that that was a good idea. When they showed their faces towards the Saracens, they pulled up and turned back. Thus did

---

261 A possible explanation of this otherwise baffling exchange is that Escarlate is the dwarf mentioned below in para. 183.

Our Lord save the Christians that day through the counsel of Hugh of Tiberias.[262]

181 The Saracens departed and went to Jaffa, and the count returned with his men to Acre. Meanwhile King Aimery sent one of his knights from Cyprus named Reynald Barlais, the father of Aimery Barlais.[263] This man came to Count Henry and on the king's behalf asked for seisin of Jaffa in accordance with the terms of the agreement. This request greatly pleased the count, and he immediately said to the envoy, 'Go off to Jaffa at once and take possession. My advice and command is that you instantly put in place all the forces that are going to be needed for the coming year, for I understand that al-Adil is going to besiege Jaffa. If he does not inflict a defeat on the Christians now, he will go back home in disgrace. So I advise you to defend Jaffa as I have said, so that if he goes there with the intention of attacking it he will be unable to do any harm and you will have your men to defend it.'

182 Reynald Barlais thereupon left the count and went off to take seisin of Jaffa. But he behaved just like a Poitevin and did not do one-tenth of what the count had advised and commanded. Instead he followed his own inclinations and was overconfident. He went to Jaffa with a small company. No sooner had he taken possession there, than al-Adil came to lay siege. Once the people of the castle were under siege and the castellan saw that he was inadequately provided with men, he sent to Count Henry asking him to send crossbowmen and troops as reinforcements, as the castle would be lost if he did not have speedy aid.

183 When the count heard this news he was extremely angry and put out, and that was not surprising. For he had advised and counselled Reynald Barlais to take pains to provide the castle with men-at-arms and the other things necessary for defence. But he had taken greater trouble over bringing his wife with him.

Meanwhile the king of Hungary had died without an heir. His wife, the queen, had been the daughter of King Louis of France and was Count

---

262 Hugh of Tiberias was one of Count Raymond III of Tripoli's stepsons. Quite why he should come to such prominence in the narrative at this point is not clear. He was, however, a figure around whom myths developed. Most notable is the story that he had knighted Saladin and thus inducted him into the mystique of western chivalric virtue.

263 The text errs consistently in referring to Reynald as William. He was a Poitevin follower of Guy of Lusignan whose son, Aimery, led the anti-Ibelin faction in Cyprus at the time of Frederick II's crusade (1228-29) and the ensuing civil war.

Henry's aunt.[264] The kingdom passed to her husband's brother, and she conceived a longing to visit the Holy Sepulchre. Because the emperor had sent such a great army, she expected that he would recover the whole kingdom of Jerusalem. So she sold her dower to her brother-in-law in return for a large sum of money. Then she took the cross and, bringing a fine company of knights, came with the Germans to Syria and arrived at Tyre. She imagined that with the arrival of the Germans, the city of Jerusalem would be won back from the Saracens. Count Henry went to Tyre to see his aunt, and he greeted her with the greatest honour. But within eight days of her arrival she died and was buried in the choir of the church at Tyre. She gave all her wealth to Count Henry because he was her nephew, the son of her sister.

After her burial the count returned to Acre and ordered sergeants and crossbowmen to be retained so that they might be sent to the relief of Jaffa. They were signed on, and they came to the courtyard of the palace to muster. He was leaning on the railings of a window and looking down. The railings gave way, and he fell to the ground. His dwarf, frightened and distressed, fell out too and landed on top of him. It was said that if the dwarf had not fallen on him he would perhaps not have died so soon. Great harm befell the Christians of the kingdom of Jerusalem that day because of his death, for he was noble and wise and he would have provided the people of the kingdom with great strength and profit had he lived longer. He was a man of excellent character, and the worst sin that afflicted him was that he was too willing to listen to flatterers. He had several times ordered the railings on this window to be repaired. He was buried in the church of the Holy Cross at Acre.[265]

184 After the count's death, al-Adil, who was laying siege to Jaffa, took it by force at the point near the sea where the patriarch Gerald had a tower built, for that was the weakest place in its defences.[266] The Saracens seized Reynald Barlais and his wife. The other people who were in the castle took up defensive positions in the church of Saint Peter, thinking they would hold out there until aid came from Acre. But he who should have helped them was already dead. The Saracens climbed up onto the church and broke down the vault above them so that most of them were killed and those who escaped were taken captive. Great tribulation and ill fortune had befallen the inhabitants of Jaffa, for the Saracens had twice

---

264 Margaret, daughter of Louis VII, was the widow of King Bela III (1173-96). Bela was succeeded by Emeric (1196-1204), his son by an earlier marriage.
265 Henry died on 10 Sept. 1197. The last two sentences are in the Florentine *Eracles* only.
266 Jaffa was captured in September 1197 and returned to Christian rule in 1204. Patriarch Gerald (1225-39) built his tower at the southern end of the town in 1229.

taken them by force, once in the time of Saladin and once in the time of Saif al-Din who was also known as al-Adil.

185 After the Saracens had won Jaffa, the Germans took counsel with the men of the kingdom as to how they could achieve something for the benefit of Christendom. The Germans left Acre and went to besiege Toron.[267] While they were besieging it, the archbishop of Mainz went to Armenia where he crowned Leo of the Mountain as king.[268] The chancellor of the imperial palace who was at the siege of Toron sent a messenger overseas to the emperor Henry, who, as soon as he came into his presence, told him that his men were besieging Toron. This greatly annoyed him and made him very angry. This should not surprise us, since it was shameful for such a mighty and powerful lord as he to have his men besieging a castle. 'What?' said the emperor, 'Isn't there a city to which they can direct their attention rather than this castle?' The messenger replied, 'Sire, there are no other cities there apart from Jerusalem or Damascus. We do not have enough men to maintain a siege and escort our caravans, for there is a very great multitude of Saracens in those parts.'

186 After the messenger had gone off to the emperor, those who were besieging Toron set sappers to work to undermine the walls. When the people inside weighed up the situation and saw that there would be no assistance from any direction, they agreed among themselves to capitulate. They sent envoys to the Germans saying that they would surrender the castle in return for their lives, their property and their wives and children, and they would release 500 Christian slaves that they held in their prison. When the Germans heard this offer, they became all the more puffed up with pride and took a hard line and told them that they would not accept these terms but that they must surrender entirely to their will. They then took the Saracen envoys to the mine and showed them what they had done and said, 'How can we accept you on these terms? You are all ours.' After that they gave them leave and let them enter the castle.

187 The Germans, who relied heavily on their strength and their imagined power, had no pity on the Christian slaves who would have been surrendered to them, nor did they see the good and honour that would come to them. For had they accepted the castle on the terms the Saracens had proposed, they would then have surrendered the castle of Beaufort,

---

267 The siege began on 28 Nov. 1197.
268 Leo's coronation, which thereby inaugurated the monarchy in Cilician Armenia, took place on 6 Jan. 1198.

which is in the land of Sidon, and other castles to them. They assailed the castle ferociously with machines and men, and the Saracens defended themselves vigorously. Meanwhile the wall which they had mined collapsed and they tried to force their way through into the castle. But the Saracens defended the entrance. When the Saracens saw the strength of the attack, they feared that they would be taken by force. They renewed the safe-conduct and gave hostages and told the Germans that they could have the castle with all its wealth and whatever they had within in return for their lives and nothing else. The chancellor received the hostages and told them that he could not take the surrender of the castle until the morning because it was Christmas night and he would keep the feast and hold court. After the Saracens had handed over the hostages, they immediately regretted doing so. For they feared the Germans' cruelty, and on the other hand they had heard tell that aid was coming from Cairo. They were moved to follow a different policy, but they had nevertheless left the hostages.

188 While the Germans were waiting to get the castle of Toron, news came to them that their lord, the emperor Henry, was dead and that relief from Cairo was coming to the people in the castle. As soon as they became aware of the relieving force, they took counsel among themselves and departed like men who, thanks to the death of their lord, had lost their hearts and wills.[269]

---

269 The siege was raised on 2 Feb. 1198. The emperor had died on 28 Sept. 1197.

Part II

Selected Sources

1. The Marriage of Guy of Lusignan and Sibylla (1180)

By 1186 Guy of Lusignan was clearly unpopular with a substantial section
of the baronage in the kingdom of Jerusalem. As regent for the ailing
Baldwin IV in 1183, he had failed to impress his critics and ended by
quarrelling with the king,[1] but his problems began with his marriage to the
king's sister, Sibylla, in 1180. As these three excerpts illustrate, the circumstances of the marriage were controversial, and Guy, a younger son
from a reasonably prominent French provincial seigneurial family, was
Sibylla's social inferior. William of Tyre (document 1a),[2] who was writing in or before 1184, damns with faint praise, describing him as 'satis
nobilis' - 'noble enough' - and ascribes the marriage to an ill-judged
pre-emptive move by the king to thwart the ambitions of his relatives,
Bohemond III of Antioch and Raymond III of Tripoli. The English writer,
Roger of Howden (document 1b),[3] has a scurrilous story that he could
have picked up from a member of Patriarch Eraclius's entourage when the
patriarch visited England in 1185 or from English crusaders who accompanied the patriarch to the East only to return home when they discovered
there was a truce with the Muslims and no fighting to be done.[4] With
document 1c[5] we have a story designed to explain the antipathy of the
Ibelins for the Lusignans. This comes from the *Chronique d'Ernoul et de
Bernard le Trésorier* and could well be part of the authentic work of
Balian of Ibelin's squire, Ernoul. Some aspects of the story - the emperor
covering Baldwin of Ramla in gold coins being the most obvious - stretch
our credulity, and it has to be said that no other source mentions Baldwin's ambition to marry Sibylla. On the other hand, some of the information can be corroborated: Baldwin did go to Constantinople to raise his
ransom; the ransom was huge, with Muslim sources putting it at 150,000
dinars; Aimery of Lusignan did marry Baldwin's daughter, and the
marriage had taken place before 1176.[6]

---

1   R.C. Smail, 'The Predicaments of Guy of Lusignan, 1183-87' in *Outremer*, pp. 159-
    72.
2   Text: *WT*, p. 1007.
3   Text: Howden, *Gesta*, 1, pp. 342-3. See J. Gillingham, 'Love, Marriage and Politics
    in the Twelfth Century' in *Richard Coeur de Lion: Kingship, Chivalry and War in the
    Twelfth Century* (London and Rio Grande, 1994), pp. 244-8.
4   See Gillingham, 'Roger of Howden on Crusade', pp. 146-8.
5   Text: *Chronique d'Ernoul*, pp. 56-60.
6   See B. Hamilton, 'Manuel I Comnenus and Baldwin IV of Jerusalem', *Kathegetria:
    Essays presented to Joan Hussey* (London, 1988), p. 372; *RRH*, no. 539.

1a   At about the same time the lord Bohemond, prince of Antioch, and the lord Raymond, count of Tripoli, entered the kingdom with their armed followers. Their coming struck fear into the lord king who was afraid that they might attempt to bring about a political upheaval: namely that they would deprive him of the kingdom and would seek to lay claim to it for themselves. For the king was afflicted by his illness worse than usual, and every day the signs of his leprosy were becoming more and more evident. His sister, who had been the marquis's wife, still remained a widow and was awaiting the duke as we have said.[7] The king was aware of the arrival of these nobles and was distrustful of it, even although each was his kinsman. He therefore hastened the wedding of his sister. She could have been given in marriage much more suitably and far more to the advantage of the kingdom, since nobler, wiser and indeed richer men could have been found either among the visitors to the kingdom or among the residents. But the king was insufficiently mindful that violent impulse serves everything badly, and for various reasons that had cropped up she was given unexpectedly to a noble enough young man named Guy of Lusignan. He was the son of Hugh Le Brun[8] and came from the diocese of Poitiers. Contrary to custom, the ceremony took place during Easter. Then the aforesaid nobles, seeing that their coming was regarded with suspicion by the king and his people, completed their prayers in the customary fashion and returned home.

1b   Meanwhile William, the count of Jaffa, died. He was the son of the marquis William of Montferrat and had married Sibylla, the daughter of King Amaury and sister of King Baldwin.[9]

After his death the king took his sister to his house to be looked after with his mother. This king was a leper and therefore ill-equipped to defend his subjects. All the same, in his time the Lord achieved many things for His people. For 'unless the Lord guards the city, he who guards it watches in vain'.[10] Moreover, this leper king had many knights in his service, one of whom was named Guy of Lusignan. He was the brother of the Geoffrey of Lusignan who had killed Earl Patrick of Salisbury during the war between the king of England and his men in Poitou.[11] Guy was handsome in his appearance and excellent in arms, and among the members of the royal entourage he was closer to the king than the others. The countess of Jaffa, the king's sister, seeing therefore that this Guy was

7 Since William of Montferrat's death in 1177, negotiations had been in motion for Sibylla to marry the duke of Burgundy. WT, pp. 996-7, 1004 (B/K, 2, pp. 436, 445).
8 Guy's father was Hugh VIII, lord of Lusignan.
9 The text has 'daughter of King Baldwin and sister of King Amaury'.
10 Cf Psalm 127 v. 1
11 In 1168. See Gillingham, *Richard the Lionheart*, pp. 55-6.

handsome, chose him to be her husband. But not daring to make her will known to her brother, she loved him secretly, and he slept with her. When he found out, the king wanted to stone him, but, after many tortures and at the request and on the advice of the Templars and other wise men, he granted life to them both. Because he had no closer heir than this sister, he allowed her to take Guy to be her husband, and he gave them the county of Jaffa on condition that the son that she had had by her first husband should succeed him in the kingdom. This duly came to pass. Shortly afterwards Baldwin the Younger, the king of Jerusalem, died, and his sister's son succeeded him in the kingdom.

1c Now I shall tell you about Baldwin of Ramla who was in prison in Damascus and who had been captured at the defeat at Beaufort.[12] The countess of Jaffa, the sister of the leper king, was a widow, and she sent to him telling him to redeem himself as quickly as he could for if he were out of prison she would get the king her brother to agree that he could have her as his wife.

So Baldwin went to Saladin and asked him to show pity and let him ransom himself. Saladin answered that he had no need of money for he was rich enough, and great honour would come his way for having such a valiant knight in his prison. For never had so good a knight as he been spoken of in Christendom or in Paynim. But Baldwin managed to persuade Saladin against his better judgement to agree to a ransom. Then he much regretted having agreed, and so he went and demanded such a high figure that even if Baldwin had sold off every last piece of his land he would not have been able to pay the tenth of it. So Baldwin said that he could not pay that ransom, whereupon Saladin, because he was so cross with himself for having agreed to it, replied that either he would pay up or he would pull out every tooth he had in his mouth. Baldwin told him to go ahead, for he could not pay. So Saladin ordered his teeth to be pulled out. They pulled two of them, at which point, so great was the pain, he cried for mercy and said that he would pay the ransom which amounted to at least 200,000 bezants. Saladin was very cross, for had he imagined that he could raise this ransom he would never have agreed to it in the first place.

While Baldwin was being ransomed and was getting the payment organized, he sent word to his brother Balian of Ibelin, telling him the terms and that for the sake of God he should help him secure his release from prison: they should borrow part of the money and for the rest they should hand over such hostages and pledges as the king of Jerusalem and the Temple and Hospital should decide. When he had finalized the arrangements for his ransom, Baldwin was let out of prison and went to the land of Jerusalem.

---

12 This engagement, usually known as the battle of Marj Ayun, took place in June 1179.

Baldwin then went to the countess of Jaffa and told her to make a request to her brother the king and arrange it so that he would have her as his wife. She replied that she would raise the matter once his ransom was cleared, for she did not want her land to be put in pledge in order to pay it; he should get it paid, and then she would talk about it.

So Baldwin went off to the emperor Manuel in Constantinople. On his arrival the emperor welcomed him with joy and made a great fuss of him. When Baldwin came before the emperor he told him that he had come to him for assistance in paying his ransom. So pleased was the emperor at his coming, that he said he would willingly help him because of the love he had for so worthy a man as he and because of his love for Balian his brother.[13] Then the emperor said that he wasn't interested in giving him the exact sum of money. He had a chair brought and had Baldwin sit on it in the middle of the room. He then had gold *hyperpyra* carried in and had them all heaped up around him until they entirely covered him and came over his head.

Thus did he help Baldwin pay his ransom. The money amounted to more than was needed, and so Baldwin had it kept in a safe place. When he had stayed there as long as he wished and was wanting to set off, he took his leave from the emperor. Manuel had galleys made ready and had them carry him to Acre.

When Baldwin came to Acre he paid over the ransom and freed his hostages and pledges. He then expected to have the countess, but it was not to be. For while he was in Constantinople getting his ransom money there was a knight in the land of *Outremer* who was married to his daughter and who was the king's constable. Many times had he had his way with the king's mother, and it was she who had persuaded the king to make him his constable. He went to the countess of Jaffa and told her that he had a brother, one of the finest knights in the world, and that if she wished he would go and get him and he could have her as his wife. He managed to persuade the countess's mother and the countess herself to promise that she would not take a husband until he returned. So he went off to his land to get his brother.

Now I shall tell you all about this constable. His name was Aimery and he was born in Lusignan, the son of Hugh Le Brun, lord of Lusignan. His prowess was spoken of throughout Christendom, so good a knight was he. He went to seek out his brother Guy and bring him back across the sea. He too was a very good knight but was neither wise nor worthy. This Guy was later king of Jerusalem. When the news reached that good knight Geoffrey of Lusignan that his brother Guy was king, he said, 'Next might he well be God, by rights!'

So the constable brought his brother Guy across the sea. After they had come to land, the constable went to the countess and her mother and they

---

13 Balian was married to Manuel's great niece.

spoke to the king. They arranged things so that the king gave his sister to be Guy's wife and made him count of Jaffa.

2. The Coronation of Guy and Sibylla (1186)

The Lyon *Eracles* describes the coronation of Guy and Sibylla at paragraph 18. Two western writers, Roger of Howden and Guy of Bazoches, both of whom were in the East during the Third Crusade and so were well placed to pick up stories of what had happened, give a rather different version of events. Roger (document 2a)[1] claims that Sibylla's accession was made conditional on her divorcing Guy - there was a recent precedent in that Amaury had been obliged to divorce his wife, Agnes, in 1163 before he could be crowned - and that Sibylla outsmarted Guy's opponents in the manner described. Guy of Bazoches (document 2b)[2] also indicates that a divorce was suggested but that Sibylla firmly rejected it. It may seem strange that the Lyon *Eracles* and the related texts, all of which are closely in parallel at this point, make no mention of a possible divorce. On the other hand, the westerners' accounts might explain why the *Eracles* texts have the patriarch inviting Sibylla to nominate her consort instead of automatically proceeding to crown Guy. As Professor Kedar has suggested, they would seem to have omitted an important element in their story of what happened.[3]

2a   In the same year there died King Baldwin (V) of Jerusalem who was the son of the count of Jaffa and who had succeeded his uncle King Baldwin (IV) the Leper on the throne. After his death the Templars and Hospitallers, the counts and barons, and the clergy and people chose the countess of Jaffa, the sister of the aforesaid Baldwin (IV),[4] as queen. This was on condition that she would agree to a divorce between herself and Guy her husband. For they were saying that although Guy was seen to be honourable in arms, he was nevertheless not her equal in the nobility of his birth; and they were saying that it was not right that she, who was the daughter of King Amaury,[5] should have a husband who was not born of the noblest stock of the kingdom. On hearing this, the countess realized that there was no way she could achieve the highest position in the kingdom unless she bowed to popular demand, and so she replied that she would grant them her consent: she would agree to a divorce between herself and Guy on condition that she should be allowed to chose whoever

---

1   Text: Howden, *Gesta*, 1, pp. 358-60.
2   Text: Kedar, 'The Patriarch Eraclius', p. 197 n. 70.
3   See Kedar, *op. cit.*, pp. 195-8.
4   The text reads 'Amaury'.
5   The text reads 'Baldwin'.

she wished as her husband. Once all this was agreed and had been confirmed under oath, she was taken to the Temple where the royal diadem was placed on her head and she was consecrated queen by the patriarch Eraclius and his suffragans. After that everyone prostrated themselves in prayer and called upon the Lord that He, the King of Kings and Lord of Lords, would provide for Himself a man who could rule His people and defend them from the enemies of the cross of Christ. When this prayer was over, the queen, invoking the grace of the Holy Spirit, spoke in a loud voice, saying, 'I, Sibylla, chose for myself as king and as my husband Guy of Lusignan, the man who has been my husband. For I know that he is a worthy man and in every way of upright character: with the help of God he will rule his people well. I know that while he lives that I cannot, before God, have anyone else, for as the Scripture says, "Whom God has joined, let not man put asunder."'[6] On hearing this many of the leading men of the kingdom were outraged. But the Templars and the Hospitallers and the others who were bound by the oath saw that she could in no way be diverted from her intention and granted their consent to her wishes. Then, in accordance with God's will, they anointed Guy as king, and the people showed their assent by their subsequent acclamation. ... Meanwhile, Raymond,[7] count of Tripoli, unhappy and saddened because Queen Sibylla of Jerusalem would not have him as her husband, plotted as much evil as he could against the kingdom of Jerusalem and other Christians. He sent envoys to Saladin, the king of Babylon,[8] and told him that he was prepared to act entirely at his command and aid him against the Christian land and people. When he heard this, Saladin was moved to invade the land of Jerusalem with a huge multitude of armed men and to conquer and destroy it, as will be recounted later.

2b On the death of King Baldwin IV of Jerusalem, the governing of the kingdom devolved upon his sister, the countess of Jaffa. Although it had been recommended to her, and permission had been granted, that she should dismiss her husband Guy of Lusignan - a noble and vigorous enough knight - because he was seen to be unequal to the heights and title of royalty, and that she should take a new husband - someone of greater authority - she replied that she refused to separate from the man whom God had joined to her. It would not be lawful for her to confer the crown that he ought to receive on anyone else, since she had promised to be faithful and had granted him power over her own body. So, by the wish and decision of his most faithful wife, Count Guy of Jaffa was crowned with her as king.

---

6 Matthew 19 v. 6.
7 The text has 'Waleran'.
8 I.e. Cairo.

3. The Battle of Cresson (1 May 1187)

This letter from Pope Urban III (1185-87) to the English clergy is an appeal for aid for the Templars and draws on an account of the Battle of Cresson which the master, Gerard of Ridefort, had sent to the pope after his defeat there.[1] It is instructive to compare the information on the battle given here with the account given in paragraphs 25-6 of the Lyon *Eracles* which by contrast has a strongly anti-Templar bias.

3a *Bishop Urban, servant of the servants of God, to his venerable brothers (Baldwin) archbishop of Canterbury, legate of the Apostolic See, and the bishops, beloved abbots and other prelates of the church in England, greeting and apostolic benediction.*

When we consider the great calamities and pressures to which the eastern church has been constantly exposed and how the wicked race of pagans labours for its destruction with all its strength, deep sorrow weighs upon our heart. For, as we say with grief, there are few Christians on this side of the seas who aid that land, the desolation of which they should dread with the greatest zeal of the Christian faith. But although the enemies of the cross of Christ are ever anxious for that land's destruction, they are now striving to attack it all the more violently since they are well aware that its rulers who ought to be defending it are held back by their own quarrels. For our dearest son in Christ, the illustrious king of the people of Jerusalem, and that noble man, the count of Tripoli, have a grave enmity for one another, and they are thought likely to come into armed conflict unless the hand of the Lord restrains them.

Recently it has come to our ears through the doleful account of our dear son the master of the house of the knights of the Temple how that when he and R(oger) of good memory, late master of the Hospital of Jerusalem, together with certain other people, were to have had a conference with the aim of restoring peace between the count and the aforementioned king, it so happened that they heard that a strong company of Turks had entered Christian territory, and, although they had only 110 knights with them, inflamed with Christian zeal they fought against 6,000 enemy. In the end, so it pleased God, the master of the Hospital and Brother Robert Frenellus the marshal of the Temple and Brother Jaquelinus together with 50 Templar knights and ten sergeants and others beside

---

1 Text: R. Hiestand (ed), *Papsturkunden für Kirchen im Heiligen Lande* (Vorarbeiten zum Oriens Pontificius 3: Abhandlungen der Akademie der Wissenschaften in Göttingen, 136. Göttingen, 1985), pp. 322-4.

yielded up their souls to the Lord,[2] while others yet living were, as we hear with great bitterness of heart, taken into Turkish captivity.

The master of the Temple states that in this battle he has suffered serious losses of horses and arms, quite apart from the loss of men, and that the evil race of pagans is inflamed to attack the aforesaid land more strongly than usual in accordance with the purposes of its iniquity. So we, to whom it especially falls to be solicitous for the safety of that land and desiring that they should be more concerned with its defence, call on you as brothers and command and order you to persuade and enjoin the princes, barons and other faithful men by frequent exhortations and admonitions so that, for the remission of their sins, for God and for their salvation, they may, by their strong hand, succour Christianity there: in their compassion they should not delay in aiding the brothers of the Temple with horses and arms whereby they may be better able to defend that land. Have such care over these things that something definite is done about it, so that both the people committed to your charge, through the contributions that they may make for that land and for the brothers themselves, and you yourselves, through your words of exhortation, may be assured of eternal rewards.

Given at Verona, on the third day before the nones of September.[3]

---

2 A letter written by Terricus, the grand preceptor of the Templars, after the battle of Hattin refers to 60 brothers of the Order killed in this engagement. See Barber, *The New Knighthood*, p. 115.

3 I.e. 3 Sept. 1187. News of the much greater disaster at Hattin just over two months later had evidently not yet reached the pope.

4. The Battle of Hattin (4 July 1187) and its Aftermath

Precisely what happened at the battle of Hattin is of enormous interest, and modern scholars have been at pains to try to reconstruct events from the surviving sources - both Muslim and Christian - and from a consideration of the terrain.[1] Document 4a is the account of the battle as given by the Colbert-Fontainebleau *Eracles*.[2] It parallels the Lyon *Eracles* paragraphs 40-2, providing details lacking from that account. Of the other narrative accounts of the battle, perhaps the single most important, the *De expugnatione Terrae Sanctae per Saladinum Libellus* has been published in an English translation by Professor Brundage.[3] News of the battle was spread by letters appealing to the West for help, and some of these clearly had a wide circulation. So far as the events of the battle itself are concerned, the most informative of these is a letter addressed to Archumbald, the Hospitaller master in Italy. This letter was evidently written before news of the surrender of Ascalon (4 September) had reached its author, and it is translated here as document 4b.[4] A letter sent to the pope by the Genoese consuls contains similar information,[5] and a third letter, written before 6 August by Terricus, the Templar grand preceptor, has been translated in full by Professor Barber.[6] More rhetorical in tone is the letter (document 4c)[7] from the patriarch Eraclius to the pope written shortly before the siege of Jerusalem began - internal evidence places it in the period 5-20 September - and here news and an appeal for aid is overlain with lamentation.

4a   Now I shall tell you about King Guy and his host. They left the Springs of Saffuriya to go to the relief of Tiberias. As soon as they had

---

1   In particular Prawer, *Crusader Institutions*, pp. 484-500; M.C. Lyons and D.E.P. Jackson, *Saladin: The Politics of the Holy War* (Cambridge, 1982), pp. 258-64; B.Z. Kedar, 'The Battle of Hattin Revisited' in B.Z. Kedar (ed), *The Horns of Hattin* (Jerusalem and London, 1992), pp. 190-207.
2   Text: 'Eracles', pp. 62-5.
3   J.A. Brundage, *The Crusades: A Documentary Survey* (Milwaukee, 1962), pp. 153-63.
4   Text: A. Chroust (ed), 'Historia de expeditione Friderici imperatoris' in *Quellen zur Geschichte der Kreuzzuges Kaiser Friedrichs I* (Berlin, 1928), pp. 2-4.
5   Not translated here. There are various Latin editions including Howden, *Gesta*, 2, pp. 11-13.
6   Barber, *The New Knighthood*, pp. 115-16.
7   Text: Hiestand, *Papsturkunden für Kirchen im Heiligen Lande*, pp. 324-7.

left the water behind, Saladin came before them and ordered his skirmishers to harass them. From morning until mid-day they rode at great cost up towards the valley called *Le Barof*, for the Turks kept engaging them and so impeded their progress. The heat was very great and that was a source of great affliction, and in that valley there was nowhere they could find water. By midday they had only got half way between the Springs of Saffuriya and Tiberias. The king asked advice as to what to do. The count of Tripoli gave him evil counsel and advised him to leave the road he was on since it was too late for him to get as far as Tiberias in view of the great attack that the Turks were making; they could not camp where they were because there was no water, but nearby, beyond the mountain to the left, there was a village named Habatin (Hattin) where there were springs of water in great plenty, and there they could camp for the night; in the morning they could go on to Tiberias in great strength. The king agreed to this advice, but it was bad. Had the Christians kept to their original plan, the Turks would have been defeated. But he accepted the count's proposal and left the road he was going and turned off to the side. In the process the Christians, out of their desire to get to water, put themselves at a disadvantage, and as a result the Turks took heart and attacked them from all sides. Also they moved on and got to the water first. So it came about that our people stopped on the summit of the mountain at the place called the Horns of Hattin. Then King Guy called on the count to advise the Christians and himself. The count replied that if the king had accepted his original advice, it would have been much to his great advantage and to the salvation of Christendom. But now it was too late: 'There is nothing for it,' he said, 'I cannot now offer any advice other than to try to make camp and to pitch your tent on the top of this hill.' So the king accepted his advice and did what the count had said. On the summit of this mountain where King Guy was captured, Saladin had made a mosque which still stands in celebration and remembrance of his victory.[8]

When the Saracens saw that the Christians were making camp they were delighted. They camped around the Christian host so close that they could talk to one another, and if a cat had fled from the Christian host it could not have escaped without the Saracens taking it. That night the Christians were in great discomfort. Great harm befell the host since there was not a man or a horse that had anything to drink that night. The day that they left their camp was a Friday, and the following day, the Saturday, was the feast of Saint Martin *Calidus*, towards August. All that night the Christians were stood to arms and suffered much through thirst. The following day they were all got ready for combat, and for their part the Saracens did the same. But the Saracens held off and did not want to engage in fighting until the heat got up. Let me tell you what they did.

---

8   See Z. Gal, 'Saladin's Dome of Victory at the Horns of Hattin' in B.Z. Kedar (ed), *The Horns of Hattin* (Jerusalem and London, 1992), pp. 213-15, cf p. 207.

There was a big swathe of grass in the plain of *Barof*, and the wind got up strongly from that direction; the Saracens came and set fire to it all around so that the fire would cause as much harm as the sun, and they stayed back until it was high terce.[9] Then five knights left the squadron of the count of Tripoli and went to Saladin and said, 'Sire, what are you waiting for? Attack them. They can do nothing for themselves. They are all dead men.' Then too some foot sergeants surrendered to the Saracens with their necks bared, such was their suffering through thirst. When the king saw the affliction and anguish of our people and the sergeants surrendering to the Saracens, he ordered the count of Tripoli to attack the Saracens for it was on his land that the battle was taking place and so he should have the first charge. The count of Tripoli charged at the Saracens. He thundered down the slope into the valley, and as soon as they saw him and his men advancing towards them the Saracens parted and made a way for them as was their custom. So the count passed through, and the Saracens closed ranks as soon as he had passed and attacked the king who had stayed where he was. Thus did they take him and all who were with him, except only those who were in the rearguard and escaped.

When the count of Tripoli saw that the king and his men were taken, he fled to Tyre. He had only been two miles from Tiberias, but he did not dare go there for he knew well that, if he did, it would be taken and he would not be able to escape. The prince of Antioch's son, who was called Raymond, and the knights that he had brought with him and the count's four stepsons escaped with him. Balian of Ibelin who was in the rearguard also escaped and fled to Tyre, as did Reynald of Sidon who was one of the barons.

4b   *We shall tell you, Lord Archumbald, master of the Hospitallers of Italy, and the brothers about everything that has taken place in the lands beyond the seas.*

You must know that the king of Jerusalem was at Saffuriya around the feast of the Apostles Peter and Paul (29 June) with a huge army of at least 30,000 men. He had been properly reconciled with the count of Tripoli, and the count was with him in the army. And behold, Saladin, the pagan king, came against Tiberias with 80,000 cavalry and captured it. The king of Jerusalem was informed, and he moved from Saffuriya and went with his men against Saladin. Saladin attacked them at Meskenah[10] on the Friday after the feast of the Apostles Peter and Paul (3 July). Battle was joined, and for the whole day they fought bitterly. But night put an end to

---

9 I.e. towards noon.

10 Here and elsewhere in the translation of this letter I have followed Prawer's identification of the various locations in the vicinity of the battlefield. *Crusader Institutions*, pp. 495-6 and map on p. 494.

the strife. With the coming of night, the king of Jerusalem pitched his tents near Lubiyah, and next day - the Saturday - he set off with his army. At around the third hour the master of the Temple charged with all his brothers. They received no assistance, and God allowed most of them to be lost.[11] After that the king with his army forced his way with great difficulty to a point about a league from Nimrin, and there the count of Tripoli came to him and had him pitch his tents near a mountain that is like a castle. They could only get three tents up. Once the Turks saw them marking out their defences, they lit fires round the king's army, and so great was the heat that the roasting horses could neither eat nor drink. At this point Baldwin of Fatinor, Bachaberboeus of Tiberias and Leisius, with three other companions, separated themselves from the army and went to Saladin and, sad to say, renounced their faith.[12] They surrendered themselves and told him the situation in the king of Jerusalem's army and its dire condition. Thereupon Saladin sent Taqi al-Din against us with 20,000 chosen knights.[13] They charged at the Christian army, and from nones until vespers the fighting was most bitter. As a consequence of our sins many of our men were killed, and the Christians were defeated. The king was captured and the Holy Cross. So too were Count *Gabula*,[14] Miles of Colaverdo,[15] Humphrey the Younger,[16] Prince Reynald who was captured and killed, Walter of Arsur,[17] Hugh of Jubail, the lord of Botron and the lord of Maraclea. A thousand more of the better men were captured and killed, with the result that no more than 200 of the knights or footsoldiers escaped. The count of Tripoli, the lord Balian and Reynald lord of Sidon got away.

After that Saladin gathered his army again. On the Sunday he came to Saffuriya and took it together with Nazareth and Mount Tabor, and on the Monday he came to Acco, which is called Acre, and the people of Acre surrendered themselves to him. So too did the people of Haifa, Caesarea,

---

11 This Templar action, unnoticed in the *Eracles* texts, is also reported in the Genoese Consuls' letter.

12 The Genoese Consuls name them as Baldwin of Fortuna, Ralph Buceus and Laodicius of Tiberias and similarly indicate that there were a further three, unnamed men.

13 The Genoese Consuls also mention Taqi al-Din's role in the battle and specify that he was Saladin's nephew.

14 Not identified. The only man with the title of count in the East apart from Raymond of Tripoli was Count Joscelin. Maybe the text has a badly garbled form of his name. It should be noted that although the Lyon *Eracles* (above para. 44) reports that he escaped the field of battle, all the other versions report his capture. 'Eracles', p. 66 and p. 68 variant; *Chronique d'Ernoul*, p. 173.

15 A royal vassal known from charters of 1181-83 and who later (1189-99) appears as a vassal of the prince of Antioch. *RRH*, nos. 606, 608, 614, 624, 680, 714, 753.

16 I.e. Humphrey of Toron.

17 Presumably the 'G. (i.e. Gualterius) de Arsuro' of Guy's charter of 1186. *RRH*, no. 650.

Jaffa, Nablus, Ramla, Saint George, Ibelin, Belfort, Mirabel, Toron, *Gwaler*,[18] Gaza and Daron. After that, just as our galley was setting off from Tyre, they sent Balian to Saladin that he might go to Jerusalem and they would surrender the city. We fled with the galley to Latakia and we heard that Tyre was to be surrendered. But these cities are still safe, and they desperately need the aid of the western church: Jerusalem, Tyre, Ascalon, Marqab, Antioch, *Lassar*,[19] Sahyun and Tripoli. But so great is the multitude of Saracens that from Tyre which they are besieging as far as Jerusalem they cover the face of the earth like innumerable ants. Unless these remaining cities and the very small remnant of eastern Christians are aided quickly, they too will succumb to the pillaging of the raging gentiles who are thirsting for Christian blood.

4c   *To his most holy lord and father, Urban, supreme pontiff of the most holy Roman church and universal pope, Eraclius, by the permission of God, miserable patriarch of the Church of the Holy Resurrection of Christ, greetings and most dutiful service in due subjection.*

The enormity of our lamentation and sorrow, Reverend Father, we are scarcely able to convey to your piety's ears. It has fallen to us to see in our days the oppression of our people, the doleful and lamentable desolation of the holy church of Jerusalem and that which is holy given unto dogs.[20] Truly, Holy Father, the anger of the Lord has come upon us and His terrors have put us to confusion.[21] His displeasure drains my spirit,[22] while He has added sorrow to our sorrow.[23] He has allowed the most holy and life-giving cross, once and only given for our salvation, to be captured by the Turks, and our venerable brothers, the bishops of Lydda and Acre who were in its service, the one to be captured, the other to die on the field of battle. Also He has given over our king and the whole Christian army into the hand of pagans, and of all those who were in the battle, some have fallen by the sword, some have been led off into captivity and just a few have escaped by means of flight. Nor are these things enough to satiate the barbarity of the enemies of the cross of Christ. Indeed, striving to blot out the Christian name from under heaven, they have captured and brought under their dominion the cities and castles of the Holy Land, namely Jubail, Beirut, Sidon, Acre, Tiberias, Nazareth, Sebastea, Nablus, Haifa, Caesarea, Arsur, Jaffa, Ascalon, Lydda, Ibelin,

---

18 Not identified.

19 Not identified. Maybe Gibelacar in the county of Tripoli is intended.

20 Cf Matthew 7 v. 6. This letter abounds in biblical phraseology, and only a few of the references are given here.

21 Psalm 88 v. 16.

22 Job 6 v. 4.

23 Jeremiah 45 v. 3.

Toron, Mirabel, Bethlehem and Hebron, and have killed almost all the inhabitants by the edge of the sword. Alas, alas, O Reverend Father, that the Holy Land, the inheritance of the Crucified, should be given into the hands of pagans. Alas, alas that the Lord has thrown away His inheritance and has not spared it, withholding His mercy behind his anger. Your piety should consider and see whether there is any sorrow like unto our sorrow,[24] and should grieve for the love of the Crucified One and ourselves in accordance with the magnitude of our grief. For the holy city of Jerusalem, which formerly was wont to have dominion far and wide over the neighbouring lands, now allows unrestricted exit beyond the walls to none of its inhabitants, as it and Tyre alone remain. But, now that we find ourselves in this final and dreaded moment of our need, unless the Dayspring from on high according to the multitude of His mercies shall have visited us,[25] and unless your fatherhood shall have compassion and, through the sending of letters and your own envoys, shall have stirred all the princes of the west to bring aid speedily to the Holy Land, we despair of being able to defend these cities at all by ourselves for half a year. Your holiness may know for certain that if the Turks, having now recently won the battle, were to come to the holy city, they would find it devoid of all human defence. Therefore, although there remains no other refuge for us apart from God, we have recourse to bring our afflictions and intolerable miseries tearfully to the feet of your holiness, like sons to their father, like the shipwrecked to a haven, that out of your paternal affection your heart may be roused on our behalf and on behalf of the holy city of Jerusalem. By this your supporting protection may the Lord be appeased for his inheritance, and may He redeem our life from death. By your counsel and aid may the Lord send us quickly what is to be sent to alleviate the needs of His land and to destroy the persecutions of the enemy that most violently afflicts it. Now Saladin in overrunning the whole land is near Jerusalem, and daily we are expecting him to come and lay siege to it. He has occupied all the archbishoprics and bishoprics of our patriarchate apart from Tyre and Petra.

---

24 Lamentations 1 v. 12.
25 Luke 1 v. 78; Psalm 69 v. 16.

5. The Repercussions of Defeat

After their victory at Hattin, Saladin's forces pressed home their advantage by occupying Acre, thus cutting the kingdom of Jerusalem in two. Saladin then marched north, and, after a military demonstration outside Tyre which he decided was too well defended to be taken quickly, he continued along the coast and occupied Sidon, Beirut and Jubail. The Lyon *Eracles* records these events at paragraph 45, but then makes a serious chronological error in having him proceed still further north to occupy towns and castles in the principality of Antioch and attempt the siege of La Roche Guillaume before returning to the south to begin the campaign that culminated in the capture of Jerusalem (paragraphs 45-6). The Colbert-Fontainebleau *Eracles* rightly locates Saladin's Antiochene campaign in 1188 and, where the Lyon text has this misplaced information, it gives an account of the death of Raymond of Tripoli and the succession to Tripoli (document 5a).[1] The Lyon *Eracles* has a detailed account of Conrad's successful defence of Tyre in the closing weeks of 1187 (paragraphs 62-5). So when Terricus, who now describes himself as the former grand preceptor of the Templars, wrote a letter early in 1188 (document 5b),[2] he was able to report the beginnings of a Christian fightback. However, he also had to relate the fall of Jerusalem, and in the process he provides corroboration for the Lyon *Eracles's* account of the Muslim purification of the Dome of the Rock (the Templum Domini) after its use as a Christian church (paragraph 62).

5a   When the count of Tripoli heard that Saladin had entered his land, he went by sea to Tripoli together with Raymond, the son of the prince of Antioch, and as many knights as he could muster. After he had arrived there he fell ill, and when he realized that he was stricken with illness and had no heir who could defend his county, he decided to entrust Tripoli to the prince of Antioch so that he would guard both lands as one. So he took messengers and sent them to Prince Bohemond in Antioch and told him to send him Raymond, his eldest son, who was his godson and bore his name, since he wanted him to have Tripoli as a godson's gift.[3] When the messengers came to Antioch and had delivered their message, the prince replied that he would not send Raymond, for he had enough to do since he would be lord of Antioch and Armenia and would have to govern

---

1   Text: 'Eracles', pp. 71-3.
2   Text: Howden, *Gesta*, 2, pp. 40-1.
3   The text has 'en filluelage'.

these two lands; instead he would send him his other son, Bohemond, who was worthy and valiant and would be well able to protect Tripoli with the aid of God and his brother. He referred to him as lord of Antioch and Armenia because, when Raymond married Isabella the daughter of Rupen who had been the lord of Armenia, he had resigned the principality of Antioch and had put him in possession and had arranged for him to receive homage and fealty from the men of Antioch. The messengers returned to Tripoli and brought Bohemond, the prince's younger son, and told Count Raymond of the prince's reply. The count, who sensed that he was dying and saw that there was nothing else he could do, received Bohemond and gave him Tripoli and the whole county with all his rights and had homage and fealty done to him. Some men say that there were certain conditions attached, but I do not know the truth of it. After the count had done this he did not live long. Some people say that he had died of the great sadness that he had because he had seen the immense loss that had befallen the Christians. Thus the county of Tripoli passed to Bohemond the younger.[4]

5b *To (Henry), by the grace of God lord king of England, duke of Normandy and Aquitaine and count of Anjou, Brother Terricus, formerly grand preceptor of the house of the Temple at Jerusalem, greetings in Him who gives salvation to kings.*

You know that Jerusalem with the Tower of David has been surrendered to Saladin. The Syrians had custody until the fourth day after the feast of Saint Michael (2 October), and Saladin himself has allowed ten brothers of the Hospital to remain in their house for a year to look after the infirm. The brothers of the Hospital at Belvoir are still resisting the Saracens very well, and already they have captured two Saracen caravans, in one of which they bravely won all the arms, equipment and supplies that had been in the castle of La Fève when the Saracens destroyed it. Also Kerak, Montreal, the Templars at Safed, Crac des Chevaliers, Marqab, Chastel Blanc and the land of Tripoli and the land of Antioch are

---

4 Aspects of this story are clearly mistaken. Raymond of Antioch did not marry Rupen's daughter (whose name was Alice and not Isabella) until the mid-1190s, and so there can have been no expectation at that time that he would rule in both Antioch and Armenia. (See above, para. 154.) Raymond of Tripoli was alive and in Tripoli in August 1187 (*RRH*, no. 662), but died soon afterwards. According to Diceto (2, p. 56) he died fifteen days after the surrender of Jerusalem (i.e. 17 Oct. 1187); cf J. Richard, 'An Account of the Battle of Hattin referring to the Frankish mercenaries in oriental Moslem states', *Speculum* 27 (1952), p. 176 (a hostile account which alleges that Raymond's body showed recent signs of him having been circumcised, evidence for his conversion to Islam and thus explaining his treachery before and during the Hattin campaign).

still resisting.[5] But after Jerusalem had been captured, Saladin had the cross removed from the Templum Domini, and had it carried for two days on display through the city for it to be beaten with sticks. Then he had the Templum Domini washed with rose water both inside and out and up and down, and had his law proclaimed above it from the four corners with an extraordinary uproar. From the feast of Saint Martin (11 November) until the Circumcision of Our Lord (1 January) he besieged Tyre, and night and day he had 13 petraries constantly hurling stones into it. But on the vigil of Saint Sylvester (30 December) the lord marquis Conrad arranged his knights and foot soldiers around the walls of the city; he had 17 galleys and ten other smaller ships armed and, with help from the house of the Hospital and the brothers of the Temple, he did battle with Saladin's galleys. He defeated them and in so doing captured 11 of them. Among his prisoners were the grand emir of Alexandria and eight other emirs. A large number of Saracens were killed. But Saladin's other galleys got away from the hands of the Christians and fled to Saladin and his army. At his order these were brought up on to land, and Saladin himself took fire and had them reduced to ashes and embers. Distressed by so much sorrow, he cut off the ears and tail of his horse and rode it through his whole army in the sight of all.

---

5 Belvoir fell to the Muslims in January 1189; Safed in December 1188; Kerak in November 1188 and Montreal in April or May 1189. See above, paras. 62, 75. Crac des Chevaliers, Marqab and Chastel Blanc (Safita) remained unconquered.

6.   The Siege of Acre (1189-91)

Guy of Lusignan was released from captivity in June 1188, and in August 1189 he embarked on what was to become the central episode in the Third Crusade, the siege of Acre. To some of his detractors his defeat and capture at Hattin entailed the loss of his kingship; indeed, in a letter to the archbishop of Canterbury (document 6a), Conrad of Montferrat could speak of him as the 'former king'. This letter is dated 20 September, and is preserved by the English chronicler, Ralph of Diceto.[1] Its editor ascribed it to 1188, but there is no particular reason to place it in that year. The reference it contains to Guy depriving Conrad of support could be an allusion to the fact that Guy had induced as many troops as he could, including the crusaders who by now were arriving from the West, to accompany him to the siege of Acre. If so, the letter would belong to 1189. There is no doubt that Conrad opposed the siege and that Guy, by embarking on this project, had wrested the initiative away from him. Nevertheless Guy was soon in difficulties and had to call on Conrad for assistance. The beginning of the siege and an engagement which took place on 4 October 1189 and which resulted in the death of Gerard of Ridefort, the master of the Templars, and heavy losses on both sides are described in an undated letter from two Italian crusaders, Theobald the Prefect and Peter son of Leo, to the pope (document 6b).[2] For another account of this episode, see above paragraphs 85-6.

The siege was to last for almost two years. The Christian forces were periodically renewed by the arrival of fresh crusaders from Europe, but the death of Frederick Barbarossa in June 1190 and the fact that both Richard of England and Philip-Augustus of France delayed their departure until the summer of 1190 meant that they lacked the ability to tilt the balance decisively in their favour. A number of English crusaders including Archbishop Baldwin of Canterbury, Hubert Walter, the bishop of Salisbury, and Ranulf Glanville, the former justiciar, arrived in the early autumn of 1190, and in October Baldwin's chaplain wrote to the monks of Canterbury telling of the situation they found (document 6c, cf above, paragraph 103).[3] Clearly they were hoping that Richard and Philip would be arriving soon. But the kings did not appear. Many crusaders succumbed to epidemics, including Archbishop Baldwin, who died on 19 November 1190. Hubert Walter, bishop of Salisbury and himself soon to become archbishop of Canterbury, was left as the senior English

---

1   Text: Diceto, 2, pp. 60-2.
2   Text: Diceto, 2, pp. 70-1.
3   Text: 'Ep. Cant.', pp. 328-9.

churchman at the siege, and his letter (document 6d),[4] written apparently in the early weeks of 1191, tells of continued stalemate with problems encountered on both sides and the long-expected kings still nowhere in sight.

The death of Queen Sibylla in the late summer of 1190 is mentioned by the archbishop's chaplain. This event set in motion a major political upheaval. As described above, in paragraphs 103-6, Conrad of Montferrat succeeded in getting the clergy at the siege to agree to the divorce of Sibylla's half-sister, Isabella, from her husband Humphrey of Toron so that he could marry her himself and through her lay claim to the throne of Jerusalem. The legal and moral issues raised by the divorce were highly controversial, and Archbishop Baldwin for one had been opposed to it. If the divorce were invalid, then the legitimacy of Isabella's child by Conrad would be in doubt. So too, as Humphrey lived until about 1198,[5] was the legitimacy of the children of Isabella's next husband, Henry of Champagne, whom she married in 1192. Henry and Isabella had three daughters, two of whom survived to maturity (see paragraph 167). The question of their legitimacy was raised early in the thirteenth century when they claimed that, as their father's heiresses, they ought to have inherited his county of Champagne. In fact Champagne had passed to Henry's younger brother, Thibaut (1197-1201), and then to his descendants. So were Henry's daughters the rightful heritors of the county? The question turned on the agreement Henry had made with his brother when he had set off for the East in 1190 - it was claimed that he had intended his brother to have the county should he not return - and on the question of whether Henry's marriage to Isabella was legal. If it was not legal, then his daughters were bastards and had no right of inheritance. In 1213 a papal legate investigating the rights and wrongs of the case took statements from a group of Champenois nobles, veterans of the Third Crusade (document 6e).[6] All were partisans of the incumbent count, and so their testimony has to be regarded with some suspicion, but what they had to say about the circumstances of the divorce is nevertheless of considerable interest.

6a   *To (Baldwin), archbishop of Canterbury, Conrad, son of the marquis of Montferrat, sends greetings ...* [7]

The holy city of Jerusalem, despoiled of its worshippers, is to be mourned and lamented. As a consequence of their sins, its inhabitants

---

4 Text: Diceto, 2, pp. 88-9.
5 This date is given in Howden, *Chronica*, 4, p. 78.
6 Text: *PL*, 216, cols. 980-1. For an account of the dispute, see J. Richard, *Saint Louis, Crusader King of France* (Cambridge, 1992), pp. 42-6.
7 An opening paragraph on the turmoil into which the losses in the East have put the Church is omitted.

have been placed under tribute to Saladin and, having paid the capitation tax, are driven far from the kingdom. The walls of Jerusalem are bereft of their hermit occupants. God has stood back as if from the defilement of our evil, and Mohammed has taken over; where Christ was prayed to day and night at the appointed hours, now Mohammed is praised with uplifted voice.

But what and how much I have achieved in Tyre for the salvation of the Christian people, I believe has been made known sufficiently to your clemency. The very fact that I have preserved and am preserving Tyre is grievous and insupportable to Guy of Lusignan, the former king, and to the master of the Temple and the magnates on this side of the sea. They begrudge me and derogate my name. Thanks to them and their supporters all help is taken away, and, what is more serious, the master of the Temple has carried off the king of England's alms. Accordingly I cannot avoid complaining in tears both to God and to you. But as for the Hospitallers, I voice my full thanks to you and to God. They have persevered that good work that they have begun, and in addition to the alms of the king of England they have spent more than 80,000 brabatines[8] of their own in the service of Tyre.

Therefore, seeing as you have deigned to have compassion on the calamities of Jerusalem, I shall not stop imploring your paternity to encourage kings and rouse the people so that the patrimony of Jesus Christ may be recovered, that the exiles and the disinherited may be restored to fullness, that the chains of the captives may be loosed, and that the sacred land, trodden the feet of the Saviour, may, by your influence and your pious eloquence, be freed from the power of the pagans. I am sending you the bearers of these letters, master Bandanus, my prudent chancellor and secretary who is my faithful retainer,[9] and John, an honourable knight and member of my household, whom you may recognize as my special envoys. You may have no hesitation in accepting what they have to say to you on my behalf as if I were speaking in person. I beseech you again for the sake of piety and out of respect for me that you will be good enough to grant them your aid and counsel.

Given at Tyre on the twelfth day before the kalends of October.[10]

6b *To the lord pope, Theobald the Prefect and Peter son of Leo send greetings.*

On the fourth day before the end of August the king of Jerusalem, the

---

8 The Latin text has 'brab.', which may be a bad reading. As the editor points out, Conrad would have been more likely to have reckoned in bezants.

9 Bandanus appears in documents as Conrad's scribe (1187) and later as his chancellor (1191). *RRH*, nos. 665-8, 703, 705.

10 I.e. 20 Sept. 1188 or 1189.

Templars, the Hospitallers, the archbishop of Pisa[11] and many Pisans, came to Acre and began to besiege it. In this they were acting against the wishes of the lord marquis and the archbishop of Ravenna[12] and other Christians. On their arrival they surrounded the city in such strength that none of the Saracens could go in or out. But on the third day afterwards Saladin arrived in force and directed his attack against the king's brother and the Hospitallers. He was able to push their battle line aside and so throw open the road leading to and from the city. Our Christians were extremely alarmed and withdrew for a while and took refuge on the top of a nearby hill. Then Saladin, with 100,000 knights, surrounded them below the hill so that they could not get off. When the king of Jerusalem realized that he was surrounded by enemies on every side, he sent envoys to the lord marquis and the archbishop and the other knights whom his action had displeased, praying that, though they had been out of sympathy with his whole undertaking, they should nevertheless immediately come to his assistance as they were hard pressed from every quarter. So the marquis, together with the archbishop, took pity on the Christians in their difficulties, and on the seventh day before the end of September came by sea to their aid with 1,000 knights and 20,000 foot men. Saladin was much alarmed at his coming and withdrew for a mile from this hill.

On 4 October, we went into battle against the Saracens. The king, with the Hospitallers and the French made up one squadron. In the second squadron was the lord marquis and the archbishop of Ravenna, and we were with them. In the third were the landgrave[13] and the Pisans and Germans. In the fourth were the Templars, the Catalans and certain Germans. The king's brother and James of Avesnes remained in the camp. All of us together amounted to 4,000 knights and 100,000 foot soldiers. But Saladin had 100,000 knights against us. We, armed with the sign of the Holy Cross, began the battle at around the hour of terce, and, with God favouring our side, we pursued them with the edge of the sword and put them to flight as far as their tents. We overwhelmed seven squadrons of the Saracen who broke ranks shamefully. We killed Saladin's son, *Baldewinus* by name, and mortally wounded *Tacaldinus*, Saladin's brother, and we understand that he is now definitely dead.[14] Five hundred of Saladin's knights were killed in addition to those mentioned. While we were fighting against Saladin, 5,000 knights came out from the city and attacked us unexpectedly. Saladin saw that his allies were thus assailing us

11 Ubaldo (1174-1206), the papal legate in the East.
12 Gerardo.
13 The landgrave Ludwig of Thuringia.
14 *Tacaldinus* would appear to refer to Saladin's nephew, Taqi al-Din, who was at the battle but certainly survived. Who is meant by *Baldewinus* is unclear, but if any close relatives of Saladin had been killed this would almost certainly have been noted by the Muslim writers. For an account of this battle, largely relying on Arabic sources, see Lyons and Jackson, *Saladin*, pp. 302-4.

and rallied his forces against ours. But we, pressed on each side, resisted Saladin and fought the others bravely. However, willy-nilly we fell back to our camp. The master of the Templars and many of our men were killed on that day.

6c *The archbishop's chaplain to the convent of Canterbury.*

I know that to satisfy your concern for the state of our lord of Canterbury (i.e. Archbishop Baldwin) and the condition of the army you need true and reliable information. Our lord of Canterbury arrived safe and sound at Tyre with his entire entourage on the Sunday after the exaltation of the Holy Cross (16 September). He waited there for some time for the kings, who have still not yet arrived, and then moved down to our army at Acre. The army is given over to shameful activity. It is with sorrow and sighs that I tell you that it indulges in idleness and vice rather than in virtue. The Lord is not in the camp: there is none that doeth good.[15] The princes envy one another and jockey for position. The lesser men are in want and find no support. In the camp there is no chastity, sobriety, faith, love or charity, and, as God is my witness, I should not have believed it had I not seen it. The Turks besiege us; daily they incite us; continually they attack us. Our knights lurk in their tents, and those who promised a speedy victory are cowardly and slothful. As if defeated, they let the insults of the enemy go unpunished. Saladin's strength grows daily; every day our army gets smaller and fails. On the feast of Saint James (25 July) more than 4,000 chosen footsoldiers were slain by the Turks. Moreover, many princes have breathed their last: (Sibylla) the queen of Jerusalem; Count Stephen, the brother of the archbishop of Reims; his nephew, the count of Bar; the earl Ferrers, brother of the earl of Clare; Bernard the younger of Saint Valéry; Ranulf Glanville and innumerable others. When the bearer of these letters left us, on the Sunday after the feast of Saint Luke the Evangelist (21 October), the kings had still not arrived, nor had the city of Acre been captured. Farewell again.

6d *To his venerable lord and father in Christ, his most dear Richard, by the grace of God bishop of London,[16] Hubert, by that same grace bishop of Salisbury, greetings and steadfastness of an affection that is as faithful as it is due.*

Your belovedness should know that the town of Acre still strongly resists us after very many assaults and cannot be taken by us because it is well defended by men, walls and machines. Saladin on the other hand has his army surrounding us as if in siege. But, as we have learned for certain,

---

15 Cf Psalm 14 v. 3.
16 Richard fitz Nigel (1189-98), author of the *Dialogus de Scaccario*.

many men have withdrawn from his army, burdened beyond measure by sickness in body, or by labour and expense; they cannot be retained any longer by entreaty or by money or indeed by threats. In that army a man could be found of some probity at one time, so it was said, whom Saladin would send into the town of Acre, so that he might bring out others who were wounded in their limbs or weak in body. From our side too men have pulled back and scattered into various places, so that they might take thought for themselves against the many damaging effects of the campaign. So, thanks to departures or deaths, the army of Christendom is much diminished. However, the Christians, trusting in the strength of Christ, hope that they can maintain their efforts and withstand the discomforts of the siege until the coming of our kings. We say this, assuming that they arrive around Easter. For if they were to put off their coming any longer, the money needed for our expenses will run out, and the hope of worldly consolation will die away. This then is the situation at the siege of Acre.

6e   *To all those who may inspect this present document, Robert, servant of the cross of Christ, by divine mercy cardinal priest of Saint Stephen* in Coelio Monte, *legate of the apostolic see, greetings in the Lord.*

You should all know that we, having taken counsel with wise men and having joined to ourselves our venerable brothers Haymard bishop of Soissons and William bishop of Meaux and other good men, have heard witnesses and have written out their depositions under our seal and those of the said bishops. We have heard what they have to say about these articles that we have explained to them: that Count Henry, about to go overseas, had his land sworn to his brother Thibaut if he should not return from the lands overseas ... and that the marquis took the queen of Jerusalem away from Humphrey of Toron her husband by violence, and, while Humphrey was still alive, Count Henry had her after the marquis's death ... [17]

Guy of Dampierre, a nobleman, took the oath and said that he was not present when Count Henry had his lands sworn to his brother Count Thibaut, but had heard it said that he did. Asked about how Henry had the queen, he replied that Humphrey, her previous husband, was living when he contracted his marriage with her, and that Humphrey had been married to her for upwards of three years. He added that he had heard Humphrey frequently complaining in the army that his wife had been taken from him by the marquis. Also that when Humphrey took her as his wife, she was

---

17 The omissions are mostly legal formulae, evidence relating to Henry's transfer of his county to his brother or statements to the effect that the particular witness said the same as the others.

18 years old.[18] All this he saw at the siege of Acre and in Tyre, and bore witness that it was public knowledge in the army that she was Humphrey's wife and that the count himself was well aware of this. He added that the count was in the company of those who seized her, and that with others the count took her so that she should be given to the marquis. This took place at Acre.

Erard, marshal of Champagne, a nobleman ... added that in the presence of the count and before many of the barons Humphrey demanded that his wife be restored to him using as his spokesman Reginald of Tiberias:[19] almost all threatened Humphrey, saying, 'Sir, you wish that we in the army should all perish by hunger on account of you alone. It is better that the lady should be given to a certain good man who may command the army lest it perishes by hunger.' ... He also added that three daughters were born to this queen in Humphrey's lifetime. This was claimed in order to secure the marriage for the marquis, and he alleged that unless he married her the army would perish by hunger.[20]

Guy of Chappes ... said that a cry went up in the army: 'O what a great disgrace has been committed in the army because they have taken Humphrey's wife from him by force!', while others said that it had been done to improve the army's market through the marquis. He added that he had neither heard nor believed that the Church had ever made a divorce between Humphrey and his wife ...

William count of Joigny ... added that he heard a big uproar often made in the army because Humphrey had lost his wife so dishonourably when she had been taken away from him by force.

Hugh of Saint-Maurice ... added that he was in the same tent with Humphrey when his wife was taken by force from a neighbouring tent, and Humphrey said to him, 'Sir Hugh, I fear that they who are with my wife will make her say something inspired by the devil.' Then came one of his knights and said to him, 'Look, they have taken away your wife.' And when Humphrey himself went after her, he said to her, 'Lady, this is not the right way to your lodging. Come to me.' But she, with her head bowed, set off in another direction ...

Oger of Saint-Chéron ... had heard the barons often say, 'Humphrey will be no use at holding the kingdom.' And so they said, 'Let us take away his wife and give her to the marquis who will rule the kingdom well and will provide a good market in the army.' ...

All agreed ... that it was being said publicly in the army that on account of that sin, i.e. because his wife had been taken from Humphrey, many evils occurred to the army. Thus on the day of the wedding many

---

18 In fact Isabella would have been 18 at the time of the divorce. See para. 104 note.

19 Perhaps Ralph of Tiberias is intended. A stepson of Raymond III of Tripoli, he was a noted pleader. Riley-Smith, *Feudal Nobility*, p. 122.

20 The order of these last two sentences has been reversed.

knights and other men were captured by the Saracens and killed; not long afterwards the marquis himself was murdered by the Assassins, and Count Henry, after he had married her, similarly fell from a window and died ...

Enacted in the year of grace 1213, in the month of October.

7. Richard the Lionheart in the Holy Land (1191-92)

Although quick to take the cross, Richard did not set off for the East until the summer of 1190. He and Philip Augustus overwintered in Sicily where events took a much more dramatic and violent turn than the *Eracles* accounts (paragraphs 101-2, 107) would suggest, and it was not until 10 April 1191 that Richard resumed his voyage. On 6 May he landed his men on the island of Cyprus at Limassol. Document 7a is the version of his conquest of Cyprus as given in the Colbert-Fontainebleau *Eracles*,[1] an account that diverges significantly from the one to be found in the Lyon *Eracles* from a point mid-way through paragraph 116. Richard's own announcement of his conquest of Cyprus as well as his success in recovering Acre are contained in a letter to his justiciar in England on 6 August 1191 (document 7b).[2] In another letter, this time addressed to the abbot of Clairvaux and dated 1 October 1191 (document 7c),[3] Richard reported on the massacre of his Muslim prisoners (see paragraphs 125-6) and his victory at Arsur (see paragraph 131). At the time of the Second Crusade, the then abbot of Clairvaux, Saint Bernard, had been the most effective crusade preacher, and it may be that Richard was hoping that the present abbot would seek to emulate his predecessor's eloquence and raise more troops and resources to sustain the crusade. Alternatively, he may have seen his letter more as part of a public relations exercise, designed to establish his credentials as the overall leader of the crusade in the eyes of Philip's subjects. Clairvaux was well away from the Angevin-controlled regions of France, and Richard could have been engaged in a piece of subtle oneupmanship at Philip's expense. In another letter dated the same day, he had some scathing remarks about the abandonment of the crusade by King Philip, and at the same time he reported that he himself had been wounded.[4]

Richard was evidently well briefed on the strategic realities of the situation in the East and, although he was to make two military demonstrations in the direction of Jerusalem itself, he made no direct attempt at capturing it. By mid-November he had come to realize that it would be necessary to carry the war to the centre of Saladin's power in Egypt and was calling on the Genoese to supply the necessary naval

---

1 Text: 'Eracles', pp. 163-9.
2 Text: 'Ep. Cant.', p. 347.
3 Text: Howden, *Chronica*, 3, pp. 130-3.
4 Not translated here. Howden, *Chronica*, 3, pp. 129-30.

support the following year (document 7d).[5] Hitherto Richard had worked more closely with their main rivals, the Pisans, but in any case it would seem that nothing came of this initiative. Although he remained in the East until early October 1192, he was never in fact in a position to launch an Egyptian campaign. However, the idea that a conquest of Egypt was a prerequisite for the recovery of Jerusalem became generally accepted and comprised the chief strategic consideration in both the Fifth Crusade (1217-21) and the first crusade of Saint Louis (1249-50).

7a   He immediately ordered his men to seize the port of Limassol and had his people made ready so that if the Greeks tried to prevent his landing he could come ashore in strength. When the Greek emperor saw the fleet coming to land at the city, he did not dare wait but abandoned the town and fled together with all his armed men. The king and his host arrived at the shore beyond the city, and, when all the knights and sergeants were on land, they started off on foot towards the town. The king himself had not landed but moved parallel in a galley with the other galleys following. Some Latins who were living in the city of Limassol came out to meet the host and said that they wished to speak with the king. They were put in a boat and taken to the galley where the king was. When they came into his presence they said, 'Sire, you can enter the city without opposition because the Greek emperor has departed with his whole army and has gone off towards the mountains. Only the ordinary people and the merchants remain, and they will willingly receive you as lord.' When the king had heard this, he took two knights and sent them to the people of the town in the company of the men who had brought him this news to tell them that they and their possessions would be safe. Then he had it proclaimed throughout his host on land and sea that no one should be so foolhardy as to do the people of Limassol any harm or wrong; he ordered that they should all camp in the gardens and that no one should camp in the town.

On the third day after he had landed, the king took some Greek monks and sent them as messengers to the emperor Isaac who was at Kilani. He told them to say that he was greatly surprised that he had abandoned his city and had avoided him; he was a pilgrim who had come from his own land in the service of Our Lord, and he was keen to see him, if he so wished, and discuss matters with him that would be to his advantage. Isaac replied that if he would send him a safe-conduct by one of his knights so that he could come in safety, then he would come to see him and speak with him. The king sent a rich man from Normandy named William of Préaux who brought him the safe-conduct he had requested.

---

5   Text: *Codice diplomatico della Repubblica di Genova*, ed. C. Imperiale di Sant'Angelo (Fonti per la storia d'Italia, 89; Rome, 1942), 3, pp. 19-21.

When he came to Kilani, the emperor received him most honourably and had him lodged sumptuously and served him richly. On his departure Isaac gave him fine gifts and told him that he would have his men draw near to Limassol and on the third day he would come to the king. William of Préaux took leave and returned to the king and informed him of the emperor's reply. As promised, the emperor left Kilani with his whole army and came down to the plain and had his men camp two leagues from Limassol at a village named Kolossi. Then, with few companions, he came to the king.

When he entered the camp, the king came a good stone's throw from his tent on foot to meet him with a large company of men. As soon as Isaac realized that it was the king who was coming out to meet him on foot, he got down from his horse. As he approached the king, he bowed down several times, and the king responded in like manner and took him by the hand and they entered the tent and sat together on a seat covered with a silk cloth. The king spoke to him through an interpreter about many things, and he to the king, and then the king said, 'Sir emperor, I am most amazed that you, who are a Christian and have seen the loss of the Holy Land in which God died and rose and the destruction of Christendom, have never sent counsel or aid there. In particular, while the siege of Acre has been in progress, the Christians have endured great hardships and have been short of both food and men, but you have done nothing to suggest that it means anything to you. Instead you have shown them enmity, for you have harmed and oppressed many of those who have gone to their aid. So I require and summon you on behalf of God and Christendom and the pilgrims that you make amends: that you come in person to the army bringing as many men as you can, and that you grant licences in your land to anyone who comes to buy food to take to the host. In this way you will do yourself honour and profit, as you will have your earthly reward for it and you will put an end to the complaints that are raised against you.'

When the emperor of Cyprus had heard and understood what King Richard had said to him, he was most put out. Nevertheless he concealed his thoughts as best he could and replied, 'Sire, I thank you for what you have said, for I see and know that it would be much to my profit and honour if I could do it. But if I were to leave this land, I should never return, for the emperor of Constantinople disputes the land with me and so the people who are here and who hold me as lord would then turn against me. But everything else I shall do most gladly: I shall send 200 men-at-arms until Acre is taken, and I shall licence all those who come to Cyprus to buy supplies.' The king said that that would suffice, but what would he do so that he could assure the pilgrims of the host? Isaac replied that he would hand over his daughter to him as a hostage and that he would send her to him before he departed. The king thought himself well satisfied. Then Isaac got up, and the king took him to a tent that he had made ready for him, and returned to his own tent. The emperor was given luxurious lodgings, and after he had eaten they made up a good bed for him and he lay down. When he sensed that all the people in the host were resting, he mounted a horse and fled still barefoot. His men went away too.

After he had reached his own army, he took a Greek monk and sent him to the king to tell him that he should leave his land, and if he would not go he would show him that he loved neither him nor his company. When the king heard this and learned what Isaac had done, he ordered the horses to be unloaded from the ships, and he marshalled his men and put them in squadrons and rode to where Isaac was. Once Isaac knew that the king was coming to fight with him, he put his own forces in order and set them to ride against him. The two armies drew near to each other and clashed together. But the battle did not last long, for the Greeks were defeated and Isaac and his people, except for those who were killed or taken, fled to the mountains. The king occupied the camp where he took great booty. Then he returned to Limassol and married the maiden that his sister had brought. At this point King Guy, who had been king of Jerusalem and who had come from the host in a galley, arrived at Limassol. Isaac left the mountains and went off to Nicosia which is the archbishopric and the chief city of Cyprus and is situated in the middle of the island. When the king of England learned of it, he ordered his march and went with his whole army by land; his navy followed the coast until it came to a town named Kiti, and from there the king headed off towards Nicosia.

When he arrived at a place named Tremetousha, he encountered Isaac who was coming to fight against him with his whole army. The squadrons assembled, but in the end the Greeks could not endure the Latins and were badly defeated. Many were put to flight and many others were taken or killed. When Isaac, who was a brave man but cruel and violent, saw that all was lost beyond recovery, in his final desperation he abandoned himself and charged into the greatest press of men until he reached the king. Isaac struck him a great blow with the mace that he was holding, but so many people closed in on him that he was brought to the ground and taken. After that the king encountered no more opposition in the land. All the castles were surrendered to him, and he had Isaac put in shackles and rings of silver and sent him and his wife and daughter to Marqab in the keeping of the Hospitallers. The king ordered the affairs of Cyprus and appointed people to guard the island. Then he departed, taking away much wealth that he had acquired there, and arrived in the host before Acre.

7b   *Richard, king of England etc., to his justiciar in England,*[6] *greetings.*

You know that we have suffered much from illness since we undertook

---

6   William Longchamp, bishop of Ely.

our journey, but by the mercy of God we are restored to full health. Enough has been told you of how divine mercy added to our honour at Messina. Then, as we were continuing our pilgrimage journey, we were diverted to Cyprus where we hoped to find the refuge of those of our number who had been shipwrecked. But the tyrant, who, revering neither God nor man, has usurped the name of emperor, hurriedly brought a strongly armed force to bar us from the port. He robbed and despoiled as many as possible of our men who had suffered wreck and imprisoned those dying of hunger. Not unnaturally we were spurred to revenge. We did battle with our enemy and, thanks to divine assistance, obtained a speedy victory. Defeated and fettered, we hold him together with his only daughter. We have subjected to ourselves the whole island of Cyprus with all its strong points. Then, happy and rejoicing, we entered the port of Acre, and not long after the arrival of the king of France and ourselves we recovered the city of Acre with the Holy Cross and took 1,700 captives. But within 15 days the king of France left us to return to his own land. We, however, place the love of God and His honour above our own and above the acquisition of many regions. We shall restore the land of Syria to its original condition as quickly as possible, and only then shall we return to our lands. But you may know for certain that we shall set sail next Lent. We order you to attend faithfully to furthering our affairs.

Witnessed by myself at Acre, on the sixth day of August (1191).

7c *Richard, by the grace of God king of England, duke of Normandy and Aquitaine and count of Anjou, to his venerable and most dear friend in Christ, the abbot of Clairvaux,[7] greetings and best wishes.*

After the tragic and universally lamented destruction of the holy city of Jerusalem, the city of the living God by which His name is invoked, the world was shaken and trembled because the King of Heaven had lost His land wherein His feet had stood. But, as your sanctity is well aware, God's blessing was spread by the Apostolic See throughout the whole world, and the friends of the cross of Christ sprang forth eagerly to take the sign of salvation on their foreheads and on their shoulders and avenge the injuries done to the Holy Cross. To serve the living God we too have accepted the sign of the cross to defend the places of His death that have been consecrated by His precious blood and which the enemies of the cross of Christ have hitherto shamefully profaned, and we have taken upon us the burden of so great and so holy a work.

Soon after the arrival of the lord king of the Franks at Acre, we too arrived there thanks to God's favourable providence. Not long afterwards the city of Acre was surrendered to the king of the Franks and ourselves on condition that the lives of the Saracens who had been stationed there to

---

7   Garnier of Rochefort, later bishop of Langres.

guard and defend it should be spared. On Saladin's behalf it had been agreed that the Holy Cross and 1,500 living prisoners would be handed over to us, and he fixed a day for us when all this was to be done. But the time-limit expired, and, as the pact which he had agreed was entirely made void, we quite properly had the Saracens that we had in custody - about 2,600 of them - put to death. A few of the more noble were spared, and we hope to recover the Holy Cross and certain Christian captives in exchange for them.

After the king of the Franks had returned to his own lands and the ruined and broken walls of the city of Acre had been repaired and the city fully fortified by ditches and a wall, we set off to go to Jaffa so as to further the affairs of Christendom and achieve the intention of our vow. With us was (Hugh) duke of Burgundy with the French under his command, Count Henry (of Champagne) with his men, and many other counts and barons and an innumerable people. It is a good distance between Acre and Jaffa and the roads are long, and it was with much fatigue and grave loss of our men that we eventually made it to Caesarea. Saladin too lost very many of his own men during that journey. After the people of God had rested there for a while, we continued on our intended route to Jaffa. Our vanguard was proceeding and was already setting up camp at Arsur, when Saladin and his Saracens made a violent attack on our rearguard, but by the grace of God's favourable mercy they were forced into flight just by the four squadrons that were facing them. The Christians chased them for a whole league. So great was the slaughter among Saladin's more noble Saracens, that he lost more that day near Arsur - it was a Sunday, the vigil of the nativity of the Blessed Virgin Mary[8] - than on any day in the previous 40 years. By the grace of God we lost no one that day except that best of men whose merits had made him dear to the whole army, James of Avesnes. He had been in the Christian army for several years in the service of the living God, and he had been like a pillar of the army, ready and devout in all holiness and sincerity of faith.[9] Then, by the will of God, we reached Jaffa. We have fortified that town with ditches and a wall, having as our plan the effective furtherance of the affairs of Christendom everywhere to the best of our ability.

Since his defeat that day, Saladin has not dared do battle with the Christians. Instead he lies in wait at a distance out of sight like a lion in his den, and he is intent on killing of the friends of the cross like sheep led to the slaughter. But he learned that we intend to make rapid progress to Ascalon, and so he has destroyed it and razed it to the ground. He is now abandoning and disdaining the whole land of Syria as if deprived of the benefit of counsel and aid. We take this as grounds for optimism that soon, by God's grant, the Lord's inheritance will be fully restored.

---

8   7 Sept.
9   Above paras. 84, 131.

Because the inheritance of the Lord is already partly recovered, and because to further its recovery we constantly endure the heat of day and have already exhausted all our money - and not only our money but both our strength and our body also - we have to tell your fraternity that we can in no way remain in Syria beyond next Easter. The duke of Burgundy, with the French under his command, and Count Henry with his men and the other counts, barons and knights have spent all their wealth in the service of God and will return to their own lands unless by the ingenuity of your preaching thoughtful provision may be made for people to popu-late and defend the land and for more money to be spent in God's service. So, throwing ourselves at your holiness's feet with profuse tears, we offer up our affectionate prayers, asking ever more earnestly that you, as behoves your office and honour, will make every effort to induce princes and nobles and the other people of God throughout the Christian world to share in the service of the living God. Call upon them that from next Easter they will uphold and defend the Lord's inheritance which we, with God's favour, will by then have fully obtained. See to it that through the watchful attention of your zeal Christendom's requirements are not lost due to your neglect. We are sending this letter concerning the affairs of Christendom to your holiness as early as this so that there is no possibility that we might be accused in any way of being lazy and negligent by failing to warn so great and holy a man as yourself about them. Like us therefore you should encourage the other people of God before the start of the passage[10] to serve of Him by restoring His inheritance to Himself. Now is the time that you should make the greatest effort to inspire the people of God to do this.

Witnessed by myself at Jaffa, on the first day of October (1191).

7d *Richard, by the grace of God king of England, duke of Normandy and Aquitaine and count of Anjou, to those venerable men and dearest friends, the archbishop, the podestà, the consuls and council and the other good men of the Genoese to whom this letter shall come, greetings.*

Since hitherto you have had more concern than all other men for the immediate needs of the holy land of Jerusalem, we have judged that those things that we are planning to do for the advantage of that land should be brought to your attention. So you should know that next summer, for the honour of God and for the confusion of the pride of the gentiles, we shall, if you are agreeable, hasten with all our forces into Egypt, to Babylon and Alexandria. And so we beg your sincerity as earnestly as we can, that you, out of regard for your sacred duty and with an eye to your own bene-fit, come with as much equipment as you can and without delay to the Christian army, secure in the knowledge that we shall fully honour the

---

10 I.e. the 1192 spring sailing.

whole agreement and covenant that we have made with you and you with us (not counting the passage after the one on which we came to Syria).

If indeed you bring your whole fleet of ships, you will receive your share of the land which, by the help of God, we shall be able to win from the Saracens in keeping with the agreement that we shall make between us.[11] But if not, you will get a share in proportion to the number of ships and people you do send. As for the galleys, you should know that from the time from which they shall set sail to come to the Christian army, we shall pay you in full half the expenses. For the rest, we are sending to you Maurinus, that distinguished man and friend of Christianity, who has been your consul in Syria, with the special request that you should trust what he, as a friend of Christianity, has to say about these proposals. We shall hold firm and valid everything that Maurinus shall say to you on our behalf or shall do as if we ourselves had been speaking in person. You may inform us through this same Maurinus without delay as to what you will do in this business and how many galleys and men you will send to the Christian army.

Witnessed by myself at Acre, on the eleventh day of October (1191).

---

11 In a second letter written on the same day, Richard spoke of giving the Genoese a third share in any conquests he might make if they promised to provide half what was agreed. *Codice diplomatico della Repubblica di Genova*, 3, p. 21.

Select Bibliography

There is no full-length study of the Third Crusade. General accounts of the Crusades to the East have chapters on the events of the years 1187-92, and of these the most dependable in English are:

P.M. Holt, *The Age of the Crusades: The Near East from the Eleventh Century to 1517* (London, 1986) (placing the crusades in the context of Near Eastern History).
H.E. Mayer, *The Crusades*, trans. J. Gillingham (2nd edn, Oxford, 1988).
J. Riley-Smith, *The Crusades: A Short History* (London, 1987).
S. Runciman, *A History of the Crusades* (3 vols: Cambridge, 1951-54).
K.M. Setton (ed), *A History of the Crusades* (6 vols: Philadelphia/ Madison, 1955-89).

There are important articles in B.Z. Kedar, H.E. Mayer and R.C. Smail (eds), *Outremer: Studies in the history of the Crusading Kingdom of Jerusalem* (Jerusalem, 1982), and B.Z. Kedar (ed), *The Horns of Hattin* (Jerusalem and London, 1992).

The best modern biography of Saladin is M.C. Lyons and D.E.P. Jackson, *Saladin: The Politics of the Holy War* (Cambridge, 1982).

On the crusade of King Richard see J. Gillingham, *Richard the Lionheart* (2nd edn, London, 1989). Also very useful are the same author's collected papers: *Richard Coeur de Lion: Kingship, Chivalry and War in the Twelfth Century* (London and Rio Grande, 1994), and the collection edited by J.L. Nelson: *Richard Coeur de Lion in History and Myth* (London, 1992) (especially J.O. Prestwich's essay, 'Richard Coeur de Lion; *Rex Bellicosus*'). C. Tyerman, *England and the Crusades, 1095-1588* (Chicago and London, 1988), has some important discussion.

For Philip Augustus and Conrad of Montferrat, see the articles by J. Richard, 'Philippe Auguste, la croisade et le royaume' in R.-H. Bautier (ed), *La France de Philippe Auguste: Le temps des mutations* (Paris, 1982), pp. 411-24, and D. Jacoby, 'Conrad, Marquis of Montferrat, and the Kingdom of Jerusalem (1187-1192)' in L. Balletto (ed), *Dai feudi monferrini e dal Piemonte ai nuovi mondi oltre gli Oceani* (= Biblioteca della Società di Storia Arte e Archeologia per le Province di Alessandria e Asti, 27) (Alessandria, 1993), pp. 187-238.

On the military matters, the classic study remains R.C. Smail, *Crusading Warfare (1097-1193)* (Cambridge, 1956; new edn 1995). For the siege of Acre see R. Rogers, *Latin Siege Warfare in the Twelfth Century* (Oxford, 1992), pp. 212-36. A sound, up-to-date survey of his subject is provided by H. Kennedy, *Crusader Castles* (Cambridge, 1994).

For the battle of Hattin, see works cited at p. 158.

On the military Orders, J. Riley-Smith, *The Knights of Saint John in Jerusalem and Cyprus c.1050-1310* (London, 1967), and M. Barber, *The New Knighthood: A History of the Order of the Temple* (Cambridge, 1994) are the standard works in English.

For the political conflict in the kingdom of Jerusalem with references to earlier work, see P.W. Edbury, 'Propaganda and Faction in the Kingdom of Jerusalem: the Background to Hattin' in M. Shatzmiller (ed), *Crusaders and Muslims in Twelfth-Century Syria* (Leiden, 1993), pp. 173-89.

On Byzantine history at this period, see C.M. Brand, *Byzantium Confronts the West, 1180-1204* (Cambridge, MA, 1968), and M. Angold, *The Byzantine Empire 1025-1204. A Political History* (London, 1984), and for Cyprus, P.W. Edbury, *The Kingdom of Cyprus and the Crusades, 1191-1374* (Cambridge, 1991).

Other sources available in English

Narrative sources composed in the Anglo-Norman realm are particularly rich for this period:

Ambroise, *The Crusade of Richard Lionheart*, trans. M.J. Hubert and J. La Monte (New York, 1941).
'De Expugnatione Terrae Sanctae per Saladinum Libellus', excerpts trans. J.A. Brundage in *The Crusades: A Documentary Survey* (Milwaukee, 1962), pp. 153-63.
Itinerarium Peregrinorum et Gesta Regis Ricardi, trans. as *Chronicle of the Third Crusade*, H.J. Nicholson (Crusade Texts in Translation 3: Aldershot, 1997).
Richard of Devizes, *Cronicon*, ed. and trans. J.T. Appleby (London, 1963).

Pope Gregory VIII's bull, *Audita tremendi* (October-November 1187) which inaugurated the Third Crusade is translated in J. and L. Riley-

Smith, *The Crusades: Idea and Reality, 1095-1274* (London, 1981), pp. 63-7.

Arabic Sources provide contrasting views of events and are often stronger on chronology. A useful anthology is available in F. Gabrieli (ed), *Arab Historians of the Crusades* (London, 1969). Two strongly partisan biographies by members of his entourage are Baha ad-Din, *The Life of Saladin, 1137-1193*, trans. C.W. Wilson (Palestine Pilgrim Text Society, 13; London, 1897), and 'Imad al-Din al-Isfahani, *Conquête de la Syrie et de la Palestine par Saladin*, trans. H. Massé (Paris, 1972). Saladin's own letter describing the battle of Hattin is translated by C.P. Melville and M.C. Lyons as 'Saladin's Hattin Letter' in B.Z. Kedar (ed), *The Horns of Hattin* (Jerusalem and London, 1992), pp. 208-12.

Index

191

Meaux, bp, see William
Medes, 133
Meskenah, 160
Messina, 93, 98, 99-100, 179
Midianites, 18
Miles of Colaverdo, 161
Miles of Plancy, 96 n.163
Mirabel, 162, 163
Moab, 41-2, 67
Mohammed, 61, 66, 72, 79, 169
Monachus, abp Caesarea, pat. Jer., 125-6, 134 n.241
Montreal, 41, 55, 67, 78, 118, 165
Mosul, 133
Mount Tabor, 161
mounted sergeants, 114
Münster, bp, see Herman

Nablus, 24-5, 26-7, 30, 32 n.52, 33, 34, 35, 43, 54, 95, 162
Navarre, k., see Sancho VI, Thibaut
Nazareth, 29, 31-4, 40, 161, 162
Negroponte, 84
Nephin, 65
Nicosia, 103, 112, 140, 178; abp, see Alan
Nimrin, 161
Normandy, 73 n.109, 102, 115 n.195, 123, 176
Nur al-Din, see al-Afdal Nur al-Din, lord of Damascus
Nur al-Din, Zengid ruler of Aleppo and Damascus, 120

Oger of St-Chéron, 173
Oliver, chamberlain of Ant., 129
Oste of Tiberias, 46
Otto of Brunswick, 124
Otto, ct Burgundy, s. of Frederick Barbarossa, 75
Outrejourdain, 24 nn.35, 37, 96 n.163; lord, see Reynald of Châtillon
Outremer, land of, 18, 24, 73-4, 114, 139, 152

Palermo, 93-4, 135, 136
papal legate, see Baldwin, abp Canterbury, Conrad abp Mainz, Robert of St Stephen, Ubaldo abp Pisa
Pardhisi, 127

Paris, peace of (1229), 7
Pasque de Riveri, 43-4
Patrick, earl of Salisbury, 150
Pella, 23 n.32
Persia, 35, 42
Peter of Angoulême, bp Tripoli, 113
Peter Brice, 49
Peter son of Leo, 167, 169
Petra, 163
petraries, 56, 59, 68, 70, 105, 116, 166
Philip II Augustus, k. France, 2, 4, 47, 76, 79, 80, 82, 91-4, 96 n.164, 97-9, 100, 104, 105-10, 111, 115, 118, 121, 123-4, 128, 167-8, 171-2, 175, 179, 179-80
Philip of Dreux, bp Beauvais, 92, 94, 96, 114-5
Philip, ct Flanders, 92, 98, 108, 110
Philip, duke of Swabia, 23, 75
Philippi, 22, 74
pilgrims/pilgrimage, 52, 74, 82, 97, 100, 101-2, 111, 176-7
Pisa, abp, see Ubaldo
Pisans, 38, 52, 53, 66, 96-7, 98, 116, 120, 124-5, 141, 170, 176
Plivain, lord of Botron, 38-9, 47, 161
Poitevins, 46, 98, 142
Poitiers, 130, 150; ct, see Otto of Brunswick; county of, 91
Poitou, 99-100, 150
polains, 45-6
Ponthieu, ct, see John
pope, 14, 25; see Alexander III, Anacletus II (Anti-pope), Celestine III, Clement III, Gelasius II, Gregory VIII, Innocent II, Innocent III, Urban II, Urban III

Qilij Arslan II, sultan of Iconium, 84-6, 87
Quafarbole, 126

Ralph Buceus, 161 n.12
Ralph of Diceto, 167
Ralph of Mons, const. Ant., 129
Ralph of Tiberias, 46, 173 n.19
Ramla, 27 n.43, 118, 162
Randolf, bp Bethlehem, 117, 118
Ranulf Glanville, 167, 171
Ravenna, abp, see Gerardo

William, abp Reims, 92, 171
William I, k. Sicily, 90-1
William II, k. Sicily, 73-5, 90-1, 93, 135, 138
William of Tiberias, 46, 116
William, abp Tyre, 3-5, 11 n.1, 12 n.4, 14 n.8, 15 n.11, 35, 42-3, 44, 96 n.165, 128 n.225, 149; Continuation of, 3, 4, 7

Würzburg, bishopric of, 75 n.113; bp, see Godfrey

Yazur, see Castle of the Plains

az-Zahir, sultan of Aleppo, 133-4